NOT SO PLAIN AS BLACK AND WHITE

ROCHESTER STUDIES In
AFRICAN HISTORY and the DIASPORA

Toyin Falola, Senior Editor
The Frances Higginbotham Nalle Centennial Professor in History
University of Texas at Austin

(ISSN: 1092-5228)

*Power Relations in Nigeria: Ilorin
Slaves and Their Successors*
Ann O'Hear

Dilemmas of Democracy in Nigeria
Edited by Paul Beckett and
Crawford Young

Science and Power in Colonial Mauritius
William Kelleher Storey

*Namibia's Post-Apartheid Regional
Institutions: The Founding Year*
Joshua Bernard Forrest

*A Saro Community in the Niger Delta,
1912–1984: The Potts-Johnsons of
Port Harcourt and Their Heirs*
Mac Dixon-Fyle

*Contested Power in Angola:
1840s to the Present*
Linda Heywood

*Nigerian Chiefs: Traditional Power in
Modern Politics, 1890s–1990s*
Olufemi Vaughan

*West Indians in West Africa, 1808–1880:
The African Diaspora in Reverse*
Nemata Blyden

*The United States and Decolonization
in West Africa, 1950–1960*
Ebere Nwaubani

Health, State, and Society in Kenya
George Oduor Ndege

Black Business and Economic Power
Edited by Alusine Jalloh and
Toyin Falola

Voices of the Poor in Africa
Elizabeth Isichei

*Colonial Rule and Crisis in Equatorial
Africa: Southern Gabon ca. 1850–1940*
Christopher J. Gray

*The Politics of Frenchness in Colonial
Algeria, 1930–1954*
Jonathan K. Gosnell

*Sources and Methods in African History:
Spoken, Written, Unearthed*
Edited by Toyin Falola and
Christian Jennings

*Sudan's Blood Memory: The Legacy of War,
Ethnicity, and Slavery in Early South Sudan*
Stephanie Beswick

*Writing Ghana, Imagining Africa:
Nation and African Modernity*
Kwaku Larbi Korang

*Labour, Land and Capital in Ghana:
From Slavery to Free Labour in Asante,
1807–1956*
Gareth Austin

*Not So Plain as Black and White: Afro-
German Culture and History, 1890–2000*
Edited by Patricia Mazón and
Reinhild Steingröver

NOT SO PLAIN AS BLACK AND WHITE

AFRO-GERMAN CULTURE AND HISTORY, 1890–2000

Edited by Patricia Mazón and Reinhild Steingröver
With a Foreword by Russell Berman

UNIVERSITY OF ROCHESTER PRESS

First published 2005

University of Rochester Press
668 Mt. Hope Avenue, Rochester, NY 14620, USA
www.urpress.com
and of Boydell & Brewer Limited
PO Box 9, Woodbridge, Suffolk IP12 3DF, UK
www.boydellandbrewer.com

ISBN: 1-58046-183-2

Support was provided by the College of Arts and Sciences at the State University of New York at Buffalo.

Library of Congress Cataloging-in-Publication Data

Not so plain as Black and White : Afro-German culture and history, 1890–2000 / edited by Patricia Mazón and Reinhild Steingröver.
    p. cm. — (Rochester studies in African history and the diaspora, ISSN 1092–5228; v. 19)
    Includes bibliographical references and index.
    ISBN 1-58046-183-2 (hardcover : alk. paper)
    1. Blacks—Germany—History.   2. Blacks—Race identity—Germany—History.   3. Germany—Race relations.   I. Mazón, Patricia M.   II. Steingröver, Reinhild.   III. Series.
    DD78.B55N68 2004
    305.896'043'0904—dc22
                                                                    2004024338

A catalogue record for this title is available from the British Library.

This publication is printed on acid-free paper.
Printed in the United States of America.

Tina Campt's essay appeared in a slightly different version in *Callaloo* 26, no. 2 (Spring 2003): 322–41 and is reprinted here with kind permission. © 2003 by *Callaloo*.

CONTENTS

v

FOREWORD

THOMAS MANN, W. E. B. DUBOIS, AND AFRO-GERMAN STUDIES

Russell A. Berman

Why Afro-German? Why Africa and Germany? As much as this coupling may seem surprising or unexpected, it turns out, on closer examination, to be uncannily familiar, sometimes a topic of explicit consideration in foundational texts, sometimes only a fragmentary reference. Yet be it as fading trace or as foregrounded topic, a linkage of the two terms shows up repeatedly in the writings of seminal thinkers. In key texts, pertinent to definitions of both Germany and Africa, the other term suddenly appears and takes on a pivotal importance: "Africa" as a referent for German self-reflection, and "Germany" as a figure in the emergence of pan-African consciousness. Despite an initial assumption to think them apart from each other, there is evidence that they tend to converge. It appears that the twain shall meet, in complex entwinements of separation and identification, dialectics of negation and appropriation, spread out through histories of subjectivity and across maps of colonialism and migration.

Consider for example Thomas Mann's novella, *Mario and the Magician*, published in 1930, the year after the author had been awarded the Nobel Prize for Literature. One of the best known works of the leading German writer of the twentieth century, it is the story of a German family's summer vacation to a seaside resort in Italy. While the first-person narration is very much unpolitical—in the mode of the "unpolitical" character of German conservatism that Mann himself had expounded in his polemical essayism during World War I—it is nonetheless perfectly clear that this travelogue is very much about politics: the story of going to the beach in fascist Italy. It is in effect a conservative description of totalitarianism, addressed to a democratic audience. In other words, Mann has fashioned a text for his readers in the Weimar Republic, Germany's fledgling democracy, that amounts to a conservative German's report on the character of life and culture under Mussolini.

Not only life and culture are at stake, however: at a crucial point Mann has his narrator, concerned like every summer vacationer with the weather, choose to describe Italian heat, oddly, as "African." Why this choice of terms, this incongruous geographical referent in the midst of this German travel narrative to Italy, which is after all the privileged site of German tourism? A close examination of this deployment of the African epithet in the text of the leading author of the Weimar Republic can help tease out some of the tensions and fault lines in the duality under question: Germany and Africa.

Part of the answer surely has to do with the subtle and only interlinear characterizations of Italian politics throughout the text. Without naming the regime or even coming close to an outwardly political discourse, Mann has his discrete and tasteful, if not overly analytical narrator describe aspects of contemporary Italy that would be read in Germany as critical comments on fascism, despite the lack of any explicitly tendentious vocabulary. Thus the reference to Africa, in this regard, names the Italian colonial legacy: the failed effort to conquer Abyssinia in the late nineteenth century, and the colonization of Libya in the early twentieth. Mann's reference was in fact tragically prophetic: by the mid-1930s, Mussolini would engage in an effort to establish a "new Roman Empire" by invading Abyssinia, one of the first steps toward World War II. Understood in this way, the usage of "Africa" in *Mario and the Magician* entails a postcolonial German perspective (Germany's colonies were lost in World War I) on the ongoing colonialism of its nondemocratic neighbor. The text, therefore, reminds the reader in the democratic Weimar Republic that Italy, a victor in the Great War, remains a colonial power and an African presence, while Germany's colonies had been confiscated and redistributed among the victors. This line of thought ends, however, ambivalently, oscillating between competing conclusions: a democratic Germany's disdain for the colonialism of authoritarian Italy or, alternatively, a German resentment that the victors could claim the spoils that a rearmed Germany might still hope to recover in the future.

Yet the characterization of Italian weather as "African" has an even more complex reverberation, because in the lines that follow immediately, Africa is explicitly contrasted with an antithetical definition of German or "northern" identity, all in the mouth of Mann's troublesomely unreliable narrator. "The heat—if I may bring it in evidence—was extreme. It was African. The power of the sun, directly one left the border of the indigo-blue wave, was so frightful, so relentless, that the mere thought of the few steps between the beach and luncheon was a burden [. . .]. The burning void of the sky, day after day, weighs one down; the high coloration, the enormous naiveté of the unrefracted light—they do, I dare say, induce light-heartedness, a carefree mood born of immunity from downpours and other meteorological caprices. But slowly, slowly, there makes itself felt a lack: the deeper, more complex needs of the northern soul remain unsatisfied. You are left barren—even it may be, in time, a little contemptuous."[1] The signifier "Africa" is evidently much more than a marker of Italian colonialism. It points instead to a substantive geography of temperament and culture, a hierarchy of regions in which a putatively African clarity, brilliant but empty, consistently external, fully enlightened and therefore leveled, is judged inferior to a North, a Germany, of complexity, interiority, and romantic soulfulness. This polarized dialectic of South and North, of enlightenment and romanticism, of terrible simplification and complex individuation would seem to suggest that our own starting point, the double exposure of Africa and Germany is unattainable: the twain may not meet after all, at least according to the assumption of Mann's vacationing narrator.

It would, however, be a cardinal critical error to regard the rhetoric of irreconcilable geographical alternatives, articulated so emphatically by the narrator, as itself the last word on the meaning of the text or the intention of the author. On the contrary, it is in the very nature of Mann's writing here and throughout much of his fiction that any explicit statement in the narrator's discourse is subject to revision due to the overriding irony of the work and, more generally, by the principled autonomy of literature. The fundamental distinction between the terms, the Africa of solar illumination and the nocturnal interiority of the German North, is written into the speech of the conservative, unpolitical narrator, whose judgments throughout the text are consistently shown to be inadequate. One gets closer to the crux of the matter by understanding that Mann's text portrays this central figure as incapable of adequate thought and, even less, of adequate action, and the meteorology passage demonstrates how his racist geography contributes to his immobility, which is both conceptual and political. The symptomatic inability to think "Africa" and "Germany" together, or rather, the inability to think of them as anything but opposites, is part and parcel of the same cultured indolence that renders him incapable—incapable like most of the public of Torre di Venere, the resort where the novella takes place—of resisting the mesmerizing power of the tyrannical magician.

Mario and the Magician is about Italian fascism, but it is also about the inadequacy of a particular German response to fascism, a response that presumes an ontological distinction between Africa and Germany. Mann suggests, *ex negativo*, the possibility of hybridity: if only the narrator's northern soul had been capable of embracing, rather than denouncing, the African light, if only being "German" did not entail hostility to "Africa," a democratic resistance to tyranny might be possible. Indeed throughout Mann's oeuvre one finds explorations of a dynamic relationship between North and South, although it is only here, in *Mario*, that this particular South, Africa, figures so prominently. Without suggesting that the biography of the author is the ultimate source of meaning, it is worthwhile recalling that Mann himself faced attacks from Nazi critics who denounced him as a "mulatto" due to his Brazilian Creole ancestry. The representative German author of the twentieth-century a "mulatto"? The prospect of an arithmetic in which "Germany" and "Africa" could be added together and tallied into something other than colonialism turns out to be less counterintuitive than first imagined.

While Mann's novella suggests this overlap of Africa and Germany indirectly in a passing remark within the mediated configurations of aesthetic form, the two regions converge prominently, boldly, and with public intention, in various writings and at several conjunctures in the thought of W. E. B. DuBois, the father of pan-Africanism. As early as 1888—he was twenty, Thomas Mann was thirteen—DuBois delivered a commencement address at Fisk on the subject of Bismarck. "This choice," he wrote a half-century later in his autobiography, "in itself showed the abyss between my education and the truth in the world. Bismarck was my hero. He had made a nation out of a mass of bickering peoples. He had dominated the whole development with this strength until he crowned an emperor at Versailles."[2] In retrospect, the democratic and progressive DuBois is apologizing for his own youthful enthusiasm for Bismarck, the conservative. Nonetheless, the recapitulation of that enthusiasm sheds a revealing light on some tenacious aspects of DuBois's political thinking, especially the admiration for leadership, the vision of unity, and a positive estimation of nationhood. Is there a Bismarckian or even Wilhelmine inflection to black nationalism as imagined by DuBois? Consider his halcyon recollection of his time in imperial Berlin, where he studied in 1892–93: "When I heard my German companions sing '*Deutschland, Deutschland über Alles, über Alles in der Welt*' I realized that they felt something I had never felt and perhaps never would. The march of soldiers, the saluting of magnificent uniforms, the martial music and rhythm of movement stirred my senses.

Then there was that new, young Emperor, '*von Gottes Gnade, deutsche* [sic] *Kaiser, Koenig von Preussen*' [. . .] who led and pinpointed the pageantry. Ever and again he came riding ahead of his white and golden troops on prancing chargers through the great Brandenburg gate, up the Linden 'With banners gaily flying, with trumpet and with drum!' I thrilled at the sight even though I knew of that shriveled left arm and of his impossible demand for supreme power. I even trimmed my beard and mustache to a fashion like his and still follow it."[3]

DuBois's positive enthusiasm for the symbols of German imperialism has an aesthetic as much as a political component, and the politics are not solely about a cult of leadership. On the contrary, he goes on in the same passage to explain that the fascination with German nationalism represents an indirect expression of his marginalization in the United States, where he felt excluded from any similarly naïve patriotism. His budding pan-Africanism could begin to mature through his German experience for two perhaps incompatible reasons. Germany was important both because of an uncritical bias toward European culture—the legacy of hegemonic American taste—which brought him to Germany in the first place, and, simultaneously and perhaps paradoxically, because Germany provided an alternative to the United States of institutionalized racism. Berlin gave DuBois a sort of Archimedean point, from which he could gain a critical leverage on the America of Jim Crow; hence his bitter regret at leaving Germany when his scholarship for study in Berlin ended and he was compelled to return to the race hatred at home.[4]

In subsequent decades, this predisposition toward a subjective identification with Germany would be framed by the complex structures of international relations and competition. For example, in 1914, even as he decided to side with the allies in World War I against Germany—by no means a foregone conclusion for an African American intellectual who would have had no obvious reason to shed tears for Belgium, given its particularly bloodthirsty colonial history in the Congo—DuBois nevertheless asserted in the pages of the *Crisis* that "the writer speaks without anti-German bias; personally he has deep cause to love the German people. They made him believe in the essential humanity of white folk twenty years ago when he was near denying it."[5] Similarly, after the war, his disappointment with the disposition of the confiscated German colonies in Africa at the Versailles peace negotiations led him toward a critique of the treaty quite congruent with the objections which were voiced in Germany. In complex ways, his subjective orientation was driven both by individual predilection and by the dynamics of larger social and political forces.

DuBois weaves Germany and Africa, or African America, together in the rich fabric of allusion and montage in his classic text, *Souls of Black Folk* of 1903. He embeds the exploration of African American identity in American history, but in Africa as well, while building on a variegated and extensive network of German references. Aside from the borrowings from Goethe and Hegel, which might be attributed to the more general neo-Hegelianism of American intellectual life around the turn of the century, there are explicit moments where DuBois establishes a double exposure of German and black identity. The choice of epigraph for chapter four, for example, implicitly transports Schiller's Joan of Arc into the life of rural blacks in the hills of Tennessee, where the young DuBois had taught school. The thirteenth chapter restages *Lohengrin* in coastal Georgia, stunningly citing the text of the wedding march, in the original German, as a prelude to a lynching, and mapping the departure of Wagner's swan-knight onto African American folklore of a return to Africa.[6] This program is made explicit in the final chapter where he establishes an identity between an African American "sorrow song" and a German folk-song, as if the two peoples suddenly became one in the spirit of music. "A black women said of the song, 'It can't be sung without a full heart and a troubled spirit.' The same voice sings here that sings in the German folk-song: 'Jetzt geh i' an's Brunele, trink aber net.'"[7] While the narrator of *Mario and the Magician*, whose credibility Mann calls into question, insists on separating the brilliant light of Africa from the romantic depth of Germany, DuBois—and in this, at least, surely quite consistent with Mann—maps a dialectical identity of romantic sensibility and enlightenment critique, a utopian point where Germany and Africa suddenly converge.

Against this backdrop of Mann, DuBois, and their constellation of Africa and Germany, the topics of the essays collected in this volume address varied aspects of Afro-German history, culture, and identity. Yet despite Mann and DuBois, despite their respective explorations of the interpenetration of what might have appeared as disparate categories in a complex social and political mediation, the contemporary emergence of Afro-Germans as a self-conscious community as well as a topic of public and scholarly recognition entails a considerable departure from past assumptions: especially in how we think about Germany but perhaps also in how we envision the African diaspora as well. To understand how and why this change came about is no easy task, nor does this volume offer a single definitive answer. Yet, as this volume shows, it is certainly the case that a central role was played, and continues to be played by the Afro-Germans themselves, the individuals of African descent in Germany, who have actively forged their own identity. Parts of this story are told in this book, and important questions are raised. Is identity invented or is it a consequence of objective conditions? Does it build on traditions or even an "essence," or, alternatively does it develop through opposition and the recognition of "others?" How do the individual self-understandings of isolated individuals coalesce into a no-longer-fragmented subjectivity? And what relationship does this new, or newly articulated collective identity have to the individuals who see themselves as part of it?

These issues, obviously, have a direct pertinence to the Afro-German population, but these are also questions that are absolutely crucial to how we conceptualize history or cultural criticism as scholarly enterprises that might tell us something about how people anywhere live and how they think about their lives. To focus solely on one aspect of the Afro-Germans that highlights a fundamental question of method: shall we think of this identity as an "invention," a new articulation by contemporary actors defining for themselves and others a new role within the larger social context—or is this primarily a matter of an objectively given historical condition, structures inherited from the past that define the conditions of possibility of any "individual" life? To argue the former implies a considerable malleability in individuals' self-understanding, while to argue the latter restricts the capacity of innovation. Presumably the answer lies in between, a balance of invention and history. Yet can one even speak of a single Afro-German history? Consider the descendants of African American soldiers, or African students, or, in the past, colonized Africans from the German empire, or, further in the past, the African Americans who came to Germany from North America with the returning Hessian mercenaries in the Revolutionary War. Is a single narrative possible, or should we hope for little more than an anthology of separate stories? The underlying question involves the relationship between identity and temporality, how subjective understandings in the present inherit the experience of the past, just as the inhabitants of this present redefine their past as memory. It is possible that the DuBoisian legacy of pan-Africanism is compelling enough, due perhaps to its own subterranean Bismarckianism, to weld the various legacies into a single account, an imaginable Afro-German nationalism. The question for historians and cultural critics, however, would be whether that amalgamation could be plausible in light of the lived diversity of experience.

Yet the standing of any identity, including Afro-German, is not only a matter of its internal logic and self-definition; it exists as well in a context of alternative identities that set limits or encourage new representations. The seminal volume *Farbe bekennen* appeared in 1986 and represents something of the founding document of modern Afro-German identity. But the vicissitudes of Afro-German identity and certainly the attention it has received in scholarship as well as in popular culture have just as much to do with the process named by the date 1989. The opening of the Berlin Wall, the unification of Germany, the collapse of the Soviet Empire, and the larger transition toward a (gradual) European unification have reframed the discussion of German nationhood and the standing of minorities within it. The dramatic political turn of 1989 involved an exploration of democracy and nationality: the change in the slogans in the East German demonstrations from "*Wir sind das Volk*," a call for popular sovereignty against the authoritarian bureaucracy, to "*Wir sind ein Volk*," an assertion of national integrity against the division of the Cold War. Whether the events in 1989 and 1990 can genuinely be attributed to a reassertion of a fundamental national cohesion—as Willi Brandt put it famously, "Es wächst zusammen, was zusammengehört"—will be scrutinized by future historians. Alternatively, one could well imagine that the primary issue was the collapse of an authoritarian regime, and only secondarily a reestablishment of national essence. In any case, the nationalist interpretation appeared to hold sway in the initial post-Wall years, just as a wave of anti-foreigner sentiment led to tragic violence and far-right agitation. Did this xenophobia confirm the anxiety that a unified Germany, because unified and, perhaps also, because German, would necessarily be hostile to ethnic or national difference? A heightened attention to these issues ensued, at least in the public sphere of the press and, gradually, in scholarship as well. More importantly, however, there was also a public response to the xenophobia, and that public rejection of *Ausländerfeindlichkeit*, typically carried more vibrantly by popular demonstrations than by the political leadership, pointed to a different, nonparochial German sensibility. A unified and democratic and increasingly European Germany was coming to grips with the importance of a differentiated understanding of what it could mean to be German. In the context of several other discussions relevant to identity diversification—the reform of the citizenship laws, the growing prominence of Turkish-German literature, the discussion of the Holocaust Memorial in Berlin, and the relationship of Germany to Europe—the new willingness to imagine "German" in different ways included the growing attention to Afro-Germans. After a decade of unification, it now appears that the consequence of the seemingly nationalistic "*Wir sind ein Volk*" does not at all necessarily include an assertion of homogeneity and hostility to difference. The one people that the Germans may have become in terms of national sovereignty and political legality has demonstrably made room for a multicultural range of self-definitions.

A primary historical component of Afro-German studies involves the history of German colonialism, especially in Africa, and in the context of the broader European colonialist period. Until recently, German colonialism was treated as a marginal phenomenon, a minor component of the Wilhelmine period. However scholarship, particularly in the United States, has begun to thematize colonialism and "postcolonial" issues, and this has come to include German colonialism as well. Important investigations of various aspects of German colonialism have recently appeared.[8] To be sure, the German colonial era, 1884–1919, was short-lived compared to the history of overseas colonization associated with England, France, and other European powers; nor was this colonial period the first encounter between Germany and Africa. It was nonetheless an important one and is very much linked to discussions about the character of German racial thinking and imperialism in the twentieth century. In particular, the question of the relationship between colonial race policies, including the war of destruction waged against the Hereros in today's Namibia, and the race policies and genocide of the Third Reich remains unanswered. It was of course none other than DuBois who insisted on thinking of European colonialism as not marginal but, on the contrary, quite central to European politics and therefore a prime source for the First World War. Was it a source of the Second as well, including the Holocaust? We are only now beginning to understand the complex fates of Afro-Germans in the Third Reich. Essays in this volume help elucidate the interplay of colonialism, racism, and genocide.

To study German colonialism today requires asking comparative questions: the similarities with and differences from the other European colonialisms. Surely the relatively brief period of German colonialism must be a relevant factor in the overall estimation of the period and its legacies. Moreover it seems likely that the logic of universalism that underwrote French and, to a somewhat smaller extent, British colonialism was even less operative in German colonialism. Were there cultural consequences? Meanwhile larger questions about colonialism in Germany remain to be posed: the relationship to Russian colonialism in the guise of the Soviet Empire—that is, the colonization of Germany itself, if that is the proper term. And what of the German "colonization" of Eastern Europe, stretching back into the Middle Ages? While it is urgent to frame the study of Afro-Germans in relationship to German colonialism of the decades around 1900, we should also not lose sight of larger and longer histories of global expansions and relations of international power.

Finally, the study of Afro-Germans is lodged in the complex terrain of the relationship between Germany and the United States. This is true on multiple levels. Multiculturalism in Germany cannot be understood solely as an American import, since it reflects the genuine diversity of German society; nonetheless much of the conceptualization and theory of multiculturalism was indeed part of a cultural transfer from North America. Similarly, the Afro-German movement toward self-consciousness, growing very much out of local roots, received important influences from the U.S., particularly through the inspiring visit of Audre Lourde. Historically, the Afro-German population has important connections to the presence of the American military, and ideologically, "race" is a field in which German-American relations have been played out in multiple ways. The American perception of an insular and racist Germany, requiring democratic tutelage from across the Atlantic, confronts the postwar German disdain for the treatment of African Americans in the United States. This dynamic is the continuation of the problematic identified in DuBois's self-positioning between German and the United States: by defining a position outside the United States, he was able to gain a critical distance.

The conclusion to draw is surely not that Afro-Germans are merely functions of a political competition between the United States and Germany. That sort of approach, blind to the integrity of lived subjectivity, is too reductionistic and cannot yield an adequately complex description. But neither should one imagine that this discussion of Afro-Germans takes place outside of a multifaceted totality of politics and power. The essays in this volume do justice to that complexity by taking up multiple aspects of the Afro-German condition. This is an important step in understanding this vital component of German and pan-African history and culture. At the same time, the contributions to the volume amount to a set of exemplary studies that shed light on the complexities of identity in the contemporary world and more generally on the matrices of subjectivity and structures, tradition and invention. Afro-German Studies can tell us much about Germans and about the African diaspora, but it can also raise urgent questions about identity formation with ramifications for the humanities in general.

Notes

1. Thomas Mann, *Death in Venice and Seven Other Stories* (New York: Vintage, 1989), 138–39.

2. W. E. B. DuBois, *The Autobiography of W. E. B. DuBois: A Soliloquy on Viewing My Life from the Last Decade of Its First Century* (New York: International Publishers, 1968), 126.

3. Ibid., 168–69.

4. Cf. DuBois, *Autobiography*, 183.

5. W. E. B. DuBois, "The World War and the Color Line," *The Crisis*, November 1914, 28–30.

6. See my "DuBois and Wagner: Race, Nation, and Culture between Germany and the United States," *German Quarterly* 70, no. 2 (1997): 123–35.

7. W. E. B. DuBois, *The Souls of Black Folk* (New York: Bantam, 1989), 184.

8. Cf. Marcia Klotz, "White Women and the Dark Continent: Gender and Sexuality in German Colonial Discourse from the Sentimental Novel to the Fascist Film," Ph.D. diss. (Stanford University, 1994); Benjamin Nicholas Lawrence, "Most Obedient Servants: the Politics of Language in German Colonial Togo," *Cahiers d'Etudes Africains* 159 (2000): 489–524; Suzanne Zantop, *Colonial Fantasies: Conquest, Family, and Nation in Precolonial Germany, 1770–1870* (Durham: Duke University Press, 1997); and my *Enlightenment or Empire: Colonial Discourse in German Culture* (Lincoln: University of Nebraska Press, 1998).

INTRODUCTION

Patricia Mazón and Reinhild Steingröver

Historical Overview

A gifted *raconteur*, Hans J. Massaquoi has lived an adventurous life. Born in 1926 as the son of a Liberian father and a German mother, he grew up in Hamburg, where he survived the war despite several close calls. Afterwards he emigrated briefly to Liberia and then to the U.S., where he made a career for himself as editor of the black magazine *Ebony*. His 1999 memoir, *Destined to Witness*, is being marketed by Harper Collins in the U.S. under the rubric of "Holocaust Studies." The publicity flyer announces the story of "a young black child growing up in Nazi Germany" and hails Massaquoi's "account of surviving the Holocaust." Massaquoi's book was also a bestseller in its German translation, which appeared as "*Neger, Neger, Schornsteinfeger!*" The German title literally translates as "Nigger, Nigger, Chimneysweep!" and sounds like a childhood taunt that Massaquoi likely endured. While the English title emphasizes Massaquoi's survival of the Nazi period, the German title points up his isolation as a black child in supposedly "Aryan" Germany. The larger question here is where Massaquoi's story belongs. Is it a Holocaust narrative, or does it belong to the growing body of literature produced by Afro-Germans? While both readings are possible, Massaquoi's story shows how Afro-German experience itself is ambiguous and open to multiple interpretations.

Contact between Germans and Africans goes back not decades but centuries. Africans were first brought to Europe beginning in the 1400s as living curiosities. In Germany they were mostly slaves, court servants, and military band drummers. Best known among these early African Germans was the eighteenth-century philosopher Wilhelm Anton Amo, who taught at the University of Halle and was brought from Ghana as a small boy. Usually blacks lived scattered across Germany, but in the eighteenth century there was at least one German village with exclusively black inhabitants, the

1

"Mohrenkolonie Mulang" near Kassel. After Germany became a unified nation in 1871, it acquired the colonies of German Southwest Africa, German East Africa, Togo, and Cameroon in 1884–85 but lost them at the end of World War I. The number of German settlers, while never as high as colonial enthusiasts might have wished, peaked at twenty thousand, and a small number of mixed-race unions took place.[1]

In the aftermath of World War I, the French occupied the Rhineland using colonial African troops, leading to several hundred children born of German mothers and African fathers. In a racist public campaign against the so-called "Black Horror on the Rhine," these children became known as "Rhineland bastards" in the 1920s. During the Weimar Republic, the government registered them in special lists later used by the Nazis to identify them as targets for forced sterilization. After World War II, a sizable number of children were born to African American soldiers stationed in West Germany and German mothers. Other Afro-Germans were African refugees, or their children, granted political asylum in West Germany. During the Cold War, both the German Democratic Republic (GDR, or East Germany) and the Federal Republic of Germany (FRG, or West Germany) hosted significant numbers of African students, some of whom stayed on; a few of the men founded families with German women. In West Germany in the 1980s, black Germans formed the "Black German Initiative" (Initiative Schwarze Deutsche or ISD) and an independent women's organization, ADEFRA, to fight for their rights.

Today Germany contains the largest and most diverse group of Afro-Germans ever, numbering approximately five hundred thousand out of a population of eighty million. This estimate includes persons of North African descent as well as those from sub-Saharan Africa; also part of this tally are those of mixed German and African or African American parentage.[2] Nevertheless, German society still sees them largely as "foreigners," assuming they are either African or African American but never German.

This volume seeks to address two interrelated sets of questions surrounding the lives and experience of Afro-Germans over the past century. The first group of questions has to do with how images of Afro-Germans have changed over time. Here the shifting ideas of race and nation in Germany are of paramount importance. In many respects these inquiries reveal more about (white) Germans than about Afro-Germans themselves. The second group of questions concerns how Afro-Germans have sought and seek to define themselves. We will explore the tension between individual identity and the attempt to build community in what has historically been a highly fragmented group.

Before the Enlightenment, Africans were regarded as a novelty in the German lands. By the late nineteenth century, when Germany had been unified as a state and began to acquire its colonies, the encounter between Germans and Africans took place in a new landscape, literally and metaphorically. New, scientifically legitimated ideas about race had formed, and Africans landed at the bottom of the racial hierarchy constructed by nineteenth-century thinkers. As Pascal Grosse has argued, at the end of the nineteenth century, Germany was in the process of transforming itself from a society based on citizenship to one based on race.[3] Much scholarly attention has focused on the role of Jews as the excluded "other" in this transformation; less attention has been given to the ways in which Africans also figured as the "other."

From this point on, Afro-Germans were seen through the prism of a racialized German national project. This was the backdrop for the debates over the legality of mixed marriages in the colonies and the outraged response to the mixed-race children fathered by French occupation forces after the World War I. During the Nazi period, the sterilization of these children was planned so as not to further "contaminate" the "Aryan" national body. After World War II, Germans on both sides of the Wall modified their views on race somewhat. West Germans switched to what Heidi Fehrenbach calls a liberal discourse of race, while East Germans layered socialist ideology on top of the old ideas. Yet while each German state sought a way of coming to terms with the Nazi past, the legacy of German colonialism and attitudes about Africans went largely unexplored. It has only been in the last decade's discussions about the possibility of a multicultural Germany that a discursive space has been opened to, and by, Afro-Germans individually and as a group. Ironically, even attempts to count the numbers of Afro-Germans have been complicated by the legacy of German racial ideology. As a reaction to the racial classification schemes of the Nazi period, the census no longer lists race as a category.[4]

The self-definition of Afro-Germans began with the search for a name. Before the 1980s, choices were limited to terms with heavy historical and political baggage. *Mischling*, or "half-breed," was clinically precise but carried echoes of a Nazi past. "Mulatto" was an even older historical label with associations left over from the days of slavery. *Farbig*, or "colored," was an improvement over these two but still somewhat vague. The coining of the term "Afro-German," on the other had, was conceived of as a deliberate positive and political act. As May Opitz (later Ayim) and Katharina Oguntoye wrote, "We want to propose 'Afro-German' in opposition to more commonly used names like 'half-breed,' 'mulatto,' or 'colored,' as an attempt to define ourselves instead of being defined by others."[5]

Agreeing on a name, however, proved only half the battle. Which individuals would choose to use it, and why? Here is where the gap between the Afro-German individual and community opened up. For many who grew up as the only mixed-race children in their area, the decision as adults to identify as Afro-German and seek out other Afro-Germans was a highly personal one, complicated by all sorts of factors, including the continuing gap between East and West Germans. Since the 1980s, the opportunities for Afro-Germans to affiliate with groups like the ISD has led to the emergence of a more visible Afro-German community that values the connection to an African diaspora that Audre Lorde once encouraged. Yet the vast majority of Afro-Germans are not politically active in this group, and many might not identify themselves as members of the African diaspora.

In some ways, Afro-Germans would now appear to occupy a paradoxical position. On the one hand, the rest of German society views them as an undifferentiated, monolithic "other." On the other hand, they may appear upon closer examination to be a "postmodern" minority group, in the sense that the group itself is composed of individuals from very diverse backgrounds and may have little in common, both in their daily lives and in terms of their connections to Germany and Africa. In today's liberal democracies, minority groups claim a place in society based, in part, on a sense of shared history. Yet even more so than most histories, that of Afro-Germans is sharply fragmented, full of ruptures and discontinuities. The African colonial experience was ended and the ties to Germany mostly severed; the whole episode remained as an afterimage on the German national imagination. The children of color left behind by the French at the end of World War I were sterilized by the Nazis. The "brown babies" born of black American G.I.s and West German women represented a new beginning after 1945 but often came of age in isolation from each other. The African students and political refugees who joined them are coming directly from a rich community life rooted in Africa. The challenge for those who would build the Afro-German community today comes from two directions, within and without. Wider pressures and prejudices in the rest of German society may help Afro-Germans forge a common position. To sustain this common identity, however, Afro-Germans must create themselves in an act of will, like any group, by engaging the past and connecting a history that, at first glance, may appear to consist solely of the isolated episodes just mentioned.

Afro-German Culture and Politics Today

On June 12, 2000, Alberto Adriano, a native of Mozambique who had lived in Germany for twelve years, was brutally attacked and killed by a right-wing youth gang in Dessau, a city in the former East Germany. His crime, as Afro-German hip-hop star Adé would later sing, was to be in the "wrong place, [at the] wrong time." This attack was only one of thousands of racist hate crimes against members of visible ethnic minorities in Germany since national unification in 1990. One response of Afro-German artists was to found the all-star band Brothers Keepers, which produced a single CD and music video in memory of Adriano entitled "Adriano (Letzte Warnung)" (Adriano [Last Warning]), released in the summer of 2001. The song's explicitly political lyrics charge white Germans with indifference regarding his murder and demand a genuine antiracist commitment from politicians as well as the full prosecution of those guilty of hate crimes. Adé sums up (in English):

> Seventh Sunday after Easter
> A fellow brother was executed in his prime
> Adriano's crime: wrong place, wrong time
> I can still hear the voice of anguish fading through the night,
> It was an unfair fight!
> Three versus one, God they caught him by surprise
> Xenophobia's on the rise, victims get dehumanised
> Procedures standardised as the land's Germanised
> Names become numbers while death is trivialised.[6]

The meaning of the CD's title, "Adriano (Letzte Warnung)," which sold 250,000 copies in the few months after its release, is explained in the lyric by rap star Xavier Naidoo: "This is something like a last warning/ Because our strike back has been long in planning" (Dies ist so was wie eine letzte Warnung/ Denn unser Rückschlag ist längst in Planung). In spite of this pledge for revenge, Brothers Keepers as an organization has so far worked mainly to defend victims of racist attacks or government discrimination as well as to raise awareness among the group's many fans. Band member Adé stated this goal clearly:

> People here [in Germany] have . . . to accept the diversity of existing lifestyles. We want to sensitize people and finally speak for ourselves. The victims are always spoken for.

> Die Menschen hier [in Deutschland] müssen . . . die Vielfältigkeiten der existierenen Lebensweisen akzeptieren und sich mit ihnen auseinandersetzen. Wir wollen die Leute sensibilisieren und auch endlich für uns selbst sprechen. Die Opfer werden immer bevormundet.[7]

Thus Brothers Keepers' lyrics describing oppression and "othering" are often followed by statements of refusal to tolerate more discrimination and declarations of resistance. In addition to these political lyrics and videos, Brothers Keepers has also organized fund-raising concerts and uses its website to disseminate information on new antiracist work and initiatives. In 2002 members of Brothers Keepers and a closely affiliated group, Sisters Keepers, an all-female Afro-German pop/rap band, toured a number of East German secondary schools to meet with students as well as refugees and antiracism activists in cities such as Rostock, Pirna, and Prenzlau. Endorsed by the president of the German parliament, Wolfgang Thierse, the musicians had to rely on police protection to fend off disturbances by right-wing youth protesters during the meetings with students and fans in Prenzlau, sixty miles north of Berlin.

A few months after "Adriano (Letzte Warnung)," Sisters Keepers produced their own single CD and music video, "Liebe und Verstand" (Love and Understanding). The video, released in December 2001, shows a predominantly black Germany, featuring black cab drivers, supermarket clerks, pedestrians, and subway riders. In a climactic moment, a police car drives up to a group of Afro-German women at a subway stop, and two Afro-German policemen emerge and check the identity papers of the sole white passenger. This reversal of the everyday reality of Afro-Germans, which May Ayim has described as being always visible and invisible at the same time, powerfully underscores the song's message:

> It's great to see you
> Come give us your hand
> We, too, were born here
> And yet foreign in our land
> We can really change things
> If we love and understand.

> Es ist schön dich zu sehen
> Komm reich uns deine Hand
> Auch wir sind hier geboren
> Und trotzdem fremd in unserem Land
> Wir können etwas ändern
> Mit Liebe und Verstand.

In contrast to the confrontational lyrics of Brothers Keepers, the emphasis here is conciliatory, with a focus on the possibility of change if blacks and whites work together. Yet the tone and message of this album raise questions about the gender politics and marketing strategies pursued by distribution companies that prefer to promote female singers in the roles of mediators and peacemakers. The participation by members of Sisters Keepers in the above-described community outreach activities underscores their involvement with antiracist activism (which, incidentally, no one would expect from a white pop band). The question raised here is how much control the artists have over their own self-presentation and how much this is influenced by the music industry's need for happy, conciliatory entertainment by beautiful women.

In September 2001 musician and actor Tyron Ricketts released his CD, music video, and short film, all entitled *Afro-deutsch* (Afro-German). The latter aired in cinemas and on television stations across Germany and was also shown at the 2002 Sundance Film Festival. The film describes Ricketts's autobiographical experience of growing up as the only black child in a small Austrian town and recounts not only the discrimination he experienced there but also his later success in show business. Ricketts's film shows him being chased by a gang of youths through a maze of streets and subway platforms. The scene clearly makes the point that being Afro-Austrian means being unsafe on the streets of one's own country. But his song lyrics also point to the media success that hip-hop artists have experienced more recently in Germany. Ricketts commented sarcastically on the "advantage" of being black, singing, "Yesterday still a bimbo—today even a movie star" (Wer gestern noch der Bimbo war—ist sogar Moviestar).[8] Nevertheless, he aims at a large mainstream audience with his message of "awareness without judgment," as he puts it. For Ricketts this means that preaching antiracism from the moral pulpit will be less effective than trying to reach black and white audiences through popular culture, including Afro-German hip-hop. Brothers Keepers star Adé points to the effectiveness of this strategy when he assesses the increasing recognition of Afro-Germans in Germany by noting that mainstream commercial television stations like RTL-2 are now using the term Afro-German on the air.[9] *Afro-deutsch* and the significant media attention that the film and CD received is yet another example of the quickly growing presence of Afro-German artists and writers in Germany.

Afro-German identity is positioned positively in these examples of cultural production. While pointing clearly to a long legacy of isolation and oppression, these hip-hop lyrics and videos manifest a new self-confidence, and they have found an audience among young Germans. Hip-hop, with its global appeal and roots in African American culture, seems a particularly appropriate medium by which to communicate this sense of identity, earning it the title of "CNN of the street."[10] Adé has described the choice of hip-hop as an almost accidental one but goes on to state that the encounter with this global phenomenon has allowed Afro-German musicians to create their own sense of identity in Germany: "Many of us came to hip-hop because it was the only place where we found a reflection of ourselves. Now we have internalized this and create our own identity within it."[11] Interestingly and somewhat provocatively for left-wing German political activists, Afro-German hip-hop artists have not only made the connection to the African diaspora (Brothers Keepers Britain, Brothers Keepers Jamaica) but have also chosen to insist on their Germanness. As Sekou puts it: "Afro-Germans were among the first to bring a new German consciousness and patriotism forward by proclaiming: I am German."[12] Adé adds, "We're stealing the issue of patriotism from the right wing by saying, we are proud to be a part of this nation, with all the responsibility that that carries."[13]

Nevertheless, some critics have observed the inherent dangers of misreading the increased media attention as signs of progress towards an increased awareness and acceptance of German society as multiethnic and multiracial. The writer and cultural critic Hito Steyerl comments:

> The mainstream culture industry is currently including select contributions by second-generation immigrants who are beginning to be noticed by the German public after having been excluded thus far. In my opinion this is a form of neo-imperialist multiculturalism. The motto of such cultural globalization is: culture yes, rights for immigrants, no.[14]

Ricketts confirms this assessment by discussing the difficulty of dealing with radio hosts, whose concern to keep their audiences happy makes them wary of overly political lyrics. For the same reason, record companies might not release a specific song as a single but tuck it away on a longer CD. Ricketts even reflects on this in his song "Afro-Deutsch," when he says, "I wonder whether radio stations will play this song, even though it is uncomfortable" (Ob Sender diesen Song wohl spielen, obwohl er unbequem ist).[15] In order to avoid such exploitation of minority culture through marketing , Ricketts points to his own modeling agency for black models and actors in Germany that refuses to sign their talents up for racially stereotypical parts in film and television, for example, as drug dealers. The founding of the independent music label Red-Black-Green by

Afrob and Sékou is a move in the same direction. Such a "re-politicization" of Afro-German hip-hop seems especially timely considering the apparent rise in right-wing bands (hip-hop as well as punk and other styles) and their influence on mainstream youth culture.

But as the example of the "Adriano (Letzte Warnung)" CD showed, some Afro-German artists speak out not just for their own rights as German citizens but also express solidarity with immigrants, refugees, and guestworkers, all of whom live in Germany today without the possibility of becoming citizens in the first place. Consequently these Afro-Germans have participated in the civil rights initiative Kanak Attak (literally, attack of the *Kanaken*, a derogatory name for dark-skinned foreigners), which debuted publicly in 2001 in Berlin with a performance about the history of immigrants' resistance to discrimination in Germany. Mobilizing immigrants, asylum seekers, refugees, and minority Germans as well as white Germans committed to antiracist work, the group staged a second national meeting in 2002 in Berlin's Volksbühne theater. Unlike earlier activist organizations, Kanak Attak has only a loose organizational structure, operates locally, and rejects any form of identity politics. As its manifesto states, "Kanak Attak does not ask for your passport or ancestry but rejects the question of passport and ancestry."[16] Kanak Attak thus works against concepts such as multicultural integration because it signifies assimilation and selective integration into the dominant white German society [*Leitkultur*] as well as the loss of individual cultural practices, languages, and traditions. Instead of promoting identity politics and pride in ethnic difference, for example, Kanak Attak sees itself as working toward a concrete political goal: the creation of antiracist awareness as well as a pro-active rejection of all forms of domination and discrimination. In a series of panels, films, performance art, and workshops, this organization challenges dominant culture with its own tools, such as the media. Thus one initiative is Kanak TV, a form of activism or protest that turns the camera (gaze) on white Germans and asks them questions usually reserved for the perceived "other": "Where are you from? When will you go back? Why do you keep to yourselves?"

While the common experience of racism that discriminates irrespective of citizenship unites Afro-Germans, immigrants, and refugees, the question of identity politics remains a difficult one. As Stuart Hall has pointed out, "The margins could not speak up without first grounding themselves somewhere."[17] It is precisely such a self-confident grounding that the ISD among others has achieved over the past fifteen years. But the grounding is also echoed by Afro-German hip-hop artists who see themselves as both

German and as part of the African diaspora. Kanak Attak's rejection of identity politics in the form of hyphenated identities or ethnic difference is based on the experience of the racist exclusion of anyone caught outside the white German and secular Christian dominant culture. It is an attempt to avoid the "identity trap," as Steyerl calls it,[18] which functions either to exclude the minority person or to assign him or her to the position of permanent "other." From such a position, the "other" is then occasionally invited for "authentic" performances of multicultural folklore. Thus Kanak Attack argues against the concept of "integration" because it is understood as the adaptable tool of a dominant culture that determines who can be integrated and who cannot. Moreover, integration challenges the "other" to adapt to the majority culture or *Leitkultur,* however vaguely defined that might be.

Kanak Attak's rejection of identity politics and integration will remain a challenge for its own political work. Its manifesto states this clearly:

> The real hierarchies of social existences and subject positions cannot be easily erased or playfully ignored. All constructions are just not the same. The project thus finds itself in the midst of irreconcilable contradictions in regard to the relationship among representation, difference and the designation of ethnic identities.[19]

But these contradictions might also be an effective form of resistance to the hegemony of dominant culture. As Popoola has put it, "Only one's own designations of the self can create an identity. They represent explicitly the reality and normality of the subject."[20]

The Afro-Germans who have participated in this kind of grassroots activity have joined those minority groups who live in Germany without the legal advantage of citizenship in demanding a reform of the citizenship laws as well as the introduction of immigration regulations. Although a few prominent Afro-Germans have achieved visibility in the mainstream media (for instance, as hosts of talk and music shows), their histories remain unknown to most, while their skin color continues to mark them as outsiders. Afro-German hip-hop artists are attempting to use the mainstream media to raise awareness of and instill a sense of normality regarding a multi-ethnic Germany in their young audiences. The new weekly television show A.B. TV (Afro Berlin Television), which was launched on the Berlin public access channel in January 2003, the ISD-sponsored youth magazine *Blite—Black and White* for black youth, which began publication in 2002, and the informative website www.cyberNomads.edu are further manifestations of the increasing presence of Afro-Germans in the media. Joining Kanak Attak in its call for action against identity politics does not devalue the work of Afro-German organizations over the past decade. But it does signal a broadening of the discussion about race and racism in contemporary German society and a radicalized consciousness among younger generations of minorities.

A more intimate look at a younger generation of Afro-German authors comes in the form of two recent autobiographies. In 2003 the more mainstream publisher Rowohlt jumped on the bandwagon and published the popular *Schokoladenkind* (Chocolate Child) by Abini Zöllner.[21] The book is noteworthy for several reasons: in the already small group of book-length Afro-German autobiographies, it is the first by an East German and Jewish Afro-German woman. Moreover, Zöllner is a generation younger than the women around Ika Hügel-Marshall and May Ayim. Unlike the authors represented in *Farbe bekennen* (Showing Our Colors), Zöllner's account of her life is written in a very light style that rarely pauses to reflect on identity issues specific to her skin color. Instead, the emphasis is on the story of her growing up and her search for happiness, friendship, and love. In her roles as model, dancer, television host, and journalist, Zöllner seems perfectly comfortable in her very public persona, an experience very much unlike Hügel-Marshall's in her autobiography, *Invisible Woman*. Zöllner does not linger on her victimization even when she relates racist experiences in the GDR. Unlike the Afro-German women of an earlier generation from the West, Zöllner does not credit her struggle to overcome racism to a network of Afro-Germans or to the larger African diaspora. Instead, her continuously optimistic narrative emphasizes a life philosophy of overcoming all odds with the strong support of her mother and friends instead of politicizing individual experiences. The book's title *Schokoladenkind*, for example, refers to Zöllner's mother's affectionate name for her daughter and is not discussed in the context of the title's potentially derogatory implications. In the second case, Thomas Usleber has written one of the few autobiographies by Afro-German men, *Die Farben unter meiner Haut* (The Colors Under My Skin, 2002).[22] Unlike Zöllner, Usleber's main focus is his identity as a black German and his increasingly estranged relationship with his mother and brother over his fight to overcome hurdles of race and class. Throughout the book Usleber, born in 1960, ponders the connections among national identity, racism, exclusion, and the individual's struggle to educate his fellows as well as to define himself in a positive way.

In a different medium, Angelina Maccarone's film *Alles wird gut* (Everything Will Be Fine, 1997) explicitly focuses on identity, with an Afro-German lesbian heroine reaching out to audiences outside the German or Afro-German context; the film was celebrated at gay and lesbian film festivals around the world. In all these cases, institutional support by publishers, universities, television and radio stations, and foundations was crucial to the process of bringing texts by black German authors to a wider audience. Orlanda Press, based in Berlin, should be mentioned here as an important early source of support.

Scholarship about Afro-Germans

These examples of a thriving Afro-German cultural production would have appeared unthinkable in 1986, when the publication of *Farbe bekennen* (Showing Our Colors) marked one of the earliest cases of Afro-Germans coming together to comment on their situation. When surveying the literature on Afro-German history and culture, we cannot overestimate the importance of this collection of scholarly research on black Germans, autobiographical accounts by different generations of Afro-German women, and poetry. Not only does the book present for the first time in print a diverse range of Afro-German women's voices, but it also signals the emerging cultural and political (self-) consciousness of Afro-German women as expressed in the designation "Afro-German" itself. In her contribution to this volume Anne Adams, who translated *Farbe bekennen* into English in 1992, explains the impact of these women's encounters with African American poet Audre Lorde in Berlin.[23]

The consciousness-raising impact of *Farbe bekennen* on feminist circles in Germany was evident in the publication of special issues on Afro-Germans by the academic journal *beiträge zur feministischen theorie und praxis* in 1990 under the title "Divided Feminisms" as well as by the newly founded East German journal *Weibblick* in 1993. Both special issues contain essays by Afro-German women, who write about the life-long discrimination against blacks in Germany in general and within feminist organizations in particular.[24] These articles give voice to the long silence that has enveloped Afro-German women and kept them isolated from each other as well as from German mainstream society. Similarly, the 1999 volume *Aufbrüche. Kulturelle Produktionen von Migrantinnen, Schwarze und jüdische Frauen in Deutschland*, edited by Cathy Gelbin, Kader Konuk, and Peggy Piesche, also illustrates the complex process of interaction among women of different ethnic backgrounds and the need for antiracism work among whites.[25] But the decade after *Farbe bekennen* also produced a number of Afro-German writers who no longer focused primarily on the critique of the dominant culture but instead on the search for their own identity, which is positively described and nourished by a new sense of community, as Peggy Piesche explains in *Aufbrüche*. In the work of Afro-German writers such as May Ayim, Olumide Popoola, and Guy St. Louis, Piesche sees a paradigm shift in their focus on defining for themselves a positive cultural identity in the African Diaspora. Piesche notes:

> While the texts of the first generation of black German women writers were still strongly influenced by their experience of "otherness". . . this process does not need to be recreated in more recent artistic reworkings of a concept of identity. These newer texts go a step further in acknowledging an everyday identity for the subject.[26]

The articulation of an identity defined by its own self-confidence and celebration of its multiple constitutive aspects is not limited to race but includes class and sexuality. Such a more fully developed concept of identity construction overcomes simplistic notions of "community," but it can be also be a complicating factor in practical terms, as Popoola describes regarding her difficulty in finding a publisher for an anthology about queer women of color in Germany entitled *Talking Home*.[27] While there might have been interest among progressive publishers in producing a volume on Afro-Germans in general, the combination of Afro-German and homosexuality proved a stumbling block in marketing the manuscript. Ultimately, the book was published by Amsterdam's Blue Moon Press.

In the United States, scholars in German Studies initially focused on examining the fascination of white German society with the mere idea of blacks. In 1982 Sander Gilman was one of the first to investigate the historical image of blacks in eighteenth- and nineteenth-century German literature and philosophy. His poignantly titled study *On Blackness Without Blacks* helps to explain the construction of race in the German national discussion at a time when relatively few blacks actually lived in Germany.[28] Gilman's work, as well as the later anthology by Grimm and Hermand, *Blacks and German Culture*, focus mainly on precolonial times, when the absence of blacks in Germany makes this sustained fascination of German writers all the more revealing.[29]

More recently, scholarly attention in the U.S. has shifted from a white fascination with imaginary blacks to "an investigation of German society as a history not of blackness without blacks but a history of blackness with blacks" and thus a focus on the twentieth century, as Tina Campt, Pascal Grosse, and Yara-Colette Lemke Muñiz de Faria write in "Blacks, Germans, and the Politics of Imperial Imagination, 1920–60."[30] This important essay highlights the intersection between fictive images of blacks in German political discourse and their social reality during the colonial period (1884–1918), the Weimar Republic, the Third Reich, and finally the immediate post-World War II period. These three scholars represent a younger generation which has in recent years pushed beyond the study of German colonial policy to its links—scientific, cultural, and political—with the broader culture of the metropole.

The important scholarship by Fatima El-Tayeb has significantly revised our understanding of the long history of racialized thinking in German scientific and popular discourse. Her study, *Schwarze Deutsche. Der Diskurs um Rasse und nationale Identität 1890–1933*, meticulously analyzes the construction of race in the colonies and in Germany and refutes the notion that there was no racist tradition, in the sense of black-white antagonism, in Germany before the Third Reich. Her contribution to this volume represents a significant excerpt from this research.[31]

Grosse's work has demonstrated the close intersection of colonial politics and discourse on eugenics in Germany that firmly established the notion of the supremacy of the white "race" in general and of the "Germanic race" in particular.[32] This powerful discourse was later used by the Nazis to justify the forced sterilization of Afro-German children between 1937 and 1940. The fate of the so-called "Rhineland bastards," the offspring of black French colonial troops and white German women after World War I, is discussed in detail in Tina Campt's contribution to this volume.

The collaborative essay by Campt, Grosse, and Lemke Muñiz de Faria mentioned above is also noteworthy for its discussion of the fate of Afro-Germans during the Nazi years. Little is available in English in this area, except for the fascinating autobiographical accounts by Doris Reiprich and Erika Ngambi Ul Kuo in *Showing Our Colors* and Susann Samples' 1996 piece, "African Germans in the Third Reich."[33] The authors discuss not only the forced and illegal sterilizations but also the so-called German Africa Shows, in which the Nazis used Afro-Germans as "native performers" of African tribal dances and drumming. The German Africa Shows were designed to maintain public support for the recovery of the lost German colonies but were cancelled when the traveling performers could not be segregated sufficiently from the local population.

Katharina Oguntoye's work provides valuable information on this chapter of Afro-German history and expands the focus from the forced sterilization to the overall persecution of Afro-Germans under the Nazis.[34] The forced sterilizations are also the topic of Reiner Pommerin's seminal 1979 book, which stills represents the only major empirical study on the subject of the Rhineland children.[35] Tina Campt's most recent work on Afro-German experiences in Nazi Germany, *Other Germans*, builds on this research and utilizes oral history as well as archival materials in search of a fuller understanding of this particular experience. This combination of historical analysis, feminist and literary theory, and black German memory narratives produces an innovative method of understanding the effects of Nazi racial policy on Germany's indigenous black population.[36] As such Campt's book not only makes an important contribution to the study of German fascism but also offers provocative new empirical material and theoretical perspectives on the black experience within a European context. Much of the research done by the above-mentioned scholars has recently been summarized by Clarence Lusane in his study, *Hitler's Black Victims: The Historical Experience of Afro-Germans, European Blacks, Africans, and African Americans in the Nazi Era* (2003).[37] Lusane's highly readable book serves as an introduction to the topic for readers who have no access to current German-language research. Unfortunately, his study presents little new information for experts in the field and at times draws mistaken conclusions.

Until recently not much was known about the experiences of the so-called "brown babies" in post-World War II Germany, that is, Afro-German children born to white German mothers and African American fathers. Yara-Colette Lemke Muñiz de Faria's book, *Zwischen Fürsorge und Ausgrenzung* (2002), tells the story of the response by the West German government and churches to the fate of approximately fifteen hundred "brown babies" in 1946.[38] Fearing racist discrimination against these children upon their entry into the public school system, child welfare agencies and church groups attempted to encourage mothers to place their children into special orphanages where they could grow up with "children like themselves." The study analyzes a wealth of official governmental correspondence and newspaper articles as well as the story of one such orphanage.

The work of Carol Aisha Blackshire-Belay has contributed significantly to the growing interdisciplinary interest in the area of Afro-German studies in the U.S. In 1992 Blackshire-Belay edited a special issue of the *Journal of Black Studies*, in 1996 her collection *The African-German Experience* appeared, and in 1998 she coedited, with Leroy Hopkins and David McBride, the conference volume *Crosscurrents: African Americans, Africa, and Germany in the Modern World*.[39] These volumes highlight the broad scope of work currently being undertaken by Germanists, Africanists, and scholars in American Studies. The topics range from colonial encounters to issues of the African diaspora. The pioneering work of Leroy Hopkins deserves special notice. His expertise in African American Studies and German Studies has informed the breadth of his numerous publications, from the experience of Africans in colonial Germany to the image of African Americans in nineteenth-century Germany to contemporary topics in Afro-German Studies.[40] Many of the articles collected in these anthologies debunk the myth of a homogeneously white German society, which supposedly came to terms with the idea of multiculturalism only after the end of World War II.

Much of the literature on Afro-German history and culture is still emerging as we write. Recent conferences on Afro-Germans, such as the one that formed the basis for this book in October 2000 at the State University of New York at Buffalo and a July 2000 meeting at the University of Leipzig, have served as forums for exchange and further discussion. As such, the works mentioned here have been invaluable to the development of this new field of research both in Germany and the U.S. Many more dissertations are now being written thanks to the inspiration that this pioneering work has provided. On the other hand, the need especially for empirical research on the living conditions, legal status, and migration of Afro-Germans over the past 120 years or so has become even more apparent. The history and experiences of Afro-Germans in East Germany, for example, remains to be researched. Peggy Piesche's work in this area is noteworthy because it analyzes the systematic policies of exclusion of black guestworkers and students from mainstream GDR society and the social isolation that Afro-German children in East Germany experienced. As a socialist society, the GDR prided itself on its antiracist foundations and saw no need to reevaluate this myth in light of its citizens' experiences.[41] An encouraging sign of increasing interest in the study of the black diaspora across Europe is represented by the anthology *Blackening Europe: The African American Presence*. Despite its awkward title, the anthology contains work that focuses on Afro-Europeans as well as African Americans, including a well-researched piece by Cathy Covell Waegner on German hip-hop.[42] Contemporary antiracism efforts in German society stand to be benefit from this growing body of research on the long history of crosscultural encounters and oppression.

Overview of the Volume

The essays in this book build on the important works sketched above. Each chapter presents original scholarship based on sources ranging from archival materials to films to interviews with Afro-German writers and activists. While all of the contributors are specialists on German issues, we, as editors, have deliberately chosen to draw on a wide range of disciplines and methodologies, among them history, literature, film studies, women's studies, and Africana studies. With such an approach, we hope to map the rough contours and stake out the boundaries of Afro-German Studies as a field, as alluded to in Russell Berman's preface. Charting such new terrain also means that it is not yet possible to assemble a comprehensive and chronological account of Afro-German history and culture. In fact, this book cannot serve that purpose. While the historical essays take us back into the colonial period around 1890, cultural production by Afro-Germans themselves is a far more recent affair that really begins, as Leroy Hopkins argues, with literature that first appeared in the 1980s, although the example of Louis Brody shows that African actors were a part of the German movie industry before 1920. Rather than present the definitive account of the relationship between Germany and Africa, we intend every chapter to be a point of departure for new questions.

The book is divided into two thematic sections: one focuses on Afro-German history, and the second concentrates on cultural representations and self-representations. Part I, "Afro-Germans in Historical Perspective," ranges over the colonial period, which started in 1884, through the end of World War II in 1945. Three historical essays tell us about the ways Afro-Germans figured in "mainstream" German society by exploring debates in science, colonial policy, and interwar politics. Part II, entitled "Cultural Representations and Self-Representations of Afro-Germans," embraces a variety of approaches to two related questions, namely how Afro-Germans see themselves and how they are seen by the wider German society. Spanning the years from World War I until today, the chapters here touch on film, literature, and community organizations both social and political.

It is precisely the idea that there is no history of German racism directed at blacks (as opposed to the well-documented history of German anti-Semitism) that is challenged in Fatima El-Tayeb's contribution.

El-Tayeb's extensive research shows how a racialized definition of "Germanness" became dominant in the late nineteenth and early twentieth centuries and how a scientifically sanctioned Social Darwinism permeated all levels of society. While focusing her discussion on Imperial Germany, the author persuasively argues that the current wave of hate crimes has deep roots in Germany, most notably in the colonial discourse of racial hierarchies. El-Tayeb's work not only unsettles long-held beliefs about Germany's supposedly minor colonial role but also presents a historiographical critique.

Krista Molly O'Donnell follows this discussion with her investigation of the fate of Afro-German children in German Southwest Africa around 1900. O'Donnell's research shows how increasing pressure was put on mixed African and German couples in the period between 1890 and 1914 in a campaign against miscegenation. This included the invalidation of marriages and the declaration of Afro-German children as illegitimate; these children could also be stripped of their rightful German citizenship. O'Donnell's research raises many pertinent questions about ethnic identity, childrearing, and race that were revisited in Germany in the post-1945 era.

Linking Afro-Germans in the colonies with those born in Germany in the early twentieth century, Tina Campt examines the public discourse regarding mixed racial heritage. The essay shows the connections between the campaigns against mixed marriages in the colonies and the fate of Afro-German children born to white German mothers and French colonial soldiers at the beginning of the Weimar Republic. In both cases, Afro-German populations were perceived as a looming specter that threatened the purity of the German "race." Campt's piece demonstrates that the Nazi persecution of Afro-Germans could already rely on a well-established tradition of racialized self-definitions of white Germans and black others.

Tobias Nagl's biographical sketch of the black actor Louis Brody opens the section on Afro-German culture. Born (Ludwig) M'beebe Mpessa in Cameroon, Brody (1892–1951) established himself as a frequent extra in many well-known Weimar films, sometimes even landing a speaking part. He continued this work during the Nazi years but also worked in a circus, as a wrestler, and as a jazz musician. Nagl's research into Brody's amazing career returns agency to one of the many black workers in Weimar and Nazi films who long remained anonymous and are largely forgotten today. The biographical sketch is framed by the larger question of the function of the "black presence" in the imagination of white German postcolonial audiences.

Following chronologically is Heide Fehrenbach's subtle examination of the cultural representation of the so-called "*Mischlingskinder*" (mixed-race children, that is, children born to white German mothers and African American G.I.s in occupied post-World War II West Germany). Departing from a discussion of the popular 1952 feature film *Toxi, die Geschichte eines Mulattenkindes* (Toxi, the Story of a Mulatto Child), Fehrenbach analyzes the cultural strategies used to construct and confront the "problem" of race and interracial reproduction in post-fascist Germany. She explores the central role accorded Afro-German children, who numbered roughly three thousand by 1950, in racial reeducation and reconstruction in West Germany.

Randall Halle then focuses on a prominent example of Afro-German cultural production: the independent feature film by Angelina Maccarone, *Alles wird gut* (Everything Will Be Fine) from 1997. Based on a script by Fatima El-Tayeb, the film deals with the trials and tribulations of Nabou, a young Afro-German lesbian in Hamburg, who is lovesick and focused on winning back her blue-haired punk ex-girlfriend. While a comedy, the film also poignantly follows the sense of displacement the main characters experience as a result of the everyday racism present in German culture. Halle's reading of this film, as well as his discussion of other Afro-German representations in mainstream German movies of the 1990s, points to the challenges they pose to the presumed homogeneity of German society. In conjunction with the film's preoccupation with race, class, and gender, Halle demonstrates how humor works as a consciousness-raising tool for mainstream audiences.

Leroy Hopkins continues the focus on artistic work by Afro-Germans today by surveying the growing body of literary texts by Afro-German writers since 1986. His discussion introduces readers to the rich and complex poetry of May Ayim, among others, and to the numerous autobiographies recently written by Afro-Germans. His insightful reading of two prominent examples, namely the bestselling *Destined to Witness* by Hans J. Massaquoi and the more complex and commercially less successful *Invisible Woman* by Ika Hügel-Marshall, investigates the texts and their different receptions in Germany. Hopkins argues that the memoir of an Americanized Afro-German (Massaquoi), while less representative of the fate of most Afro-Germans is more palatable today, to mainstream white German audiences.

In the concluding chapter, Anne Adams examines the emergence of an organized Afro-German community since the mid-1980s. Her essay, grounded in both research and her own personal experience, describes the various institutions built by previously isolated and marginalized individuals. Adams argues that community experience is a crucial element in Afro-Germans' identity formation and is connected to interactions with a larger African diaspora linking Africa, black America, the Caribbean, and more historically rooted Afro-European communities. Adams concludes by emphasizing the contributions by Afro-Germans to new ways of imagining the black diaspora.

Looking at Afro-Germans or how Africans are perceived in Germany has much to tell us about Germany and modern Europe in general. The experience of Afro-Germans and Africans in Germany provides insight into contemporary Germany's transformation, willing or not, into a multicultural society. Our discussion is especially timely in light of the wave of violence against foreigners and persons seen as such since German unification in 1990. Sadly, one posthumous success of Hitler seems to be the conviction of many Germans today that they are a biologically homogeneous group. When the Nazis set out to "purify" the German people, they also managed to erase much of the popular memory of Germany's multicultural past, which included Poles, Jews, Sinti and Roma, and others, not to mention some Afro-Germans. It is against this backdrop that our volume has taken shape. With this work we hope to raise broad questions and to avoid facile conclusions.

Notes

1. Sara Friedrichsmeyer, Sara Lennox, and Susanne Zantop, "Introduction," in *The Imperialist Imagination: German Colonialism and its Legacy*, ed. Sara Friedrichsmeyer, Sara Lennox, and Susanne Zantop (Ann Arbor: University of Michigan Press, 1998), 11. See also essays by El-Tayeb and O'Donnell in this volume.

2. Personal communication from Fatima El-Tayeb and Tina Campt.

3. Pascal Grosse, *Kolonialismus, Eugenik und bürgerliche Gesellschaft in Deutschland 1850–1918* (Frankfurt: Campus, 2000), 245.

4. Personal communication from Fatima El-Tayeb and Tina Campt.

5. May Opitz, Katharina Oguntoye, and Dagmar Schultz, "Editors' Introduction," in *Showing Our Colors: Afro-German Women Speak Out*, ed. May Opitz, Katharina Oguntoye, and Dagmar Schultz (Amherst: University of Massachusetts Press, 1992), xxii–iii.

6. "Tonträger & Video," http://www.brotherskeepers.de, accessed 17 June 2004. The Brothers Keepers homepage also contains information about the charitable and activist branches of this organization.

7. Adrian Tischler, "Kern ist die Angst vor dem Fremden, Interview mit Adé und Torch," *Der Rechte Rand* 72 (2002), accessed 17 June 2004, http://www.der-rechte-rande.de. All translations are ours.

8. Lyrics to song "Afro-deutsch" from the CD entitled *Lightkultur*, listed under "Tonträger & Video" at www.brotherskeepers.de, accessed 17 June 2004.

9. "Wir sind stolz, Deutsche zu sein. Interview with Adé and Abi Odukoya," *die tageszeitung*, 7 December 2001.

10. "Microphone Mafia: Denkmal (2002)," http://www.kanak-attak.de/news/dunkel.htm, accessed 7 January 2003.

11. "Viele von uns sind zu hip-hop gestossen, weil das damals das Einzige war, in dem wir eine Reflexion unseres Selbst gesehen haben. Jetzt haben wir es verinnerlicht und kreieren damit unsere eigene Identität." Ibid.

12. "Die Afro-Deutschen sind die ersten, die ein neues deutsches Bewusstsein und einen Patriotismus an den Start bringen konnten, indem sie sagen: Ich bin Deutsch." "Brothers Keepers, Sisters Keepers; Ich bin kein Rassist, meine Frau ist doch Jugoslawin," interview with band members, http://www.rocklinks.de/gruppen/brotherskeepers/intro1201.html, accessed 7 January 2003.

13. "Wir nehmen den Rechten das Territorium des Patriotismus weg, indem wir sagen: 'Wir sind stolz, Teil dieser Nation zu sein, mit der ganzen Verantwortung, die dazu gehört." Ibid.

14. "Der Mainstream Kulturbetrieb wird derzeit durch ausgewählte Beiträge von MigrantInnen der zweiten Generation ergänzt, die die deutsche Öffentlichkeit nach bisheriger Ausgrenzung wahrzunehmen begonnen hat. Es handelt sich meines Erachtens um das Modell eines neo-imperialistischen Multikulturalismus. Die Formel dieser kulturellen Globalisierung lautet: Kultur ja, Rechte für Einwanderer nein." Quoted in Cathy Gelbin, Kader Konuk, and Peggy Piesche (eds.), *AufBrüche. Kulturelle Produktionen von Migrantinnen, Schwarzen und jüdischen Frauen in Deutschland* (Königstein: Ulrike Helmer Verlag, 1999), 159.

15. See note 8.

16. "Kanak Attak fragt nicht nach dem Paß oder nach der Herkunft, sondern wendet sich gegen die Frage nach dem Paß und der Herkunft." Manifesto dated November 1998, www.kanak-attak.de/manifest/manif/dt/htm, accessed 7 January 2003.

17. Stuart Hall, "The Local and the Global: Globalization and Ethnicity," in *Dangerous Liaisons: Gender, Nation, and Postcolonial Perspectives*, ed. Anne McClintock, Aamir Mufti, and Ella Shohat (Minneapolis: University of Minnesota Press, 1997), 185.

18. Gelbin et al., *AufBrüche*, 168.

19. "Die bestehende Hierarchie von gesellschaftlichen Existenzen und Subjektpositionen lässt sich nicht einfach ausblenden oder gar spielerisch überspringen. Es sind eben nicht alle Konstruktionen gleich. Damit bewegt sich das Projekt in einem Strudel von nicht auflösbaren Widersprüchen, was das Verhältnis von Repräsentation, Differenz und die Zuschreibung ethnischer Identitäten anbetrifft." Manifesto dated November 1998, www.kanak-attak.de/manifest/manif/dt/htm, accessed 7 January 2003.

20. "Nur die eigenen Selbstbezeichnungen sind identitätsstiftend, wobei diese ausdrücklich die Realiät bzw. Normalität darstellen." Gelbin et al., *AufBrüche*, 199.

21. Abini Zöllner, *Schokoladenkind. Meine Familie und andere Wunder* (Hamburg: Rowohlt, 2003).

22. Thomas Usleber, *Die Farben unter meiner Haut* (Frankfurt: Brandes and Apsel: 2002).

23. Katharina Oguntoye, May Opitz, and Dagmar Schultz (eds.), *Farbe bekennen* (Frankfurt: Fischer, 1986). The translation by Anne Adams appeared as Opitz et al., *Showing Our Colors*.

24. *beiträge zur feministischen theorie und praxis* 27 (1990), special issue, "Geteilter Feminismus: Rassismus, Antisemitismus, Fremdenhaß." *Weibblick* 13 (1993), special issue, "Schwarze deutsche Frauen, Rassismus in der Sprache, weiße Frauen mit schwarzen Kindern."

25. See for example the work of Lida van den Boek, *Am Ende der Weißheit— Vorurteile überwinden. Ein Handbuch* (Berlin, 1988).

26. "Während noch in den Texten der ersten Generation Schwarzer deutscher Autorinnen der Identitätsbegriff stark von der Erfahrung des Andersseins beeinflusst war . . . muß dieser Verarbeitungsprozeß in den neueren künstlerischen Verarbeitungen von Identität wohl nicht mehr bewältigt werden. Vielmehr gehen diese Texte einen Schritt weiter und erkennen dem Subjekt eine ganz alltägliche Identität zu." Gelbin et al., *AufBrüche*, 198.

27. Olumide Popoola and Beldan Sezen (eds.), *Talking Home. Heimat aus unserer eigenen Feder. Frauen of color in Deutschland* (Amsterdam: Blue Moon Press, 1999). See Olumide Popoola's article in *afro-look* 27 (1998): 28–31, about her experience with the ID Verlag.

28. Sander L. Gilman, *On Blackness Without Blacks: Essays on the Image of the Black in Germany* (Boston: G.K. Hall, 1982).

29. Reinhold Grimm and Jost Hermand (eds.), *Blacks and German Culture* (Madison: University of Wisconsin Press, 1986).

30. Tina Campt, Pascal Grosse, and Yara-Colette Lemke Muñiz de Faria, "Blacks, Germans, and the Politics of Imperial Imagination, 1920–60," in Friedrichsmeyer et al., *The Imperialist Imagination*, 206.

31. Fatima El-Tayeb, *Schwarze Deutsche. Der Diskurs um Rasse und nationale Identität 1890–1933* (Frankfurt: Campus, 2001).

32. Pascal Grosse, *Kolonialismus, Eugenik und bürgerliche Gesellschaft in Deutschland 1850–1918* (Frankfurt: Campus, 2000).

33. Doris Reiprich and Erika Ngambi Ul Kuo, "Our Father Was Cameroonian, Our Mother, East Prussian, We Are Mulattoes," in Opitz et al., *Showing Our Colors*, 56–76. Susann Samples, "African Germans in the Third Reich," in *The African-German Experience*, ed. Aisha Carol Blackshire-Belay (Westport: Praeger, 1996), 53–70.

34. Katharina Oguntoye, *Eine afro-deutsche Geschichte. Zur Lebenssituation von Afrikanern und Afro-Deutschen in Deutschland von 1884 bis 1950* (Berlin: HoHo Verlag, 1997).

35. Reiner Pommerin, *Sterilisierung der Rheinland-Bastarde. Das Schicksal einer farbigen deutschen Minderheit 1918–1937* (Düsseldorf: Droste, 1979).

36. Tina Campt, *Other Germans: Black Germans and the Politics of Race, Gender, and Memory in the Third Reich* (Ann Arbor: University of Michigan Press, 2004).

37. Charles Lusane, *Hitler's Black Victims: The Historical Experience of Afro-Germans, European Blacks, Africans, and African Americans in the Nazi Era* (New York: Routledge, 2003).

38. Yara-Colette Lemke Muñiz de Faria, *Zwischen Fürsorge und Ausgrenzung. Afrodeutsche "Besatzungskinder" im Nachkriegs-Deutschland* (Berlin: Metropol, 2002).

39. *Journal of Black Studies* 23, no. 2 (1992); Carol Aisha Blackshire-Belay, ed., *The African-German Experience* (Westport: Praeger, 1996); Carol Aisha Blackshire-Belay, Leroy Hopkins, and David McBride (eds.), *Crosscurrents: African Americans, Africa, and Germany in the Modern World* (Columbia: Camden House, 1998).

40. Leroy Hopkins, "'Fred' vs 'Uncle Tom': Frederick Douglass and the Image of the African American in 19th-Century Germany," in *etudes germano-africaines* 9 (1991): 67–78; "Speak, So I Might See You! Afro-German Literature," in *World Literature Today*, 69:3 (1995); "Who is a German? Historical and Modern Perspectives on Africans in Germany (AICGS, 1999); "Einbürgerungs-Akte 1154: Heinrich Ernst Wilhelm Anumu, African Businessman in Imperial Hamburg," in *Die (koloniale) Begegnung AfrikanerInnen in Deutschland 1880–1945. Deutsche in Afrika 1880–1918*, ed. Marianne Bechhaus-Gerst and Reinhard Klein-Arendt (New York: Peter Lang, 2003).

41. Peggy Piesche, "Black and German? East German Adolescents before 1989— A Retrospective View of a 'Non-Existent Issue' in the GDR," in *The Cultural After-Life of East Germany: New Transnational Perspectives*, ed. Leslie Adelson (AICGS: Washington, 2002).

42. Heike Raphael-Hernandez, ed., *Blackening Europe: The African American Presence* (New York: Routledge, 2004).

PART I

Afro-Germans in Historical Perspective

1

DANGEROUS LIAISONS

RACE, NATION, AND GERMAN IDENTITY

Fatima El-Tayeb

Among the various rituals constructing and reinforcing group identity, sports are certainly central. Germany, as one could witness during the recent world championship in Japan and Korea, is a soccer-crazy nation. Soccer is the number-one national sport and accordingly a central source of pride and identification. Thus to learn about German notions of race and nation, it might be telling to look at the public response to the "first" black soccer player named to the prestigious national team in May 2001. The selection of Gerald Asamoah caused much comment in the press, and indeed race and nation figured prominently. Asamoah is a German national, but he was born in Ghana, of Ghanaian parents, who migrated to Germany when he was a child. This is an important piece of information in a nation that still deeply mistrusts the possibility of assimilation. While Ukrainian-born U.S. swimmer Lenny Krayzelburg, for example, was hailed as an American hero during the 2000 Olympics in Sydney, in Germany the possession of "German blood" is traditionally seen as a necessary prerequisite of proper national belonging. A sympathetic article in a liberal German newspaper praising Asamoah's selection as a signal against the soccer world's notorious racism, nevertheless managed to refer to him as "Ghanaian" five times and "African" three times, twice mentioning his "tribal origin."[1] Once he is described as a "holder of a German passport," but never as "German."[2] In other articles as well, Asamoah is unambiguously identified as "black," whereas his status as "German" (as opposed to "German passport holder") seems doubtful. But he is not the only member

27

of the national soccer team born outside of Germany. Miroslav Klose is an *Aussiedler* (an Eastern European "ethnic German" with an automatic right to German citizenship) and spent the first years of his life in Poland, while Oliver Neuville, a Swiss with a German father, did not speak a word of German when he joined the team. In contrast to the immense attention Asamoah's ethnicity attracted, these players' non-German background is hardly ever mentioned. They do possess German blood, after all, and more important, as I will argue, they are white.

There is another twist to this story: there already have been two black players on the German soccer team, both in the 1970s, Erwin Kostedde and Jimmy Hartwig. They, however, are not African by birth but were born in Germany, of white German mothers and (soon absent) African American fathers. Contemporary media responses, while not directly questioning the men's Germanness (there was no other nationality available, after all) downplayed it by always primarily identifying them by their color, emphasizing their "exotic" background and their singular status as blacks in the national team.[3] Both players were mentioned in all articles dealing with Asamoah. But interestingly, while a few authors referred to them as his predecessors, most did the opposite, calling Asamoah the first "African-born," "truly black," "really colored" national player, thereby setting him apart from the merely "colored" or "dark-skinned" Kostedde and Hartwig.[4] The shift in the latters' status (from the embodiment of exoticism to "not quite the real thing") might be partly due to the current political climate in Germany. In the face of rising racist violence, heated debates about the introduction of an immigration law (built on the myth of being a "non-immigration nation," the Federal Republic does not have one yet), and a new definition of citizenship that finally departs from an exclusive *ius sanguinis*, Asamoah has a much higher symbolic value than Hartwig or Kostedde had—and more so if he can be called the "first black," indicating a new, multicultural Germany. Colorism could be at work here as well; Kostedde and Hartwig were seen as black, until the much darker Asamoah appeared.

I propose, though, that the treatment of the handful of black German soccer players reflects a deeper level of the dominant national attitude towards race and nationality, an attitude which presumes that "real blacks" cannot be Germans and Germans cannot be real blacks. Asamoah's blackness can be filed under established categories. He was born in "black Africa" (the exclusive term for sub-Saharan Africa in German) and later emigrated to Germany. His primary (discursive) identity therefore is and will always be African/immigrant. His predecessors on the team, though, were born in Germany, which in fact makes them a non-entity: black

Germans. This category is not publicly recognized, as it is not supposed to exist. The schizophrenic German relation to "race," moving between denial and obsession, has been projected onto Afro-Germans for the last hundred years. It will likely seem drastic to speak of "obsession" in this context, especially when one is not only referring to the period up to 1945, but as I will show, there are indications that this term might be quite accurate. There is no doubt that blacks and blackness are central points of reference in German culture. For generations, children have grown up with the song of the "Ten Little Negroes" and the Struwelpeter's sad story of the Moor, they play "Who's Afraid of the Black Man," and their favorite sweets will likely be "*Negerküße*" (Negro Kisses), "*Mohrenköpfe*" (Moors' Heads) or "*Eisneger*" (Ice Negroes). "Negro jokes" are an ever-popular genre, and menial, dull work is often called "*Negerarbeit.*" If you ask a favor from a German, she or he could indicate her or his unwillingness by stating that she or he is "not your Negro." But if you ask someone thus socialized about a racist tradition in Germany, she or he will likely answer that there is no such thing, often adding that Germany never had any contact with blacks, so how could there be racism?

This tension between the central metaphorical presence of blackness and a simultaneous denial of the existence of actual blacks within the nation is crucial to the perception of black Germans, who are under constant pressure to explain, or rather, redefine, their existence, expected to be something they are not and not allowed to be what they are.[5] Being nonexistent in the public mind, African Germans are not granted the role of active subjects within public discourse—in fact, not even if they are its object. The refusal to grant black Germans the right of self-definition is most strikingly reflected in the field of naming. While the term *afrodeutsch* (Afro-German) is almost unanimously used as self-reference by those black Germans who participate in political and cultural discourse, white Germans at least as unanimously reject it in favor of "colored" (a liberal version) or *Mischling* (mixed-race, also mongrel).[6] Supposed to be whatever the majority sees in them, black Germans are simultaneously invisible (there is no black minority in Germany), hyper-black (in contrast to "real Germans"), and not-really black (compared to "real Africans"). In this context, the episode about the soccer players illustrates how African Germans are never granted both parts of their identity: if their blackness is recognized, their Germanness is not and if they are allowed to be German, they are not so black, after all.

Consequently, even though blacks have lived in Germany at least since the fifteenth century,[7] "black German" still seems like a contradiction in terms to the nation's white majority.[8] The connection between race and nationality in German culture has been almost completely ignored, both inside and outside of academia. Therefore, it is highly important to analyze not only the origins of this construct but also its ongoing anchoring in the German mind and the consequences this had and has for the lives of black—and other nonwhite—Germans.[9] Yet this article cannot attempt such a wide-ranging analysis.[10] Rather, I will sketch some of the conditions that led to a consolidation of racialized notions of national identity in early twentieth-century Germany. In doing so, I will focus on the Social Darwinist sciences dealing with race, and more specifically with "racially mixed" Germans, namely the eugenic and social anthropologist movements. While perceived as too radical or "race-obsessed" by some other disciplines, their findings on race matters possessed a largely unquestioned authority inside and outside of academia. Social Darwinism is not only important in this context because of the way its ideas permeated academic thinking, though, but also because it shows that German scientists were involved in an international discourse on race that shaped Western thinking on the subject for a long time to come. Last but not least, Social Darwinism is central to the questions discussed here because of its decisive role in German colonialism. It was arguably the late start of the German colonial endeavor, coinciding with the height of Social Darwinist thinking in the last decade of the nineteenth century, that led to an especially symbiotic relationship between the two projects.

This symbiosis is personified in the anthropologist Eugen Fischer, who rose to fame after he published a study conducted on a "bastard population" in German Southwest Africa—a study he concluded with explicit political advice to the German authorities about how to deal with the colonial "bastard question." Fischer continued to pursue the subject throughout the Weimar Republic as head of the influential Kaiser Wilhelm Institute for Anthropology, and during National Socialism, when his institute offered scientific support to the secret, forced sterilization of several hundred black German teenagers.[11] While Fischer's career, continued in the Federal Republic, indicates the consistency of anthropological approaches to race through the decades, it might also be considered typical for the entanglement of the political right and Social Darwinist science (though Fischer considered himself a moderate conservative). But this entanglement stretched to other segments of society as well, which I illustrate with a look at the Social Democratic Party's ambiguous relationship to colonialism and the Protestant and Catholic missions' equally inconsistent attitudes towards interracial marriages in the colonies.

In conclusion, I will tie the above strands together by showing how they affected the perception and living conditions of black Germans from the early years of the twentieth century to the post-World War II period. Thus, looking specifically at the role the Social Darwinist sciences and colonial politics played in this consolidating a racialized concept of Germanness, I argue that the fact that Afro-Germans have never become an accepted or at least a recognized part of German society is less due to their relatively small numbers than to this racialized definition of nationality. A definition that became central at the turn of the last century was practiced in the extreme under National Socialism and has not entirely been overcome in the present.[12]

Over the last decades, a number of groundbreaking studies have analyzed the strict and systematic race hierarchy that was brought about by the new world view of the Enlightenment. The impact German philosophers such as Kant or Hegel had on this development is well known by now.[13] Less well known, however, is the role of German scholars within the movement of Social Darwinism, which at the end of the nineteenth century gave a new quality to the racist ideology. Charles Darwin's theory of evolution not only revolutionized the natural sciences but was also instrumentalized by those interested in presenting social structures as natural laws. If the existence of all living things was the result of a merciless fight for survival that left only the fittest in the game, human societies could be no exception. The ideological construct of the inequality of races, with the resulting need to fight for white domination, could now be presented as part of an inevitable natural process. Race, class, and gender hierarchies appeared as the final product of a millennia-long process, the mechanisms of which were beyond human control. With the immense progress of natural sciences in the wake of Darwin's findings, this "Social Darwinism" rapidly gained ground in all nations of the West as well.

The German Social Darwinist movement can roughly be divided into two influential groups: social anthropologists and eugenicists. Differences between the factions were partly ideological, partly scientific, and partly caused by personality conflicts. Studies of the movement long separated populist, fanatic supporters of race theories, the social anthropologists, from eugenicists, who were infected by ideas of "purification" but basically apolitical and devoted to scientific methods.[14] Although there certainly were differences between the two groups, such a clear division into "racists" and "scientists" does not seem justified, as the factions' disagreements certainly did not include their view of the "race question." Both based their theories

Ich rate Dir, Du Jammerlappen
Ziel: nach dem fernen Afrika
Hier bekommst Du doch kein Mädchen
Vielleicht ist dort was für Dich da.

Figure 1.1. Colonial Postcard.
Courtesy of Sammlung Weiss, Hamburg www.postcard-museum.com.

on the belief that there were clearly separable races with distinct characteristics and dissimilar abilities, and accordingly they worked from a common
body of literature.[15] Less than movements that came from different directions and finally melted in the national socialist ideology, the groups represent gradations within a single ideology that was able to combine science
and racism, supposed opposites. The founding of the world's first "eugenic

society" by Alfred Ploetz in 1905 was an attempt to anchor eugenics within the international scientific community. Like social anthropologists, eugenicists were convinced that their discipline was the basis of all human sciences and should be granted proper recognition. To achieve this, the society, emphasizing its scientific orientation and the members' academic background, distanced itself from dubious predecessors such as Arthur de Gobineau and concentrated instead on authorities such as Darwin and Francis Galton. This attempt at inclusion in the circle of respectable sciences was successful indeed,[16] but the group around Ploetz wanted more. Like all other Social Darwinist disciplines, eugenics attempted a practical implementation of its findings. Research was no end in itself; rather, it delivered guidelines for a politics to order human societies according to scientific principles. Moreover, a science that did not regard the individual but the race as the smallest relevant unit, in fact having the race's "optimizing" as its sole purpose, had to believe in clear distinctions between the races, in differences and inequalities. Indeed, German eugenicists did make quite clear which group they considered superior:

> [T]he hygiene of the whole human species . . . is identical with that of the Aryan race that, apart from some small ones, such as the Jewish, which probably in its majority is Aryan anyway, is the cultured race par excellence, to promote it means to promote humanity as a whole.[17]

Contrary to the social anthropologists, though, the eugenicists saw Europeans as an "Aryan unit," whose rapid "degeneration" was mainly due to social factors, not to a mixing with "inferior foreign races."[18] The two groups met again ideologically in their rejection of the "racially dangerous" social hygiene.[19] Also, the relatively little attention eugenics paid to races other than the "Aryan" cannot be equated with greater tolerance. The Eugenic Society, for example, was open to members of all parties and confessions—but only if they were white.[20]

The second group of Social Darwinists preoccupied with questions of race, the social anthropologists, belonged to the larger group of historical anthropologists, distinguishing themselves through an attitude that was much more aggressive than that of academic anthropology. The movement, which revolved around the physician Ludwig Woltmann and his journal, the *Politisch-anthropologische Revue* (hereafter *PAR*), longed to be included in the university curriculum, which meant not only the institutionalization of "political anthropology," but in fact a reorganization of the humanities according to its theories, in which the past, present, and future of humanity

Figure 1.2. Colonial Postcard.
Courtesy of Sammlung Weiss, Hamburg www.postcard-museum.com.

were seen in exclusively racial terms. Within the social anthropologist world view, race was the basis of all politics, and that necessarily meant direct political influence for "race scientists." Since the genetic predisposition of the races was undisputed, socialization, economic, or cultural factors could have no influence whatsoever on the static "racial character" and were merely perceived as causing a disturbance of "natural developments." Instead, social anthropological studies concentrated on the "racial stratification" of the European nations, on the "colored peoples" and their relation to the "white race" and, again and again, on the dangers of "racial mixing."

These topics were not uncommon in themselves; the existence of races with distinctive physical and mental characteristics was taken for granted in German academic circles in the early twentieth century. Not only anthropology, ethnology, and eugenics, but history, political economy, sociology, and philology as well based their judgment of non-Western societies on theories of the races' different stages and abilities of development. There was dissent, however, regarding the treatment of the "white" and "yellow" races. Taking the most radical stand, the social anthropologists denied that the "colored races," including Asians, were able to produce any form of civilization, and furthermore divided Europeans into three "subraces," Nordic, Asiatic, and Mediterranean, of which only

Figure 1.3. Colonial Postcard.
Courtesy of Sammlung Weiss, Hamburg www.postcard-museum.com.

the first was classified as truly white and therefore civilized, the others being tainted by "yellow" and "black" blood.[21] This position was rejected by most of the German academic community, which not only had a much higher esteem of Asian civilization (at least where the distant past was concerned), but also insisted that the white race, superior and therefore above racial limits, had to be analyzed in light of economic, social, and political considerations.[22] Academia did not doubt, however, that "race" itself was a useful category in analyzing historical and social processes, and the Social Darwinists' placement of the black race at the bottom of the racial hierarchy was not challenged. Even harsh critics of racist ideology merely insisted that blacks could reach the intellectual level of the other races if moved to the right, that is, "civilized," environment.[23]

By the early twentieth century, the notion that Africans constituted the most primitive kind of humanity, separated from civilized Europeans by a wide biological gap, had been well established.[24] From its beginnings, the concept of race had been based on a black-white antagonism. The position of the "intermediate" groups could vary widely. China moved between admired "refined civilization" and despised "yellow peril"; Jews, to whom German race scientists paid relatively little attention before 1914, were fashioned as the most dangerous "racial enemy" after World War I. The opposite

Figure 1.4. "Rheinland Campaign."
Photo courtesy of Sammlung Weiss, Hamburg www.postcard-museum.com.

positions of whites and blacks remained unchanged, though. The first group represented mankind in its most perfect form, the latter in its most primitive. All the positive qualities the race scientists attributed abundantly to the white race were missing in the black one, which in turn abounded in negative characteristics.[25] In his description of the human races, Ludwig Wilser, one of the main editors of the *Politisch-anthropologische Revue*, summarized this attitude: "The black race (Homo niger) includes the darkest and in their physical and mental development most retarded humans."[26]

In scholarly studies of the various academic disciplines, there was no differentiated analysis of African societies and cultures. Instead, following Hegel's judgment, Africa was considered a barbaric unity and blacks by definition unable to produce culture. After all development on the African continent had been attributed to Aryan, Semitic, or Hamitic invaders, the proponents of Social Darwinism turned to the next scientific question: how did the lowest members of the human species react to being exposed to civilization? In answering this question, the European colonies, Europe itself, but most of all the United States were fields of study. An astonishing number of German articles and books dealt with blacks in the U.S.[27] The aim of all these studies was to show nature's complete dominance over nurture—that is, the impossibility of influencing a genetic racial disposition.[28] Using the North American example, but claiming universality, social anthropologists as well as eugenicists insisted that the "Negro's peculiarities" resisted all civilizing influences. Unable to handle political independence—an often-used example was Haiti[29]—he might show a certain progress, if guided rightly, but would never reach the cultural level of whites. The German authors' arguments betrayed a detailed knowledge of American racist literature,[30] a literature, of course, that itself was inspired by European race theories. The image created there, of blacks who were useful and content if controlled by whites, but showed their animalistic nature whenever this guidance was missing, was of obvious usefulness for German colonial politics, which accordingly quickly incorporated Social Darwinist ideas. In 1907, the German Secretary of Colonial Affairs, Bernhard Dernburg, commented on the "uplifting of the Negro race":

> That this is one of the most difficult problems to be solved is shown by the history of the United States. There since a hundred years you have a black population, taken mostly from the west coast of Africa, where our colonies Togo and Cameroon are. Since the year 1864 those Negroes possess the full civil rights of a republican community; they have been practicing them for forty years now. But when one asks today what could be a danger to the North American republic and its political structure, one is pointed unanimously to the mass of these nine million half- and quarter-educated [*halb- und viertel-gebildete*] Negroes, who did not lose their hereditary characteristics and only took on those aspects of civilization that increased their rights and whose self-confidence is in opposite proportion to their intelligence and achievement; and these are all third- or fourth-generation Christian Negroes and second-generation free Americans.[31]

German race scientists constantly fed this line of argument, which allowed the negation of all social and economic factors. The exclusion of African Americans from many professions was caused by their inability to perform skilled work, segregation of public transport was due to their "intolerable odor," etc.[32] Accordingly, complete separation was hailed as the "natural solution" to the "American problem"—and not only in America. The scientific justification of racist measures was even more important for the introduction of a strict segregation in the German colonies that took place in the first years of the twentieth century.

While a teleological argumentation, which explained all social inequality with the inequality of the races, was typical of race theories in general, it was applied most strictly towards blacks. The idea of a static race hierarchy demanded that there be no way of ascendance for those at its bottom. Social change and political theories built on factors other than "race" therefore were extremely threatening.[33] The greatest danger to the hierarchy, however, was represented by "mongrelization." The Social Darwinist world view needed races with fixed positions and duties, determined by biological givens. "Mongrels" (*Mischlinge*), who did not fit into one of the categories, were an unwanted and dangerous disturbance. Their existence proved the dogma of unrelated, opposite, and incompatible "races" to be absurd, a dogma, after all, on which the whole Social Darwinist philosophy was built. Accordingly, persons of mixed "racial" ancestry were pathologized and marginalized as "unnatural" and "degenerate." In the last consequence, following Gobineau, Social Darwinists considered "mongrels" responsible for all evils of the modern world, since it was the dominance of the "raceless element" that led to the destruction of the race hierarchy, of the "natural order."[34] While the disastrous effects of "heterogeneous mixing"—that between "races" as opposed to that between "subraces"—were exemplified historically by the downfall of the Egyptian and Persian empires, the United States and Latin America supposedly were present locations of such mingling.[35] The U.S. system was perceived as enacting the appropriate measures: a strict segregation of whites and blacks was regarded as the only thing that could prevent "the complete mixing of the two races, which, according to all men of standing, would mean the total destruction of all civilization and culture on the American continent."[36] The Latin American situation on the other hand, associated with political chaos, was routinely used as an illustration of the catastrophic consequences of racial mixing.[37] In the first decade of the twentieth century, though, a shift in perspective occurred. The hideous effects especially of "black-white mixing" were not primarily illustrated with reference to the Americas anymore, but in relation to the German population itself. Two developments caused this shift: a German anthropologist's innovative studies on "racial crossings" and the colonial wars in German Southwest Africa, which drew the German public's attention to the biracial population there.

The German colonial project started late and hesitantly, but from the 1890s onwards, Bismarck's successors at least verbally committed themselves to a politics aimed at achieving world power status that had military power and colonial possessions at its center.[38] This direction was enthusiastically supported by a rising middle class, which increasingly compensated for its nonrepresentation within government with organized nationalist agitation outside of it. While this unrestricted nationalism had an extremely destabilizing effect on Germany and Europe in the long run, in the short term, "colonial enthusiasm" channeled tensions within society by creating a harmonizing common interest and by stigmatizing oppositional forces, namely the Social Democratic Party (SPD), as "unpatriotic" outsiders. This process of polarization showed similarities to the Social Darwinist approach, which indeed had created the prerequisites for its success. The scientific division of "civilized" and "barbarian," "developed" and "underdeveloped" nations, "superior" and "inferior races" had made sure that Germany's position as a leading colonial power did not need to be explained. The German colonial secretary Wilhelm Solf built on a common understand of the hierarchy of races when he proclaimed "the duty to confirm the dominion of the developed races in order to gradually lead the underdeveloped peoples . . . to higher levels of intellectual and moral development. It is the right and duty of all great cultured nations [*Kulturstaaten*] to participate in this duty of civilization [*Kulturmenschheit*]."[39]

Along this line of argument, the exploitation of humans, land, and resources seemed a just payment for the deliverance of civilization's blessings. And the more primitive the recipients, the higher the price they had to pay. The extremely brutal proceedings of the German colonial power in Africa thus became merely part of the process of "natural selection." Not only the colonial policy but the propaganda within Germany as well were building on a Social Darwinist foundation, while the race scientists themselves saw colonialism as a historical necessity, whose particulars were to be determined by their expertise: "The races are not made for the same accomplishments and tasks in history, and the lower races have to serve the interests of the higher ones. The interests of the higher ones are 'the aims of humanity,' since only in them does the human potential fully bloom."[40]

The numerous Social Darwinist studies of the "eternal war of the races" and "Germanic superiority" formed the ideological base of the colonial organizations' agitation.[41] The urban middle class, product of Germany's modernization and excluded by a ruling class that clung to feudal structures, had an economic interest in a colonial empire, but it also believed in imperialism as a modernizing force that would lead to changes within German society, changes that would grant the middle class a direct political influence that matched its economic importance. Skillfully using the possibilities of the newly developing mass media, the nationalist movement included "the common man," and to a lesser extent "the common woman," in a political process that had formerly largely been limited to a Prussian aristocratic elite. Thereby the nationalists gained a popularity that was only rivaled by that of the Social Democrats.

The SPD, whose influence could be limited neither by bans nor by parliamentary isolation, was styled as the bogeyman of revolution by both the traditional conservatives and the modern ultranationalists. The SPD's radicalism was thus exaggerated, and internal conflicts around central questions were underestimated. While the SPD was the only influential political group in Imperial Germany that held anti-imperialist positions, its attitude towards colonialism and scientific racism was not one of fundamental opposition. Under Eduard Bernstein, one of the party's two leading theorists, the SPD's revisionist faction rapidly gained influence. The revisionists' propagation of gradual reform and rejection of a socialist revolution also included a general acceptance of colonialism. The latter had to be cleansed of its worst capitalist excesses, but was a fundamentally positive development. The revisionist organ, *Die Sozialistischen Monatsblätter*, stated in 1907 that "as we have learned that in many areas there is a solidarity of interests between peasants and industrial workers, so we must learn to understand that in some areas, for example in colonialism, there is a solidarity of interests between the bourgeois and the proletarian."[42] Where the "black race" was concerned, many socialists were caught within the constraints of the dominant racial ideology, unable to extend political concepts and analyses meant to emancipate "the whole of humanity" onto the African peoples. Instead of practicing class solidarity, socialists asked the European worker to share the "white man's burden": "To accustom the Negro to regular activity is cultural work, after all, and it is the Social Democrats' duty to actively participate in this task."[43]

In 1912, when the SPD celebrated its greatest electoral victory thus far, the revisionist position had become dominant. In 1919, when the party gained control of the government for the first time, the idea of a "socialist colonialism" had so completely replaced any criticism of the oppression of non-European peoples that the SPD, without any sense of irony, could demand the return of the colonies lost in the war.[44] There always was an anti-imperialist wing within the party as well, though significantly weakened by August Bebel's death in 1913. It must be considered, nevertheless, that the SPD as the central progressive force in Imperial Germany did not consistently oppose the growing scientific racism but increasingly identified with its contents.[45]

For the vast majority of Germans, though, there was never any doubt about the nation's "moral right" to govern a colonial empire that was four times as big as the motherland and had twelve million inhabitants. The latter were granted no rights, sometimes not even that of mere survival. The colonial masters were unable to perceive the "natives" as independent human beings; they were of importance exclusively in relation to German interests. A complete appropriation of Social Darwinism by colonial politics defined the treatment of the colonized. As Paul Rohrbach, former colonial inspector turned successful writer, explained:

> In the context of world history, only the necessity to give up their free national barbarism and to become a class of servants to the whites gives the natives the right to exist. As for individuals, so it is for peoples that the useless have no right to live and that an existence is the more useful the more important it is for the general development.[46]

That quotation, one of many similar ones, indicates how readily colonial authorities and settlers took over the language and ideas of the race scientists. These, on the other hand, eagerly used the possibilities the colonies offered for their studies. No one was more successful in doing this than Eugen Fischer, professor of anthropology in Freiburg, whose 1913 publication *Die Rehobother Bastards und das Bastardisierungsproblem beim Menschen* (The Rehoboth Bastards and the Problem of Bastardization in Humans) made him an internationally renown expert on the "mongrel question."[47] In his study of the Rehoboth population, conducted in 1908, Fischer used Mendel's laws, which, having been rediscovered only a few years earlier, led to numerous new biological insights. Fischer rightly assumed that they would give his study additional authority as well.[48] Qualitatively, his presentation of "mongrels" as genetically inferior, "lost between the races" and "disharmonic" hardly differed from earlier "findings" that still identified the blood as the carrier of the racial character. But as a professor of anthropology, Fischer belonged to the circle of "respectable" race scientists who distinguished themselves from the social anthropologist "laymen" through a supposedly strict methodology. This professed respectability was rather helpful for Fischer's academic career—though it did not prevent him from keeping close ties to the group around Woltmann.[49] After Fischer's "bastardization" study, his influence steadily grew. In the Weimar Republic, he became head of the world's largest center for anthropology and eugenics, the Kaiser Wilhelm Institute for Anthropology, Human Heredity, and Eugenics in Berlin, a center that under his leadership gained a key position in National Socialist eugenics. Fischer ended his career as a respected professor in the Federal Republic.[50]

Fischer's attempt to present the first truly scientific study of "racial mixing" was considered a complete success.[51] This was largely due to his "objective," measured attitude that clearly set him apart from the social anthropologists' populist racism. And indeed he harshly criticized earlier texts on "racial mixing" as prejudiced and not up to scientific standards. Nevertheless, he did much to solidify exactly those prejudices by rephrasing them in acceptable "scientific" language.[52] Fischer's study not only included the outcome of his extensive anthropological measurements, the genealogical trees of all Rehoboth inhabitants (Mendel, and an assessment of their psychological states, it also devoted its final chapter to the political consequences of a possible "invasion" of the German nation by black blood. While they were passive objects of (his) science, Fischer could approach the "mongrels" in a seemingly disinterested and objective manner. When they threatened to become active social subjects, however, the tone changed. Outside of the clear scientist-object hierarchy, in social and political interaction, the supposed assault of the faceless mass of inferior coloreds on German blood justified the neglect of all "civilized" norms:

> If there is the *probability*, or even the mere *possibility* that bastard blood is damaging our race . . . *any absorption must be prevented.* I take this to be so absolutely obvious that I can consider any other point of view only as that of complete biological ignorance. . . . [T]his is about the *survival*— I choose my words consciously—of our race; this has to be the main criterion; ethical and legal norms just have to be secondary to that.[53]

These political recommendations, authorized by the scientific "facts" preceding them, had a concrete reference: the implementation of anti-miscegenation and "native" laws in Germany's largest colony, German Southwest Africa (see Krista O'Donnell's essay, chapter 2, in this volume). Following the bloody suppression of an uprising, the African population there was reduced to a state of virtual slavery through expro-priation, deportation, and forced labor. "Natives" were defined through a strict "one-drop rule" as all persons with a "native" ancestor, however far removed, and marriages between them and Germans were outlawed. These regulations legally connected the categories of "German" and "white" for the first time. Within German Southwest Africa, one could not be German if one were not white, which led to a number of Germans with "native blood" being expatriated.[54] The scientific obsession with the dangers of "racial mixing" was both reason and justification for this colonial racism. Science had made it possible to present any "mixing" as a threat to Germany's "racial survival" and measures such as those implemented in German Southwest Africa as a reasonable self-defense, a biological "instinct of survival." To make the system work in practice, however, its ideological justification had to be accepted by all forces involved in the construction of a German Southwest Africa: the colonial bureaucracy, the settler popula-tion, and the Christian missions.

In his memoirs, Albert Schweitzer, symbol of selfless Christian aid to Africa, asked rhetorically, "Shall a missionary have a thorough education?" justifying his emphatically positive answer by claiming "the more devel-oped the intellectual life and interests of a person are, the better he can stand Africa. In the other case he will easily, as they say here, become 'niggerized' [*verniggern*]."[55] This gives an indication of the complicated relationship between Christianity and Social Darwinism in the colonial context. The majority of race scientists rejected religion as an obstacle to the realization of their perfect society based on eugenic demands.[56] Nevertheless, the churches absorbed large parts of Social Darwinist thought. There were some fundamental disagreements between religious dogma and Social Darwinism, but the "race question" was not one of them.[57] The genetic inferiority of the black race was as self-evident for the German churches as it was for state officials.[58] The colonial administration in Berlin was aware of the important role the missions played in the colonies.[59] But the discourse on "mongrels" and "miscegenation" again showed the conflict arising from the churches' support of colonialism and its racist justifications on the one hand and the insistence on certain Christian "basic values" on the other. The colonial governors worked on constructing a society that contained two groups having no connection whatsoever beside the master-servant relationship: privileged whites and powerless "natives." This project was actively supported by the majority of the missionaries, who justified not only the "native laws" but also the anti-miscegenation legislation by declaring that "[t]he state has the right and duty to probe the relations of its subjects as to whether they fulfill its demands on matrimony. Only if these are fulfilled can it recognize them as marriages and grant the protection of families and the resulting children. How it defines these demands is its field of authority[. . .]"[60]

The missionaries' superiors in Germany, however, were not quite happy with this extreme loyalty to the local governments. Objections to the legislation were practical as well as ethical. There simply were not enough white women in the colonies, church leaders argued, so white men had to turn to African women and if white men did so, then better in the legitimized form of marriage than by living in sin.[61] But the missions' resistance was also a fight for territorial rights. The German Southwest African governors had outlawed not only civil but also religious marriage ceremonies. This was trespassing into a space that the churches considered exclusively their own. Accordingly, they remained uncompromising in their demand for a legalization of "intermarriage," but were ready to grant the government's right to strip this legality of its most important consequences:

> Christian morality demands—our opponents might say—that the colored wives and mulatto children acquire the German nationality with all legal consequences, [that] Christian morality wants to force the bastardization of the German nation! No, that is not the conclusion. Christianity simply demands that a possible relation between the white [man] and the colored woman should be legitimate; it does not judge on its legal position. Should the German government think it wise to refuse the colored elements entry into the community of citizens, Christianity will not protest.[62]

In the question of the colonial anti-miscegenation legislation, the churches used the right of moral intervention, which was a central part of their definition of the relationship between state and church. But the churches explicitly did this in a manner that left the racist base of the colonial system untouched. By leaving unchallenged the connection of nationality to race, which went beyond the limits of colonial legislation, the churches even went considerably further and generally accepted the legitimacy of laws based on "racial" considerations.

Another public force that saw itself as a moral authority was the rapidly growing popular press. While left and liberal papers clearly did not consider the colonies a topic of central interest, the conservative German press followed the colonial developments closely.[63] The "purity of the Germanic race," which had to be kept intact through all conquests, was a dominant topic from the beginning, and it soon became clear that the majority of the mainstream media supported the racist policies. Already in 1906, the *Leipziger Neuesten Nachrichten* commented favorably on the exclusion of African Germans from the white community in German Southwest Africa, stating that "these measures deserve the highest praise as an infallible sign of dutiful racial pride; any other solution is quite impossible to imagine. Better to cut off a limb in time than to intersperse the organism with foreign matter that later cannot be removed."[64] The references to the language of scientific racism are obvious. At the turn of the last century, a reference to "the latest scientific discoveries" was a necessary ingredient in public discussions of the ever-present "race question." Claims that had been developed by Social Darwinists and used by colonial administrators to justify their proceedings had found their way into the daily press. The theories of the new scientific racism that had easily permeated academia through the colonial debates became part of a public consensus that in turn facilitated the practical implementation of these theories in the colonies. Decisive criteria and justification for the treatment of Germany's black subjects were the scientific "facts" produced by Social Darwinism. Native and anti-miscegenation laws that went beyond the regulations of all other colonial powers and the discourse around them clearly betray a German racism that affected the public consciousness as well as political strategies in the confrontation with "inferior races." Common opinion demanded strict segregation, and sexual relationships between members of different races were unacceptable. Inconceivable, even, was a population that combined a German and an African heritage; after all, the incompatibility of these groups' biological and cultural identities was one of the foundations of the race hierarchy. That such a population existed nevertheless could no longer be denied after the colonial wars, so instead it was ideologically eliminated through a discourse taking place in the colonies and Germany itself. In this discourse, the duty to "protect the purity of the German nation" was constructed as superceding the limits established by existing laws and social conventions of the civic community. "Racial maxims" informed political and ethical norms. This was true for political decision-makers as well as for a large part of the public, a public that through the new mass media and political societies had gained an unequaled influence. Forces within society that could have stopped this development, and should have, according to their own self-images, namely the Social Democrats and the churches, had internalized the racial thinking to such an extent that they either supported measures based on it or only ineffectively resisted them.

The confrontation with a black race defined as completely "other" and "inferior," and yet its "unnatural, dangerous mongrels" defined not as scientific objects or colonial subjects but as potentially part of one's own community led to an intensification of the racist ideology based on a broad social consensus. Sanctified by "respectable" scientists such as Eugen Fischer, the equation of the terms "people" (*Volk*) and "race" became increasingly common. Since the cultural definition of *Volk* was gradually replaced by the biological one of race, the actual existence of "racially foreign," that is, non-"Germanic" Germans could be negated through the postulation of their genetic, metacultural "foreignness." In the eyes of the race scientists, each relation of a "Germanic" individual with a "foreign racial element" was an "infection" of the national body (*Volkskörper*) with "bad blood." The national body was the smallest independent unit, the individual only a correlative part of it. Within the logic of this analogy, only a complete prevention of such relationships could save the "German race" from the assault of the "colored masses." The construction of the race hierarchy necessarily put the "superior" whites on the defensive, since the "inferior races" were always in the majority and had to be held back on all fronts and by all means. Genocide and oppression as practiced in German Southwest Africa could thus be reconstructed as mere self-defense.

African Germans combined what was supposed to be separate. In the colony, the group was legally defined through the one-drop rule and subjected to the same strict regimentation as the rest of the "native" population. Within Germany, though, belonging was constituted not by race but "German blood," granting citizenship to all legitimate descendants of German men, independent of their racial designation. But the deep-set connection of tropes of "blood" and "race" made the German status of nonwhites a very tentative one.[65] The social anthropologists, for example, advocated black Germans' exclusion from the metropolitan society as well, claiming their irrevocable "foreignness": "Apart from differences in the psychic energy itself . . . the Negro, Chinese, Jew, and English possess a different *kind* of mental attitude that also shows when they outwardly have taken on the same culture and language."[66] The presentation of races, ethnicities, and nationalities as exclusive categories already implies that there cannot be any such thing as a black Chinese or an English Jew. In the same manner the association of "Germanness" with "blood" and "race" presented the combination "black" and "German" as an impossibility, not only in the colonies, but in general. This reasoning quickly entered mainstream thought: "The German Empire will have many colored subjects in the future, but colored Germans there will never be, since color and other signifiers mark the human bastard with the inextinguishable sign of its descent and according to these signs, it will be named and ethnologically classified."[67]

Humans thus objectified and pathologized could not be seen as equals, as fully entitled citizens, and least of all as "Germans." The living conditions of blacks in Germany were vastly affected by these scientific and political discourses. Their congruous biologist definition of Germanness, which not only marginalized nonwhites but also completely judged them by supposed "racial characteristics," necessarily led to social discrimination. While legitimate children of German men and African women were legally "German" as long as they lived in Germany and not in the colonies, this was different for African Germans whose fathers were African and extended their nationality, or lack of it, onto their wives and children.[68] In accordance with its general colonial policy, the German government tried to prevent its colonial subjects from coming to the motherland at all.[69] Those who did overcome the bureaucratic obstacles often belonged to their home countries' elite and intended to study or learn a trade in the metropole.[70] But if they remained in Germany after they finished their education, they almost always ended working as musicians, circus artists, or waiters. The Social Darwinist conviction that blacks, due to their genetic inferiority, had to form the underclass of any white society worked as a self-fulfilling prophecy, and African immigrants could get only those jobs that were considered appropriate for them.[71] The same mechanism worked in other areas. A local magistrate in the Weimar Republic rejected an African's request for naturalization, claiming that "direct citizenship should be granted only to those natives who in their educational and economic level and in their morals deserved the civil and legal equality with non-natives" and that no "full-blooded native" could fulfill this prerequisite.[72] German colonial subjects had no claim to German citizenship. Instead they were given "certificates" of their colonial status that legally left them without nationality.[73] With the end of World War I and the loss of the colonies for Germany, former colonial subjects living in Germany officially became stateless. In other respects as well the shift from monarchy to democratic republic failed to improve the situation of the nation's black inhabitants.

Already in colonial times, sex and gender stereotypes had structured the discourse of racial exclusion. The ban on interracial sex was relevant for white men only if they threatened the established order. German society opposed those relationships that gave black women a position not granted to them in the race hierarchy, while prostitution and the rape of

African women by white settlers and soldiers, widespread in the colonies, went largely unremarked.[74] White men became "race traitors" not through sexual but through legal relationships with black women. During the colonial debates it had become obvious that this "treachery" was less disturbing for the German public than the opposite case, namely relations between white women and black men. The latter were not considered "real men" within the dominant discourse, supposedly lacking the intellectual and moral superiority used to justify patriarchal rule. But at the same time, they symbolized the essence of maleness, an exaggeration of men's "natural" sexual aggressiveness—and one that was necessarily directed against white women. A reference to black men's "natural" drive to rape white women was mandatory whenever white aggression had to be presented as self-defense. Far from seeing relationships between black men and white women as private, German media, government, and political parties and societies in rare unity saw it as their national task and patriotic duty to prevent such relationships by all possible means.[75] The loss of the colonies affected this stance as little as did the newly installed Social Democratic government. On the contrary, the early years of the Weimar Republic saw a racist campaign that far exceed that against intermarriage.

In a Germany that had been roughly awakened from its dream of empire, the presence of several thousand African soldiers among the French troops that occupied the Rhineland became the symbol of a world turned upside down. Outside of the colonial context, beyond the German "master's" control, serving the French archenemy instead, the Africans, inferior in the best of cases, now were completely turned into beasts by German propaganda, which presented pictures of captured "cannibals" and stories of "savages who . . . walked around with necklaces from which hung up to 30 ears of 'dirty boches'" and "boasted with the cut-off head of a German soldier."[76] The Germans, who were for the most part unable to accept their defeat in the war and who regarded the loss of the colonies as strictly temporary, saw the African troops as a tremendous provocation. The government initiated a campaign against them largely financed by the heavy industry and soon resting on a broad public alliance of political parties (excepting only the communists), nationalist groups, women's and professional organizations, and the churches.[77] Blacks had such an enormous symbolic power for Germans that reality was superceded. While a substantial part of the French colonial force was made up of Asian soldiers, these were ignored by the propaganda that exclusively focused on the Africans.[78] The image of the black as master rather than servant unleashed all fears and fantasies that had been projected onto him.[79] An interpellation in 1920 of all members of the National Assembly (except the USPD)[80] quickly came to the heart of the matter:

> After the peace treaty, the French and Belgians continue to use colored troops in the occupied territories of the Rhineland. The Germans feel humiliated by this abusive use of the coloreds and see with growing indignation that these have sovereignty in German civilized territories. For German women and children—girls and boys—these savages are a gruesome danger. Their honor, body and life, purity and innocence are destroyed. There are more and more known cases of colored troops violating German women and children, hurting, even killing those who resist. Only a small part of this hideousness is becoming known. Shame, fear of brute revenge close the mouths of the unhappy victims. The French and Belgian authorities installed public houses in the territories occupied by them, in front of which colored troops huddle; there, German women are relinquished to them! These conditions are shameful, humiliating, unbearable![81]

Similar, though much more detailed, claims were made in endless pamphlets, books, flyers, and postcards that often verged on the pornographic. Even a play and two films on the subject were produced.[82] The government propaganda concentrated on the rape of German women and culture by black troops, excluding the subject of "mongrelization," since a survey among women who had borne children by African soldiers revealed that only one of them had been raped, a fact that seemed better left unpublished.[83] On the other hand, nongovernment organizations in and outside of Germany emphasized the threat of "mongrelization" from the beginning, exploiting modes of thought that had been activated at least a decade before and were still widespread. The *Ärztliche Rundschau*, a medical journal, asked rhetorically: "Shall we silently endure that in future days not the light songs of white, beautiful, well-built, intelligent, agile, healthy Germans will ring on the shores of the Rhine, but the croaking sounds of grayish, low-browed, broad-muzzled, plump, bestial, syphilitic mulattos?"[84]

Within the Social Darwinist system of logic, the mere existence of African Germans was a threat—and what else could these hybrid creatures, "half Negro, half German," be? They were invested with an enormous power; even though they were few in number, they could destroy the German nation by tainting its still "pure blood." This was a topic that had already dominated the discourse around the colonial "mongrel race," but grew even more important now that the enemy within, "the mongrel," had penetrated the heart of the national body and was about to poison it.

"In the long run, this is about the survival or ruin of the white race!"[85] A widespread fear of "degeneration," mixed with visions of doom that appeared plausible after the experience of the world war, was fueled further by the economic depression. Simultaneously, there was a naive and optimistic belief in the omnipotence of scientific progress. Only the modern sciences were believed to be able to prevent a catastrophe of their own invention. Social anthropology, sexual science, criminology, and eugenics biologized all aspects of society and thereby strengthened the claim that their findings must be the basis of political decisions. "Born criminals," "anti-socials," "perverts," and the "racially inferior" were the enemy within, trying to destroy the German nation by attacking its gene pool. That a scientific, disinterested analysis of society seemed to be at the root of the eugenic measures deemed necessary made them acceptable across political, national, and academic borders. Eugenics flourished in the Soviet Union and Switzerland, Sweden and the United States.[86] Progressive sexologists demanded eugenic sterilizations as did Protestant clergy, feminists, and nationalist politicians.[87]

The propaganda against the African troops in the Rhineland had made the image of the "syphilitic mulatto" commonplace. In connection with the discourse on degeneration, she or he became the symbol for the conjunction of the "inner and outer fight for survival,"[88] for the menace inner and outer "race enemies" posed to the German people. In 1923 the Weimar government initiated a list of all African German children in the Rhineland (and not only those fathered by soldiers). While it was not clear what one was to do with them, the government apparently did not doubt that a "solution" had to be found. Several possibilities were discussed and rejected as impracticable: send all the children to Africa (but there were no colonies available) or sterilize them so they could not further poison the German nation (but the mothers did not consent). While in the end, no measures beyond registration were taken, it is important that in the late Weimar Republic the sterilization of humans on "racial grounds" was entirely imaginable for the state as well as for science. Indeed, it was the politicians, not the scientists, who for egotistical reasons shied away from a practical implementation. It was science with its unrestrained promotion of the idea of rapid "degeneration" that worked towards an escalation.[89]

While the national and international accountability of the democratically installed Weimar government prevented a realization of these scientific ideals, the situation changed radically with the National Socialist ascension to power. Already in 1929, the eugenicist Fritz Lenz had called Adolf Hitler "the first politician of real influence who has understood that racial hygiene is a central task of all politics and who actively supports it."[90] The high esteem was mutual. During his prison term in the 1920s, Hitler had studied standard eugenic works and faithfully reproduced their theories on "miscegenation" in his *Mein Kampf*.[91] His position did not differ qualitatively from the consensus on the inferiority and dangerousness of "mongrels" prevailing in Imperial Germany and Weimar. The Rhineland occupation fit into this pattern as well, now as a means to connect racism and anti-Semitism. Already in the 1920s, the proponents of the campaign against the African troops had claimed that the Africans, too primitive to act independently, were used by others to "destroy the German race." While most authors had blamed the French, Hitler accused a group that by now had become the "mongrel race" par excellence: "Jews were and are the ones who bring the Negro to the Rhine . . . to destroy, through the inevitable mongrelization, the hated white race, to fling it from its cultural and political height and to themselves become their masters."[92] The "mongrelization of the German nation," a staple topic for decades, now became one of the "Third Reich's racial problems." The eugenic movement gave its unconditional support to the new regime.[93] Contrary to popular myths, it did not merely follow orders more or less reluctantly, but frequently initiated measures.[94] Within the international Social Darwinist community, the consensus was that only a population policy based on eugenic principles could solve humanity's pressing problems. That the "social value" of a person or group largely depended on its "genetic quality" and that this again determined its "right to live" was a conviction that far exceeded the borders of national socialist Germany, and the latter was often perceived as an ideal field of experimentation.

The African Germans registered in the Weimar lists soon became objects of eugenic studies assessing their genetic inferiority. In 1937, a commission consisting of members of key departments, such as interior and foreign affairs, and well-known "race scientists" such as Alfred Ploetz, ordered their forced and secret sterilization.[95] Apart from this measure that explicitly singled out black Germans, African Germans were affected by a number of laws aimed at "Jews and other foreign elements [*Artfremde*]," for instance, expatriation and second-class citizenship. Additionally, the exclusion from public and religious organizations was part of black Germans' daily life, as were bans on using public transport and attending public events. The loss of citizenship, the exclusion from schools, universities, and professions, and the forced sterilizations had changed the status of African Germans from outsiders to that of persecuted minority. Since their "non-Aryanness" was obvious at first glance, there was not only state prosecution but also violence from compatriots who did not need the fascist propaganda to believe in the inferiority of the "mongrels."[96] Overall, the fate of black Germans during National Socialism was inconsistent. While some paradoxically survived in relative security, as they were needed as extras for the colonial movies that were supposed to prepare Germans for their future world empire, others were deported to concentration camps.[97]

Already in Imperial Germany, Social Darwinism's racial component had become consensual to such a degree that it almost exclusively determined most Germans' attitudes towards blacks. Developments in the Weimar Republic can be seen as a consistent continuation of this ideology's implementation. The transition from monarchy to democracy, which brought numerous social and political changes, did not affect the dominant view on race. This is clearly mirrored in the Weimar government's serious consideration of a sterilization of black Germans on "racial grounds." The actual elimination of the unbearable discord African Germans embodied for the white majority, through sterilization, expatriation, and internment, cannot be accounted for by a sudden growth of racism caused by the Nazi propaganda. Rather, it was the zenith of a development that had been vital since the turn of the century, and that did not end in 1945. The persecution of African Germans under National Socialism was discussed neither in the immediate postwar period nor later. Indeed, the fate of this part of the population was so thoroughly erased from the public mind that a 1960 study on Germany's "colored children" could merely conclude that "after the First World War, about 800 children of colored French soldiers were born in the Rhineland. Only a few of them still live in Germany. Many seem to have left or died young."[98]

Those who had survived could expect neither compensation nor any recognition of their suffering. The often painful and slow process in which African Germans had to fight for the return of their German citizenship instead shows that the Federal Republic was as unwilling to see them as part of the nation as were all governments before. The unwillingness of politics, population, and science to deal with this part of German history meant that the tradition that had determined the treatment of black Germans since the late nineteenth century could survive into postwar Germany. Ignored again when the German *Volk* was defined, they nevertheless soon returned to the center of public interest, again, not as part of normal life, but as symbols of the exact opposite, the occupation of Germany by the Allies (see Heide Fehrenbach's essay, chapter 5, in this volume). While the term "black Germans" seems a contradiction in terms to many even today, *Besatzungskind* (occupation baby) is still part of the common vocabulary—used exclusively for blacks, even though more than 90 percent of the children fathered by Allied soldiers were white.[99] A strictly temporal perception of black Germans in the context of "states of emergency" made it possible to use them as symbolic presences and at the same time define their factual presence as merely temporary and "abnormal." African Germans were perceived as a group *only* when they were to signify a (violent) disruption of normalcy, a danger to Germany's homogeneity and sovereignty. Their group identity thus was always complementary to "real Germans," and it is not surprising that phases of heightened interest in them did not result in a heightened acceptance. Rather, they were returned into nonexistence and, all proof to the contrary, again and again defined as "exotic" exceptions. While the inclusion of Gerald Asamoah into the German national soccer team might be a hopeful sign of a more inclusive, less race-conscious Germany, the fate of Erwin Kostedde and Jimmy Hartwig indicates that the now-celebrated "first black" member of the national team might soon be completely erased from the public mind. The mechanisms of exclusion are still intact, and will likely continue to be so, until their existence is first admitted and then thoroughly analyzed.

Notes

All translations from the original German are the author's.

1. For a thorough overview of racism among soccer fans and clubs in Germany (and Europe), see the exhibition "Tatort Stadion," published online at www.tatort-stadion.de and as a booklet by BAFF (Hamburg, 2002). See also "Otto Addo kann nicht tanzen," interview with Gerald Asamoah and Afrob, *jetzt* (supplement to the *Süddeutsche Zeitung*) 33 (2001): 18–22 and "Lockerheit muss sein," interview with Gerald Asamoah, *Hamburger Abendblatt*, 8 June 2002, 28.

2. "Tore für Deutschland und gegen Rassenhass," *Hamburger Morgenpost*, 29 May 2001, 28–29. The article tells more about good intentions and their limitations. The unnamed author also states that Asamoah laughs all the time and plays "instinctively."

3. On Erwin Kostedde see also Ingolf Gritschneder's documentary *Erwin im Abseits* (Westdeutscher Rundfunk [WDR], 1998).

4. See "Tore für Deutschland und gegen Rassenhass;" Bernd Müllender, "Blondie für die Merkels," *die tageszeitung*, 22 March 2001, 18; "Asamoah winkt die A-National-mannschaft," *Extra Zeitung*, 29 May 2001, n. p.; "Entscheidung für Deutschland," *Spiegel Online*, 19 March 2001, n. p., http://www.spiegelonline.de, accessed 19 March 2001; Christoph Dannowski, "Asamoah trägt den Adler," *Neue Presse*, and "Rudi Völler will 'Aufsteiger' Asamoah holen," *RPOnline*, 6 May 2001, both accessed through http://www.rponline.de, 6 May 2001.

5. Again, this might seem too generalized a statement. It has become obvious, though, from the literature by black Germans that there are a number of invariable constants in their perception by the white majority—through the decades and across the East-West divide—central among them the stubborn conviction that black Germans must "really" come from either Africa or the Americas. See Jeanine Kantara, "Schwarz. Und deutsch. Kein Widerspruch? Für viele meiner weißen Mitbürger schon," *Die Zeit* 37, 7 September 2000; Olumide Popoola and Beldan Sezen (eds.), *Talking Home: Heimat aus unserer eignene Feder—Frauen of color in Deutschland* (Amsterdam: Blue Moon Press, 1999); Cathy Gelbin, Kader Konuk, and Peggy Piesche (eds.), *Aufbrüche: Kulturelle Produktionen von Migrantinnen, Schwarzen und jüdischen Frauen in Deutschland* (Königsberg/ Th: Ulrike Helmer, 1999); Katharina Oguntoye, May Opitz, and Dagmar Schultz (eds.), *Farbe bekennen* (Berlin: Orlanda Frauenverlag, 1986). While in the 1980s poetry was the major field of expression for Afro-German artists, over the last decade hip-hop has become the artform in which black Germans are most visible, even exerting a certain dominance. The experience of growing up black in Germany is a recurring topic in the works of such hip-hop artists as Afrob, Samy Deluxe, Skillz en Masse, Moses Pellheim, and Advanced Chemistry, and their songs often reflect exactly the same prejudiced reactions as the poems of their predecessors twenty years earlier. See, e.g., Advanced Chemistry, "Fremd im eigenen Land," (1992); Afrob, "Made in Germany," (2001); Brothers Keepers, "Lightkultur," (2001).

6. None of the articles on Asamoah, Hartwig, or Kostedde mentioned above uses the term "afro-deutsch"; all of the literature by black Germans listed in the preceeding note does. The project "Brothers Keepers," a group of Germany's most important black hip-hop artists, was founded in 2001 to mobilize against the normalization of racist violence and received immense media attention. When asked about the effect of his work, founder Adé Odukoya listed the use of "afro-deutsch" by at least some of these media as a big success. Daniel Bax and Joshua Aikins, "Wir sind stolz, Deutsche zu sein," *die tageszeitung*, 7 December 2001, 15.

7. Peter Martin, *Schwarze Teufel, edle Mohren. Afrikaner in Bewußtsein und Geschichte der Deutschen* (Hamburg: Junius, 1993).

8. See Kantara, "Schwarz. Und deutsch."

9. Half of the Turkish national team, to return to the soccer world once again, consists of young men who were born and raised in Germany, still live there, and speak German far better than Turkish but who lack "German blood" and therefore possess only the Turkish nationality of their migrant parents.

10. Such analyses have been attempted, of course. Over last decade, a few scholars have published book-length studies on the Afro-German experience, following various approaches, looking for material evidence of the role blacks played historically in Germany, trying to reconstruct their living conditions, looking for the relation between images of race and gender, between science and colonialism or, in my case, between race and nation. Significantly, most of these scholars are American and African German. It should be mentioned though, that the first steps towards rediscovering the buried Afro-German history were made by black German activists rather than the academic community. Ethnic diversity is still not part of German universities' curricula. History, sociology, and German studies for the most part still assume a clear division between (implicitly white) Germans and "foreigners," which leaves no space for the study of German minorities (which, of course, include not only blacks, but also Turkish Germans, Sinti, or German Jews). See

Martin, *Schwarze Teufel*; Katharina Oguntoye, *Eine Afro-Deutsche Geschichte* (Berlin: Hoho Verlag, 1997); Pascal Grosse, *Kolonialismus, Eugenik und bürgerliche Gesellschaft in Deutschland 1850–1918* (Frankfurt: Campus, 2000); Fatima El-Tayeb, *Schwarze Deutsche* (Frankfurt: Campus 2001); Clarence Lusane, *Hitler's Black Victims* (New York: Routledge, 2002); and Yara-Colette Lemke Muniz de Faria, *Zwischen Fürsorge und Ausgrenzung* (Berlin: Metropol, 2002).

11. See Reiner Pommerin, *"Sterilisierung der Rheinlandbastarde:" Das Schicksal einer farbigen deutschen Minderheit 1918–1937* (Düsseldorf: Droste, 1979).

12. Only in 2000 did Germany depart from a citizenship law based exclusively on *ius sanguinis*, "the law of blood," a construction that necessarily depends on a problematic construction of nationhood. Its point of reference is a mythical prenational community embodying a nation's essence, and therefore only the descendents of this community are granted an unqualified right to citizenship. See Helga Schultz, "Mythos und Aufklärung. Frühformen des Nationalismus in Deutschland," *Historische Zeitschrift* 236:1 (1996), 31–67.

13. George L. Mosse, *Towards the Final Solution* (Madison: University of Wisconsin Press, 1978); David T. Goldberg, *Racist Culture: Philosophy and the Politics of Meaning* (Cambridge, Mass.: Blackwell, 1993); Sara Lennox, Sara Friedrichsmeyer, and Susanne Zantop (eds.), *The Imperialist Imagination: German Colonialism and Its Legacy* (Ann Arbor: University of Michigan Press, 1998). For the effects on blacks in Germany, see Martin, *Schwarze Teufel*.

14. Jürgen Kroll, "Zur Entstehung und Institutionalisierung einer naturwissenschaftlichen und sozialpolitischen Bewegung. Die Entwicklung der Eugenik/ Rassenhygiene bis zum Jahre 1933" (Ph. D. diss., Tübingen, 1983), 2. Peter Weingart, Jürgen Kroll, and Kurt Bayertz, *Rasse, Blut und Gene. Geschichte der Eugenik und Rassenhygiene in Deutschland* (Frankfurt: Suhrkamp, 1996), 41.

15. Central for German Social Darwinists were the works of Charles Darwin, Francis Galton, Arthur de Gobineau, Georges Vacher de Lapouge, and Otto Ammon.

16. See Weingart et al., *Rasse, Blut und Gene*.

17. Alfred Ploetz, "Der Konflikt zwischen Individualhygiene und Rassenhygiene," in Günter Altner (ed.), *Der Darwinismus: Die Geschichte einer Theorie* (Darmstadt: Wissenschaftliche Buchgesellschaft, 1981), 125. The quotation mirrors the race scientists' undecided attitude towards "the Jewish race." While a nationalist anti-Semitism was flourishing at the turn of the last century, Social Darwinists still wondered whether Jews were an especially "pure" or extremely "mongrelized" race or no race at all, and if so, whether that was good or bad. While all scientists agreed on the "black race's" complete inferiority, a number of them (rapidly dwindling after 1914) saw Jews as part of the "white race."

18. This does not mean however, that the eugenicists did not pay attention to the dangers of "racial mixing." They attempted among other things an "eugenic assessment" of miscegenation using practical examples from the German colonies. Bundesarchiv Berlin (Federal Archive, Berlin, hereafter BAB), Bestand R 1001 Reichskolonialamt, 5417/1, 210.

19. "Social hygiene" means all state measures aimed at the well-being of a general population, i.e. health care, social security, etc., as opposed to measures aimed at only the "racially superior material" within a given population.

20. See Kroll, "Zur Entstehung und Institutionalisierung." The society's envisioned international branches were to be limited to "white nations" as well, and its head, Alfred Ploetz, had been a member of a "Germanic" secret society since his student days. Weingart et al., *Rasse, Blut und Gene*, 93.

21. The leader of the social anthropological movement, Ludwig Woltmann, devoted two books, *Die Germanen und die Renaissance in Italien* (1905) and *Die Germanen in Frankreich* (1907), to the theory that every European "genius," from Homer to da Vinci, had been of purely Nordic stock.

22. Wilhelm Schallmeyer, *Vererbung und Auslese in ihrer soziologischen und politischen Bedeutung* (Jena, 1903).

23. Friedrich Hertz, *Rasse und Kultur. Eine kritische Untersuchung der Rassentheorien* (Leipzig: Kroener, 1915).

24. Probably nothing was more damaging here than Georg Wilhelm Friedrich Hegel's judgment of Africa as "the continent without history." In effect it placed Africans outside the realm of humanity but nevertheless for almost two centuries was not really called into question. G.W.F. Hegel, *Vorlesungen über die Philosophie der Geschichte* (Stuttgart: Reclam, 1961), 153.

25. This does not mean that blacks necessarily were the focus of the worst racist attacks, intellectually or physically. Other "races," such as the "Slavs" and of course the Jews, at times took center stage in the twentieth-century German discourse on race, but blacks never lost their status as "the lowest race."

26. Ludwig Wilser, "Die Rassengliederung der Menschheit. Die modernen Rassen," *PAR* (1906/7), 438–46, here 438.

27. See e.g. W. von Polenz, *Das Land der Zukunft* (Berlin, 1906); "Lage und Charakter der Neger in Nordamerika," *PAR* (1905/6), 486–87; Hermann Gerhard, "Die Negerfrage in den Vereinigten Staaten," *PAR* 5, no. 5 (1906), 268–81; Hans Fehlinger, "Die Neger in den Vereinigten Staaten," *PAR* (1907/8), 363–79.

28. Of course the "nature vs. nurture" debate was a heated one in other areas as well, with Social Darwinists invariably arguing that the genetic disposition of certain subordinated groups such as women, the working class, and the mentally ill assigned them a natural, unchangeable place within society. See Heidrun Kaupen-Haas and Christian Saller (eds.), *Wissenschaftlicher Rassismus. Analyse einer Kontinuität in den Human- und Naturwissenschaften* (Campus: Frankfurt, 1999).

29. Gerhard, "Die Negerfrage." Erwin Baur, Erwin, Eugen Fischer, and Fritz Lenz, *Grundriß der menschlichen Erblichkeitslehre und Rassenhygiene* (München, 1923), 151.

30. Such as, for example, Hans F. K. Günther, *Rassenkunde des deutschen Volkes* (München, 1926).

31. Gustav Schmoller, Bernhard Dernburg, Walter Delbrück, et al., *Reichstagsauflösung und Kolonialpolitik* (Berlin: Wedekind, 1907), 7.

32. Gerhard, "Die Negerfrage," 277.

33. Those theories were often immediately racialized. Liberalism and socialism, for example, were interpreted as typical products of the Jewish and Slavic races' mentalities. See Baur et al., *Grundriß der menschlichen*, 425, 432.

34. Ludwig Woltmann, *Politische Anthropologie* (Berlin: Ludwig Diedrichs, 1903). See Baur et al., *Grundriß der menschlichen*.

35. Ludwig Schemann, *Die Rasse im Schrifttum der Neuzeit* (München, 1931).

36. Gerhard von Skal, "Die Rassenfrage in den Vereinigten Staaten," *PAR* 5, no. 1 (1906), 53–54.

37. "Folgen der Blutmischung," *PAR* (1909/10).

38. Wolfgang J. Mommsen, *Der autoritäre Nationalstaat. Verfassung, Gesellschaft und Kultur im deutschen Kaiserreich* (Frankfurt: Fischer, 1990).

39. Wilhelm Heinrich Solf, *Kolonialpolitik. Mein politisches Vermächtnis* (Berlin: Reimar von Hobbing, 1919), 56.

40. Ludwig Woltmann, "Die Klassen- und Rassentheorie in der Soziologie," *PAR* 4, no. 8 (1905), 415–24, here 424.

41. The most important of these organizations were the Alldeutscher Verband (Pan-German Legue), the Flottenverein (Navy League), and the Deutsche Kolonialgesellschaft (German Colonial Society). See Arthur J. Knoll and Lewis H. Gann (eds.), *Germans in the Tropics: Essays in German Colonial History* (New York: Greenwood Press, 1987).

42. Joachim Kranold, reprinted in Alfred Mansfeld (ed.), *Sozialdemokratie und Kolonieen* [sic] (Berlin: Sozialistische Monatshefte, 1919), 32.

43. Jansson, ibid., 29.

44. Johannes Schippel (1919), ibid., 9.

45. The most striking example is Ludwig Woltmann, leader of the radical social anthropological faction of Social Darwinism. While many of his colleagues politically leaned to the far right, he was a loyal member of the SPD and close ally of Bernstein. Many of his books and articles were devoted to developing a racist Marxism. While his theories were disputed even among the most procolonial socialists, neither he nor his critics saw them in necessary contradiction to the party's ideology. See Ludwig Woltmann, *System des moralischen Bewußtseins* (1898); *Die Darwinsche Theorie und der Sozialismus* (1899); *Der historische Materialismus* (1900); "Die wirtschaftlichen und politischen Grundlagen des Klassenkampfes," *Sozialistische Monatshefte* (1901); "Die Klassen- und Rassentheorie in der Soziologie," *PAR* 4, no. 8 (1905), 415–24; "Marxismus und Rassentheorie," *PAR* 6, no. 5 (1907), 268–79.

46. Paul Rohrbach in Theodor Grentrup, *Die Rassenmischehen in den deutschen Kolonien* (Paderborn, 1914), 101.

47. The German Southwest African Rehoboths (known also as "Rehoboth Basters" and discussed further in the next chapter) were descendents of Nama women and Dutch and German settlers and had lived in relative isolation for some decades. During the first years of German colonization, settlers had been encouraged by the authorities to marry Rehoboth women, both because they were not "full-blooded Africans" and because they possessed considerable farmland. When German rule had been established and policies shifted from negotiation to violence, the Rehoboths' status deteriorated. See Solf, *Kolonialpolitik*.

48. Race scientists up until then had been limited to extensive measurements of bodies, developing endless types of face and brain indices unanimously "proving" the white male's superiority. Fischer's "anthropobiology" aimed at introducing new, genetic methods. While his Mendel-based "discoveries" were extremely limited, race science did indeed shift from traditional anthropology to human genetics. Eugen Fischer, *Die Rehobother Bastards und das Bastardisierungsproblem beim Menschen* (Jena: Gustav Fischer, 1913), 65. See also Karl-Heinz Roth, "Schöner neuer Mensch. Der Paradigma wechsel der Klassischen Genetik und seine Auswirkungen auf die Bevölkerungsbiologie des 'Dritten Reichs,'" in Kaupen-Haas and Saller, *Wissenschaftlicher Rassismus*, 346–424.

49. Ludwig Schemann, *Neues aus der Welt Gobineaus. Echos auf ein Buch* (Hildburghausen, 1912).

50. Benno Müller-Hill, *Tödliche Wissenschaft. Die Aussonderung von Juden, Zigeunern und Geisteskranken 1933–1945* (Reinbek: Rowohlt, 1984).

51. And not only by his contemporaries. See Franz-Josef Schulte-Althoff, "Rassenmischung im kolonialen System. Zur deutschen Kolonialpolitik im letzten Jahrzehnt vor dem Ersten Weltkrieg," *Historisches Jahrbuch* 105 (1985), 52–94.

52. See El-Tayeb, *Schwarze Deutsche*, 84–93.

53. Fischer, *Die Rehobother Bastards*, 303, emphasis in the original.

54. For example, see "Urteil des Obergerichts Windhuk im Fall Karl Ludwig Baumann," 12 March 1913, BAB, R 1001, 5424, 51 and Willy Krabbenhöft to the president of the *Fortschrittliche Volkspartei* (Progressive People's Party), 18 September 1913, BAB, R 1001 Reichskolonialamt, 5418/2, 331–35.

55. Albert Schweitzer, *Zwischen Wasser und Urwald* (Bern, 1923), 143.

56. Alfred Ploetz, *Ziele und Aufgaben der Rassenhygiene* (Braunschweig, 1911); Ludwig Woltmann, "Grundfragen der Rassenpsychologie," *PAR* 6 (1906/7), 99, 100f.

57. Apart from the churches' rejection of the theory of evolution, conflicts arose mainly around the question of "eugenic" sterilizations. Protestantism, the dominant faith of the rising bourgeoisie (and of 80 percent of German settlers in German Southwest Africa), was generally more willing to compromise on these issues than Catholicism.

58. For an overview of contemporary Protestant and Catholic positions on this topic see Grentrup, *Die Rassenmischehen*.

59. Local authorities and settlers, often less pragmatic and more racist than the colonial bureaucracy in Berlin, were less trusting of the Christian missions' work. Especially during the colonial wars between 1904 and 1907, they accused missionaries of secretly supporting the African uprising, seeing the churches' "mellow" attitude on the race question as the motive for this treachery.

60. C. Mirbt, "Mischehen zwischen Europäern und Eingeborenen," BAB, R 1001 Reichskolonialamt, 5418/2, 390. Similar positions were held by the majority of missionaries in all German colonies. See "Aufzeichnung über die Lösung der Mischehen- und Mischlingsfrage," 12 November 1912, BAB, R 1001 Reichskolonialamt, 5418/2, 25.

61. Grentrup, *Die Rassenmischehen*, 56–61.

62. Ibid., 90–91; see also 111f, 116, and 121f.

63. From 1904 onwards, colonial magazines were a central stage for the discourse on the danger of a "bastardization" of Germany through a colonial "mongrel population." The debate involved local authorities, the imperial colonial office, the churches, nationalist societies, and lawyers (since legal precautions were a central topic). In 1912, after heated debate, the German parliament rejected anti-miscegenation laws but accepted the possibility of limited citizenship rights for Germans of African descent. See Fatima El-Tayeb, "'Blood Is a Very Special Juice': Racialized Bodies and Citizenship in 20th-Century Germany," *International Review of Social History* 44, Supplement 7 (1999): 149–69 and *Schwarze Deutsche*.

64. 8 March 1906, in BAB, R 1001 Reichskolonialamt, 5423/1: Mischehen und Mischlinge in rechtlicher Beziehung, Mai 1887–Dezember 1912, 77.

65. El-Tayeb, "'Blood Is a Very Special Juice.'"

66. Ludwig Woltmann, *PAR* (1907/8), 101, emphasis in the original.

67. *Leipziger Neueste Nachrichten*, 8 March 1906.

68. There were official attempts, though, to reclassify African Germans living in Germany as "natives" and to expel them. See BAB, R 1001 Reichskolonialamt, 5423/1: Mischehen und Mischlinge in rechtlicher Beziehung, Mai 1887–Dezember 1912, 210; BAB, R 1001 Reichskolonialamt, 5424, 79–81.

69. BAB, R 1001 Reichskolonialamt, 7562, 23.

70. Oguntoye, *Eine afro-deutsche Geschichte.*

71. See Baur et al., *Grundriß der menschlichen*; Oguntoye, *Eine afro-deutsche Geschichte.*

72. BAB, R 1001 Reichskolonialamt, 4457/7, 64. A number of Africans succeeded in acquiring the citizenship of the German state they were living in, which indirectly granted them the German nationality. Oguntoye, *Eine afro-deutsche Geschichte.*

73. BAB, R 1001Reichskolonialamt, 5577/7, 105.

74. An exception was Gustave Noske, *Kolonialpolitik und Sozialdemokratie* (Berlin: Dietz, 1914), 87–88.

75. And not only in Germany itself. German farmers in Cameroon, for example, still controlling the ex-colony's economy, refused to allow the return of Cameroonians who had married European women. See BAB, R 1001 Reichskolonialamt: 61 Kol DKG 1077/1: Deutsche Kolonialgesellschaft, 86.

76. Heinrich Distler, *Das deutsche Leid am Rhein. Ein Buch der Anklage gegen die Schandherrschaft des französischen Militarismus* (Minden: Koehler, 1921), 20.

77. Camille Fidel, *Die Widerlegung des Beschuldigungsfeldzuges gegen die farbigen französischen Truppen im besetzten rheinischen Gebiet* (n.p., n.d.).

78. The African troops were Moroccan and Senegalese. While Moroccans are perceived as "Arabs" rather than "Africans" by contemporary Germans, after both the First and the Second World Wars, they became embodiments of Africa's worst imagined excesses: bloodthirsty, unpredictable, and sexually out of control. Rosemarie Lester, *Trivialneger. Das Bild des Schwarzen im westdeutschen Illustriertenroman* (Stuttgart: Heinz, 1982).

79. Black women were objects of projection and obsession as well. In fact, most scientific studies of "black bodies" were conducted on women and especially their genitalia, to which they were largely reduced, equating black women with (pathological) sexuality. Siobhan Somerville, "Scientific Racism and the Emergence of the Homosexual Body," *Journal of the History of Sexuality* 5, no. 2 (1994), 243–66.

80. Soon renamed the German Communist party (KPD), the USPD was formed by a group of radicals within the SPD, who had left the party in protest over the SPD's support of the war.

81. Quoted in Pommerin, *Sterilisierung*, 16.

82. Following E. D. Morel's articles in the British *Daily Herald*, the campaign soon generated a large international following. Initiatives against the "Black Horror on the Rhine" existed in Holland, France, England, Italy, Sweden, Denmark, Hungary, Czechoslovakia, Poland, Norway, New Zealand, Peru, Argentina, and the United States. Robert C. Reinders, "Racialism on the Left: E. D. Morel and the 'Black Horror on the Rhine,'" *International Review of Social History* 13, (1968): 1–28.

83. See Pommerin, *Sterilisierung*.

84. *Ärztliche Rundschau* 47 (1920), reprinted in Distler, *Das deutsche Leid am Rhein*, 56.

85. J. Lang, *Die Schwarze Schmach, Frankreichs Schande* (Berlin: Berliner Verlags- und Treuhandgesellschaft, 1921), 16.

86. See Weingart et al., *Rasse, Blut und Gene.*

87. See Somerville, "Scientific Racism," and Kroll, "Zur Entstehung und Institutionalisierung."

88. Ploetz, quoted in Altner, *Der Darwinismus*, 122.

89. Roth in Kaupen-Haas and Saller, *Wissenschaftlicher Rassismus*, 404.

90. Pommerin, *Sterilisierung*, 40.

91. Adolf Hitler, *Mein Kampf* (München: Zentralverlag der NSDAP, 1940), 314, 324.

92. Ibid., 357.

93. The Kaiser Wilhelm Institutes, national centers of scientific research, dismissed their Jewish employees in 1933. See Müller-Hill, *Tödliche Wissenschaft*. According to the Berlin Document Center, 90 percent of the known anthropologists and eugenicists were members of the Nazi Party, 36 percent belonged to the SS, and 26 percent to the SA. See Benoît Massin, "Anthropologie und Humangenetik im Nationalsozialismus oder: Wie Schreiben deutsche Wissenschaftler ihre eigene Wissenschaftsgeschichte?" in Kaupen-Haas and Saller, *Wissenschaftlicher Rassismus*, 12–64.

94. See Kaupen-Haas and Saller, *Wissenschaftlicher Rassismus*.

95. See Pommerin, *Sterilisierung*.

96. In April 1933, the department of the interior expelled non-German blacks on a large scale. Paulette Reed-Anderson, *Eine Geschichte von mehr als 100 Jahren. Die Anfänge der afrikanischen Diaspora in Berlin* (Berlin: Die Ausländerbeauftragte des Senats, 1995). The department of foreign affairs was concerned with the negative effect Germany's racist policies might have on the country's colonial future and in 1934 initiated a survey of the situation of Africans from the former colonies who had become German citizens. While admitting that their expatriation and ensuing statelessness caused severe problems (namely, the impossibility of leaving the country), the report concluded that not official measures but the population's aggressive racism had the worst effects. See BAB, R 1001 Reichskolonialamt, 7540: Bevölkerungs- und Rassenfragen in den deutschen Schutzgebieten, September 1934 Dezember 1940, 9.

97. El-Tayeb, *Schwarze Deutsche*.

98. Klaus Eyferth, Ursula Brandt, and Wolfgang Hawel, *Farbige Kinder in Deutschland und die Aufgaben ihrer Eingliederung* (München: Juventa, 1960), 11.

99. See ibid.

2

THE FIRST *BESATZUNGSKINDER*

AFRO-GERMAN CHILDREN, COLONIAL CHILDREARING PRACTICES, AND RACIAL POLICY IN GERMAN SOUTHWEST AFRICA, 1890–1914

Krista Molly O'Donnell

Germany has forgotten the origins of its first generation of Afro-German children. In the years following the German military suppression and occupation of Namibia, then called German Southwest Africa, following the Herero and Khoi (Nama) uprisings of 1904 to 1907, an upsurge in miscegenation entailing several hundred births each year took place in the colony until 1914 and likely continued even afterwards. Germans in the metropole and especially German settlers in German Southwest Africa fretted anxiously over the citizenship, welfare, and upbringing of Afro-German children abandoned by their soldier fathers and in some cases their mothers as well. Like the Afro-German children born in the wake of the post-World War II U.S. occupation of West Germany, the problematic "fatherless" biracial children of German Southwest Africa were a powerful and highly visible symbol for Germans attempting to come to grips with their national identity as well as racial and gender ideologies, and therefore the source of significant discussion and policymaking. Unlike the Afro-Germans of the 1950s, however, the earlier generation of occupation children (*Besatzungkinder*) experienced racial segregation and suppression of their ties to German culture and identity, and in some cases of their African heritage as well. Unable to resolve the ambiguities of these children's identity, Germans instead erased the

61

Afro-German population in the colony from their consciousness and their categories of citizenship.

From the very inception of German rule in 1884, the German colonial population in German Southwest Africa included large numbers of Afro-Europeans whose genealogy traced back over centuries of interracial contacts throughout Southern Africa. The most prominent of these belonged to a group known as the Rehoboth Basters, who possessed a fused Anglo-Dutch-African culture and accumulated wealth from agriculture and trade that made them attractive marriage partners to hardscrabble German settler artisans, traders, and ranchers on the colonial frontier. The Baster population, as well as Afro-European individuals of other ethnicities, held an ambiguous position somewhere between the two starkly defined legal categories of privileged "whites" and subordinate "natives" in the colony. Throughout the early nineteenth century, European men in German Southwest Africa and neighboring regions had intermarried with Afro-Europeans and Africans. By 1891, the first date for which we have colonial census figures, records indicate that 41 of the 246 male colonists (16.7 percent) in German Southwest Africa were wed to women labeled "African," many of whom were Baster or of other biracial heritage. The number of Afro-European marriages in the colony remained nearly constant at around 40 during the era of German rule, although the European settler population surged to over 14,000 by 1914. Soon after, Germans lost possession of the colony permanently in the wake of World War I.[1]

At first, the legal Afro-European unions proved most controversial in pre-World War I German Southwest Africa because their offspring appeared to have airtight claims to a European nationality and thus "white" legal status. Nonetheless, German officials in the colony, and many Germans in the metropole as well, were especially reluctant to recognize legitimate Afro-German colonials' citizenship as German and thereby accord them and their offspring the full status and rights of other Germans. To recognize Afro-Germans, even in far-off German Southwest Africa, it seemed, would cast doubt on the "whiteness" of the German nation as a whole. Nonetheless, as the settler population grew, the numbers of Afro-German children born out of wedlock eclipsed the numbers of legitimate offspring. Although illegitimate children also had legal claims to German citizenship, their "fatherless" status quickly became a convenient excuse for denying their German identity and indeed that of all Afro-Germans.

In 1905 at the height of the colonial wars with the Herero, the governor of German Southwest Africa, Friedrich von Lindequist, decreed that marriages between colonists and persons with any African heritage

Figure 2.1. "Karte des Kriegsschauplatzes." This map indicates the major battle sites of the Herero-Nama Wars as well as the locations of key German communities. German settlers in outlying areas accused the Herero of staging treacherous surprise attacks on isolated homesteads early in the conflict, and German countermeasures grew steadily harsher as the war dragged on, culminating in the infamous Battle of Waterberg.

Source: *Kolonie und Heimat*, no. 38, v. 3 (1909–1910).

would henceforth be illegal and, in 1907, the administration ruled that existing unions also were invalid. Although this act contradicted German civil
and constitutional law, it effectively rendered Afro-Germans "illegitimate."
Nonetheless, in many instances, the formerly legitimate Afro-German individuals and families continued to exercise their previous rights without challenge. Those individuals who took their claims to court could find their legal
status as whites in the colony stripped from them. The absolute question of
the legitimacy of these marriages and those of their progeny was by no
means ever fully resolved in the courts or the German administration; however, the marriage ban, as it has come to be known, drew attention to what
for many was the even more insidious problem of illegitimate Afro-German
births. These births were more numerous and more worrisome because they
represented allegedly fatherless children whose upbringing and racial
heredity undermined their ethnic ties to Germany, but whose legal claims
to German citizenship were significant. In the homeland, a number of
Germans of varying political backgrounds argued that the marriage bans
were hypocritical because they would have little effect on reducing the overall number of mixed-race children in the colony. Some critics feared the bans
might actually increase Afro-German births by minimizing paternal responsibility for them. This concern was one of the reasons why the German
Reichstag voted to end all German colonial interracial marriage bans in May
1912. The German administration did not choose to enforce the decision
and continued the ban's effects until the end of colonial rule in 1915.[2]

As the resident German population grew in German Southwest
Africa, the settler population itself became more and more agitated about
the "question of racial mixing" (*Mischrassefrage*), although their concerns did
not always coincide with those of the German public in the metropole. The
immense violence of the German wars of 1904 to 1907 in German
Southwest Africa provoked settlers' fears of and demands for the suppression
of the African population, and brought the perceived problem of miscegenation to new consequence. Unified settler concern over the racial dimen-
sions of reproduction in German Southwest Africa first became apparent
within the colonial community in its associational and institutional life, particularly those realms controlled by prominent middle-class settler men.
Colonial social clubs, an important arena of male-dominated bourgeois
sociability in German Southwest Africa, as in Germany, took the lead in
expressing community censure against mixed-race marriages. In 1906 a territorial newspaper, the Deutsch-Südwestafrikanische Zeitung, reported that
the Windhoek gymnastic society (*Turnverein*) and district farmers' association (*Verein der Farmer*) had begun to deny new memberships to colonists

married to persons of color. According to the piece, the local Gibeon District Settler Society (*Bezirksverein*) went still further, barring the membership of settler men who "appeared to have sexual relations with native women." Since the German colonial administration already had banned mixed-race marriages and police aggressively separated mixed-race couples who were unmarried, these measures likely had little practical application for current or even potential members. Still, these public displays offered a significant symbolic demonstration of united settler support for the 1905 marriage ban, however meaningless the provision proved in actual social practice.[3]

Beneath the apparent popular drive toward social conformity displayed through such measures, strong factions of dissenting colonists continued to voice opposition. The establishment of the controversial paragraph 17f in the 1909 charter for limited settler self-rule in German Southwest Africa, which excluded German men married to or cohabiting with women of color from suffrage, quickly led other organizations to impose similar membership restrictions in their own constitutions. This new attack on German men's traditional patriarchal rights underscored the seriousness of racial anxiety in the colony. Carl Becker, a German farmer married to a Baster wife, commented on the peer pressure exerted within these clubs that compelled their membership to ratify the restrictions unequivocally, despite lingering individual misgivings:

> Soon the veterans', district, rifle, and gymnastic societies hurried to take up this paragraph [§17f] in their charters as the highest moral achievement [*höchste sittliche Errungenschaft*]. The adoption invariably took place, according to newspaper reports, unanimously, although many members scarcely were able to take part in such a vote due to their absences. Thereby, the following occurrence took place: a man married to a Baster wife (A) meets a friend (B): A: "So, you also voted for this fine paragraph!" B: "Yes, but you should not take offense with me. I know your wife to be a very upstanding woman. But they all stood up, so I did too." The case is typical.[4]

Becker's descriptions serve to reinforce the conclusion that the general impulse toward establishing rigid racial boundaries within the German settlers' associations still posed great complications within settler society in the colony as a whole, even though these institutions claimed unanimous support for community enforcement of racial segregation. The new club membership restrictions gradually took on more bite for prominent propertied colonists like Becker, particularly as the more stringent rules now singled out mixed-race couples and families who, until this point, had participated as "respectable," if lesser, members of the European social order in German Southwest Africa. Afro-German children arguably suffered more immediate and more practically from the segregation of private institutions in the colony. In 1906, Windhoek's Lutheran parish expelled "half-white" children from the parish kindergarten, as did the local private school. The state obligation to educate legitimate Afro-German children remained in force. As we shall see, however, many settlers demanded their segregation from white classrooms. Illegitimate children enjoyed no such claims to a public education.[5]

Settler newspapers evinced even more acute anxiety toward the many new births of illegitimate Afro-German children in the wake of the colonial occupation force. After the bloody wars with Herero and Khoi insurgents, some settlers feared discontented biracial individuals would sow the seeds for future uprisings and the potential loss of the colony. Metaphorically, the children's very existence was a betrayal of their fathers' intentions as well as a condemnation of their fathers' moral and sexual conduct, so the children's potential for instigating disorder in the colony was innate. Some German newspapers apparently confused the much larger number of Baster children in German Southwest Africa with the numbers of Afro-German births. As one German newspaper exclaimed, the eight hundred Basters born in 1909 represented "considerably more births of mixed-race children [*Mischlingskinder*] than those of German parents [in the colony]." The colonial newspaper, *Südwest*, however, responded that Basters should not be "thoughtlessly confused with the genuine progeny of a white father and colored mother, the *real Mischlingen* [half-breeds]."[6] The German term "*Mischling*" (someone of mixed ancestry) was racially pejorative, as witnessed by its later use in the Nazi era to delegitimize individuals of combined Jewish and non-Jewish heritages. Thus the statement, with its peculiar emphasis on the new population of Afro-German individuals as distinctly anomalous and threatening to the social order, underscores how the births resulting from the colonial wartime occupation exacerbated the already heightened concern of German settlers over miscegenation. The newspaper went on to cite Professor D. Haußleiter of Halle of the German missionary movement, who identified Basters as loyal to the colonists and opposed to insurrection. By contrast, he estimated only three to four hundred "half-white children to speak of, who run around in the colony fatherless." Of these, he reported that the Protestant Rhenish Mission cared for eighty-four. The problematic "fatherless" Afro-German children of this occupation, ready to betray and destroy their paternity, bear much comparison in both symbolism and fact with the prominent concern over Afro-German children born almost a half-century later during the American occupation following World War II.

There are many similarities between the origins of these two Afro-German populations. In the final years of German colonial rule in German Southwest Africa, from 1908 to 1914, roughly two thousand German troops were garrisoned in the colony, especially around Windhoek and the other larger towns. There, the German occupational force supposedly was forbidden access to the indigenous ethnic populations, housed in native districts known as *werfs*, which fell under police control. We have anecdotal evidence, however, that sexual contact was frequent between German forces and African women. For example, colonial health officials noted an epidemic of sexual infections among colonial soldiers, which they attributed to sexual intercourse with African women. Likewise, the Otavi Mine in Tsumeb, with another largely male population, reported comparable rates of infection among their European mineworkers, which bureaucrats also ascribed to their sexual relations with African women in the bush and to those working in single male colonists' households as domestics. The officials asserted that the African women who engaged in sex with German men were prostitutes, and the authorities hoped to prohibit the women's employment in bachelor men's houses and to increase police oversight of them with curfews and punishment. The *werf* system and other forms of repression, however strictly applied, appear to have failed miserably to prevent German men's sexual unions with African women and subsequent Afro-German births. German men seemingly acted with impunity. By contrast, it is notable that German administrators strictly and seemingly successfully forbade European prostitutes' clientage with African and Baster men under threat of deportation. No German woman was ever reported to have given birth to an Afro-German child in the colony.[7]

Rape and coercion of African women were rarely acknowledged to be a significant cause of interracial births. Nonetheless, the violent sexual climate was such that African women had little or no recourse against German men's predations. In one of the rarely reported instances of colonial rapes, 1912 settler newspapers related how two fugitive German murderers named Sommer and Falk captured and subsequently bludgeoned to death a fifty-year-old Herero woman and her nine-year-old granddaughter in the bush, allegedly while in search of "concubines." Only a few months prior, drunken German policeman Sergeant Odenwald in the city of Keetmanshoop invaded the local *werft*, abducted and raped an eleven-year-old Khoi girl from her sickbed, who then died from the assault. A second police sergeant was convicted of conspiracy in the attack. Disturbingly, the

Lüderitzbuchter Zeitung commented in light of the incident that African women commonly experienced unwanted sexual approaches from German men:

> The population has already complained for a long time that their female domestic employees have been seized and pestered by soldiers in the evenings on their way home. On more than one occasion, some employers have felt compelled to accompany their female servants, who did not want to go home without protection, to the *werf*.[8]

The report went on to assert that the understaffed German police patrols were needed elsewhere for more pressing matters! Under such circumstances, the inevitable conclusion is that German men's rape of African women was largely ignored and likely a frequent cause of Afro-German births. I have argued elsewhere that German settler mistreatment and sexual assault of African women was pervasive in the wake of the uprisings in German Southwest Africa; the level of such violence seems to have outstripped the deplorable tolerance for rape of women of color that typically characterized colonial societies at this time.[9]

Although rape likely accounted for the origins of many Afro-German children, Germans were remarkably unsympathetic toward the mothers of these children. Unlike the immediate post-World War II relaxation of abortion laws in Germany, especially in cases involving African American soldiers, Germans in the colony more strictly repressed abortion during the occupation.[10] Indeed, because of the trauma such rapes would have produced, many of the pregnancies that stemmed from African-German intercourse may well have been terminated before birth. Colonial administrators publicly fretted over African women's extensive knowledge of and easy access to indigenous herbal abortifacients. Although abortion was illegal under German colonial law, African birthrates declined precipitously during the postwar German military occupation. African women's alleged "birth strike" worried German administrators so much that they blamed interracial sexual unions in part for the population decline, although without citing rape as a factor. The governor of German Southwest Africa, Theodor Seitz, speculated that added restrictions against miscegenation inevitably would restore the African birth rate:

> The disorder of concubinage between white men and black women, too, has an unhealthy effect over the increase of the natives. A black woman, who in the course of a year has not one, but many white "lovers," naturally is not inclined to allow the embryo to develop, and instead eliminates the

fetus through abortion. Here, the measures with regard to combating the problem of miscegenation undoubtedly will have a beneficial effect.[11]

While Seitz sarcastically refers to African women's "many white 'lovers,'" he portrays their unwanted pregnancies as the result of female promiscuity rather than rape. The difficulties in assessing with any accuracy how the rape and coercion of African women by German men figured into the interracial birth rate under German military occupation are insurmountable. Nor can scholars easily ascertain how African women and local communities perceived these Afro-German births. What is more certain is that German policies sought to make absolute social chaos of indigenous African societies, first through military atrocities and subsequently through harsh postwar occupation. German sources suggest the rate of abandonment of these children to the care of the colonial state was perhaps as high as one in four.[12] The German colonists were responsible for creating an increasingly hostile environment into which new Afro-German children were born.

Many of the conditions African women experienced closely resemble and even surpass the difficulties of life for women in Germany after World War II and contributed to fraternization with occupying forces.[13] Just as postwar Germany was predominantly a society of the elderly and women, the same population distortions characterized the Africans in German Southwest Africa after the Herero and Khoi insurgencies of 1904 through 1907. Only about 30 percent of the prewar male population remained in the colony after wartime German atrocities, and many of the men who surrendered after the ceasefire subsequently died in the intolerable suffering of German prison camps. During much of the brutal campaign, Germans actually took no prisoners and even shot women and children refugees on sight. In the ensuing civilian flight from the German forces, couples and families were separated, some never to regroup or even to learn each other's fates. Noninsurgent ethnic groups including the San (Bushmen) and Damara suffered great casualties as well, with only the remote northern Ovambo and more recognizably Europeanized Basters escaping massive depopulation. Moreover, African combatants lost all traditional tribal lands and their herds, which not only represented the basis for all traditional economic life but also for their social organization and practices, and thus served further to undermine indigenous culture and identity. Africans now submitted to relocation and forced labor in German enterprises, particularly mines, railroads, and farms. Pass controls that compelled these laborers to reside in *werfs* local to their employment further separated some of the families of mines and railroad workers. Adding to the social disruption, the shortage of African men workers led German employers to demand that African women now assume the burden of traditional men's work, thus preventing many female workers who were also mothers from caring for their children during the day. The contract labor system also set minimal dietary provisions and pay scales for workers and their families, making hunger and malnutrition pervasive and compelling the theft of German foodstuffs and livestock.[14]

African women's paid work led them to enter German cities, residential areas, and homesteads and brought them into greater contact with German men as employers and overseers, as well as making possible more casual contacts in the streets and public places. Not only rapes resulted. Hunger and powerlessness apparently forced some African women into relations of concubinage, regular prostitution, or more informal or infrequent sexual relations with settler men and soldiers, sexual connections that relied on ambiguous degrees of female consent. Still worse, German officials and settlers blamed and punished African women caught in such situations for their alleged seduction of white men and took the subsequent births of biracial children as evidence against them. It is little surprise then, that these women chose to abandon their Afro-German children in growing numbers. The unfortunate result of this trend could only be deprivation and neglect for the children and lack of identification with their mothers' cultures. Indeed, historian Gesine Krüger documents that in general, African children in the colony suffered from high rates of parental death, abandonment, dislocation from families, and forced labor in the years of occupation.[15]

German authorities now began to debate the appropriate social policies to handle the growing orphaned Afro-German population. In Germany, for example, the Central Assembly for Domestic Missions in the German Territories (*Zentral-Ausschuß für Innere Mission in den deutschen Schutzgebieten*) publicly advocated that the colonial authorities forcibly remove illegitimate biracial children from their African mothers and fund an expensive Christian orphanage system to raise the unwanted and potentially subversive offspring. Other critics feared that this system of European orphanages would only serve to undermine Afro-Germans' association with Africans, suggesting their Africanness was their more definitive genetic heritage and more innate cultural identity. Some suggested the newborns could be given over to the Baster population to raise as their own.[16]

Increasingly the costly care for the illegitimate Afro-German children became a public policy issue for the colonial state in German Southwest Africa with broad implications for legitimate Afro-European children and adults in the colony. One popular colonial newspaper's

Figure 2.2. "Nun setzen die Herero zum Sturme an." Postwar German representations of colonial warfare highlighted the animal ferocity and base betrayal of the Herero troops and served to justify the heavy suspicion, repression, and mistreatment that colonial Germans continued to heap on the African population in German Southwest Africa long after formal hostilities had ended.
Source: *Kolonie and Heimat*, no. 44, v. 4, (1910–1911).

article describing Afro-German orphanages readily blamed the German fathers for their neglect of the children and failure to provide for them or give them an upstanding education (*regelrechte Erziehung*). The article, presented with a highly critical disclaimer by the editorial staff to the effect that "*Mischlinge* should be brought no closer to the whites than absolutely necessary," depicted the controversial Rhenish mission orphanages for Afro-German children in Okahandja and Keetmanshoop. The Okahandja installation was headed by a German schoolteacher and his wife who acted "in place of parents to the children" and gave them elementary education instruction in German. The author represented the Afro-German children as hereditarily unsuited to a European education:

> It is an arduous labor undertaken there, and it means much patience with the weak little heads and the inborn mediocrity of character. Yet the thought of giving these poor abandoned children a home spurs those involved forward and gives them the courage to carry on and to fight against the lies and the laziness that infects these children's blood only too greatly.[17]

Despite the emphasis on instruction in German, Afro-German mission schools appear to have been trade schools, their focus on imparting carpentry and other craft skills, which raised the specter of competition with local German workers. Nonetheless, by producing furniture and other goods for sale to settlers, the schools could defray some if not all of their expenses.

Alternately, Governor Seitz suggested collecting alimony from the culpable fathers, as a form of punitive tax at the very high rate of one thousand marks per child. These moneys could then fund the costs of raising the children as befitted their anomalous position in colonial society. As part of their consideration of Seitz's proposal, settler representatives debated whether the children should be raised to identify as Africans or Europeans. Attendance in the German school system was crucial in developing children's Germanness, especially because sharp colonial restrictions on African access to vocational training and literacy were intended to instill permanent subordination. Establishing new legal provisions to provide for the colony's growing young African-German population raised other ticklish issues as well. For instance, the governor's plan could give rise to criminal proceedings in which indigenous women accused settler men of paternity, an impermissible arrangement within the confines of the racist colonial judicial system.[18] In 1912, the settlers' elected colonial council unanimously upheld in principle the notion of establishing such a fund to be collected from all German men found to be engaging in sexual relations with women of color, to be used to raise the territory's mixed-race children to identify with indigenous, non-European cultures.[19] Nonetheless, the decision effectively and permanently relegated Afro-German children to non-German status in German Southwest Africa because it kept them at the very least from German language instruction.

Part and parcel of the shift in official thinking was the reworking of colonial census practices to register racial categories more exactly. In accordance with this newly recognized necessity, in June 1912, the governor for the first time ordered the listing of all future births involving a European father and indigenous or mixed-race mother in a separate registry. For the first time, illegitimate and legitimate Afro-European births in German Southwest Africa were to be recorded together in their own ledger. Such a comprehensive listing naturally would have enabled administrators to keep Afro-German children born after 1912 from entering the schools.[20] The decree made no explicit demand that paternity be established in such incidences, which indicates the new registry was intended to distinguish the separate racial identity and citizenship of persons of mixed-race descent and provide for the government's capacity to identify these individuals. In this manner, colonial authorities could trace the incidence of miscegenation regionally over time, punish the offending mothers, and permanently record the ancestry of persons of partial-African descent. Because Governor Seitz and his underlings viewed the reproduction of white, indigenous, and mixed-race children as interrelated, official accountings of these births would allow the government to trace the effects of their anti-miscegenation policies on the growth of the ethnic African and European populations.

Certainly the records might have allowed officials to take custody of all Afro-German children in the colony, but such a campaign did not take place before the end of German rule in the territory in 1915. Had Germany not lost German Southwest Africa, eventually such records might have provided the basis for determining the legal rights of future generations, allowing the government to research the racial background of all territorial residents as necessary and ascertain the degree of their African ancestry, perhaps according some of them naturalized German citizenship.[21] Still, the decree also reflected the colonial state's recognition of the growing consensus among extreme racial separatists in the colony who urged their government to establish boundaries for the upbringing of the young generation of German-African children, which physically and culturally distanced them from "white" children.

Indeed, as we have already seen, the education of children stemming from mixed-race marriages throughout German Southwest Africa had begun to pose a vexing ideological problem for the settler community. Although some colonists still openly protested the validity of mixed-race marital unions in the colony, their logic had always rested on the cultural attainments of such households, that is, their "European-" or "Germanness." As late as 1912, one individual employing the pseudonym "Justice" insisted of a mixed-race family reclassified by the German court system as native that "[t]hese people have enjoyed a very good school education and are married to white, pure-blooded women; their conduct of life is absolutely at the same height as that of a white . . ."[22] By this point in time, however, vocal settler demand for strict segregation within the German colonial public school system threatened to undermine permanently the educational opportunities for young children of partial African descent whose families could not afford to pay for private schooling. The movement to bar mixed-race children from German schools seemed to recognize that failing the continuation of past provisions for their co-education as Germans, these young mixed-race children's cultural upbringing would forge their permanent identification with the indigenous population, eliminating all possibility of naturalization as Germans.

At the turn of the decade, a number of outspoken settlers, shored up by German popular sentiment at home, had begun to object to the presence of mixed-race students in their children's classrooms. In November 1910, the manager of a business in Swakopmund named Behncke was charged with insulting an official, the head teacher of the Swakopmund district school (*Realschule*). Behncke alleged in self-justification that a pupil at the school named Fritz Krenz had sent his daughter a note containing "lewd remarks" (*unzüchten Bemerkungen*). The accused particularly stressed his concern that Fritz Krenz had some African blood; his father was German and his mother Baster. After some delay, the district court (*Bezirksgericht*) ruled for the defendant:

> The person administrating the school was responsible to see to the removal of the student Krenz, after receiving word of his ancestry. It cannot be expected of the citizens of Swakopmund, that they allow their children to go to the same school with not-purely white offspring of a mixed marriage. The danger for the moral well-being of the children is too great, as it is known that children from mixed marriages inherit the bad traits of the natives and especially their lax understanding of sexual matters.[23]

The judicial decision employs language strikingly similar to the rationales that former Governor Theodor Leutwein originally presented for constructing a kindergarten in Windhoek, which would distance "white" children from the sexual contamination of African youths. Again, the expression of the "moral danger" seems linked to anxiety over African heritage itself, as a signifier of immorality. Surprisingly enough, the higher court (*Obergericht*) overturned this ruling on appeal, upon documentary evidence that Frau Krenz and her children had obtained naturalized German citizenship in

1900, subsequently reaffirmed by governor's order in 1909. Furthermore, the school dormitory head presented a testimonial of the youth's good conduct, whereupon the Swakopmund elected parish council and District Officer Weber recommended leaving the boy in school and hushing up the affair.[24] Nonetheless, the case is strong evidence a few extremists had begun to exploit community concern for the chastity of "white" children to resolve all future questions of racial citizenship.

The ongoing debate over the legitimacy and citizenship of German-African youths resurfaced even more strongly in the wake of the Reichstag vote in May 1912 to again legalize mixed-race marriages in the German colonies. The question of mixed-race children's upbringing became an important weapon for winning popular consensus in favor of the continued prohibition against these marriages, because it invariably reinforced the need for continued state- and community-enforced racial segregation in the interests of protecting the chastity of German girls.[25] This anxiety was particularly pronounced in German Southwest Africa in the spring of 1912, following an infamous court case, the subject of numerous conflicting rumors in the colony between February and July 1912.

The notorious affair, which German language newspapers labeled simply the "Omaruru Case," in reference to the city where it occurred, involved a fifteen- or sixteen-year-old Herero servant named "Friedrich" employed by a city official and an unnamed four- to five-year-old German girl living under local guardianship in the wake of her mother's death. The Herero youth reportedly molested the girl sexually, thereby infecting her with gonorrhea. The local district officer and two of his assistants handled the investigation quietly, giving rise to a variety of wild rumors and obscuring the material evidence behind the charges. Unsubstantiated rumors at first led one newspaper account to misreport the age of the purported victim as twelve. Other unreliable allegations also surfaced, including charges that other perpetrators may have been involved and that similar incidents had occurred in other locales, that continually marred newspaper coverage of the facts, and demonstrate the considerable public discussion which surrounded the case.[26]

Published opinions on the affair shifted perceptibly over time. Initially, general reactions addressed the need for settler men to protect their wives and children from lascivious African servants. One paper even remarked that the sullied girl would have to leave the territory because she could no longer be permitted in the company of other settler children as classmates, but recanted this notion when apprised of her true age.[27] After several weeks, public concern began to center on the community's responsibility for preventing such incidents. Published remarks now expressed regret over the girl's orphaned status, which had robbed her of fatherly protection, chastised the poor supervision of the foster system, and regretted the tendency of lax settler parents who seemed to allow their children too much unsupervised contact with African retainers.[28] As public reflection over the Omaruru case broadened, the topic offered a discursive arena for troubled members of the German settler community to debate their recommendations for resolving a number of interrelated racial and sexual concerns. The state's handling of the sordid affair, however, also established the administration's sensitivity to extremists' pressures, when these took the form of exaggerated concern for "white" children's welfare. In the wake of the case, the colonial public continued to employ its reading of the events in Omaruru to establish subsequent demands on the imperial state to enact policies ensuring the strict racial segregation of "white" children in the interests of the public good. The ensuing debate over mixed-race boys' presence in the German colonial school system thus reflected the evocative power of the Omaruru "scare" to reshape the imperial state's racial-reproductive policies suddenly and dramatically in the final years of German rule in German Southwest Africa.

Less than a year after this first affair finally was settled by permitting an Afro-German boy to remain in the Swakopmund schools, two months after the infamous Omaruru case, other colonists began voicing objections to biracial children's presence in another colonial school. A letter to the editor of the territorial newspaper *Südwest* from a southern region of the colony now evoked concern as far away as Germany, where the *Staatsbürger Zeitung* reprinted excerpts from the original newspaper piece.[29] Again, the charges served as part of a larger condemnation of miscegenation in the colony. Now, however, the moral danger to children appeared too great to ignore:

> It likely is not known to you that the [name deleted] school is visited by several mixed-race children, who also receive government stipends, just as the children of pure white parents. That the mothers of the white children now are seeking out other instructional options, is completely understandable. . . . Among the mixed-race children found visiting the school, some are even *illegitimate*! They are, like their fathers, well known to me. . . . Now, the apple does not fall far from the tree [*Nun, wie die Alten sungen, so zwitschern ja bekanntlich auch die Jungen*], and one can only think that this coeducation of mixed-race children with the whites in the given school poses a moral danger to the children of white mothers. I myself often have heard white women complain about it.[30]

Although the angry letter places the concern for the "white" students' moral well-being on women colonists' shoulders, the author appears to have been male, and his outrage centers on protecting "white" children from sexual contamination, while also implying that the current situation represented a dishonor to German motherhood. Furthermore, the text seeks to establish the flawed paternity of the mixed-race children, particularly illegitimate children at that, undermining their legal claims to state-funded education or admission to German schooling.

The newspaper report prompted an official investigation from the governor's office in Windhoek. Bethanien Regional Officer Böhmer reported on the situation at the school in question, in Aus (Lüderitzbucht District). Three "not pure white" children received five-hundred-mark stipends from the district council (*Bezirksrat*) to cover the cost of their room and board. Böhmer explained that the parents of one of the children in question "are regarded here as white" (*gelten hier als Weisse*). Furthermore, he described making scrupulous prearrangements before permitting the child's residence in the school dormitory:

> Before I took the son of Colemann in the dormitory in Aus, I personally ascertained quite carefully that the residents of Aus took not the slightest objection to this. In this case, personally handled by me, I made an exception in full awareness to the principle of the admission of white children, in accordance with the provisions of the government and colonial council.[31]

Böhmer's justification also suggests that the accusations were raised by a local enemy of one of the families, who was known for prevarication. Böhmer's depictions serve to demonstrate how legal exceptions that rested upon the personal reputations of well-regarded members of the settler community, when viewed outside the intimate setting of Aus, became the subject of great concern for settlers in other areas and outraged readers in Germany as well.

Bourgeois opponents to the joint education of mixed-race children formulated their challenges in terms of national and class pride. A letter to the editor of the Swakopmund newspaper circulated the story of an unnamed, lowly Afrikaner who refused to enroll his thirteen-year-old daughter in the new government school out of concerns for her welfare:

> When asked for the reason, he replied, "I shall *not* have my daughter brought among all these *Baster boys*."—Even this simple peasant saw the shame immediately, while many of us Germans pass this by without concern.[32]

The general tale, perhaps even untrue, craftily invokes the subordinate social position of Afrikaners in the German colony, which served to inflame the matter further, as well as hinting at the dangers of biracial youths' attentions to a young and presumably sexually inexperienced adolescent German girl. Such passionate appeals to readers' emotions no doubt did much to coerce state officials to reconsider their handling of mixed-race school attendance.

The concern over the education of these few part-Baster children, now redirected colonists' expressions of concern over protecting the "chastity" of their children from racial contamination, offered compelling justification for tightened state restrictions on interracial reproduction in German Southwest Africa. The Omaruru case provided incontrovertible proof of hidden sexual dangers in the colony. The incident not only served to reaffirm the demoralizing effects of mixed-race unions, but also established an increased need for community involvement in overseeing the care of "white" children for the sake of the public, imperial welfare.

The context and timing of the Omaruru case suggests its similarity to the contemporary "Black Peril" scares of neighboring British colonies in Southern Africa, yet Germans' anxieties, as evident in their descriptions of the incident, were more remarkable in their divergence from this pattern. The youthful ages of the alleged perpetrator, an adolescent, and his victim, a much younger girl, suggest settlers' concern centered most directly on preserving the morality of German settler children from contamination by their young Afro-German peers, rather than mature African men. Elsewhere, reports of racial "peril" identified the adult male subject population at large as the principle source of latent sexual danger and particularly singled out indigenous servants within European households as the greatest threats to their mistresses.[33] Nonetheless, the logic of the scare urged the separation of the races at any expense. For Germans in German Southwest Africa, this meant the permanent denial of Afro-German's identity, citizenship, and legal rights as Germans.

Moreover, the move toward the deliberate segregation of Afro-German children in specialized institutions and their agonized removal from German schools, practices consciously rejected during the 1950s and 1960s in Germany, could only create an anomalous population in German Southwest Africa that was not fully African nor permitted to be German. Indeed, these practices were so successful that a generation of Afro-German children of the German occupation of Namibia is largely forgotten in Germany. Remarkably, Brigitta Schmidt-Lauber describes even the contemporary Afro-German population in Namibia as possessing a "non-identity."[34] Unlike the more liberal postwar era in which the adoption of Afro-Germans represented the rebirth of masculine responsibility, when the German authorities in German Southwest Africa took guardianship of the "fatherless" biracial children, the colonial state did not assume this role itself nor act in loco parentis for them. Instead, Germans worked to create institutions that perpetuated Afro-Germans' isolation. Wherever possible Germans worked both actively and passively to make "fatherless" Afro-German children motherless as well, and stateless and invisible in the bargain.

Notes

1. This study is based on European published sources and archival records from Namibia and Germany. All translations from the original German are the author's. Karen Boge Smidt, " 'Germania führt die deutsche Frau nach Südwest': Auswanderung, Leben und soziale Konflicte deutscher Frauen in der ehemaligen Kolonie Deutsch-Südwestafrika, 1884–1920" (Ph.D. diss., Universität Magdeburg, 1995), 431 table 1b.

2. Helmut Walser Smith, "The Talk of Genocide, The Rhetoric of Miscegenation: Notes on Debates in the German Reichstag Concerning Southwest Africa, 1904–1914," in Sara Lennox, Sara Friedrichsmeyer, and Susanne Zantop (eds.), *The Imperialist Imagination: German Colonialism and Its Legacy* (Ann Arbor: University of Michigan Press, 1998), 107–24; Dr. Georg Hartmann, "Die Mischrassen in unseren Kolonien, besonders in Südwestafrika," in *Verhandlungen des Deutschen Kolonialkongresses 1910* (Berlin: Dietrich Reimer, 1910), 908–32; Lora Wildenthal, "Race, Gender and Citizenship in the German Colonial Empire," in Frederick Cooper and Ann Laura Stoler (eds.), *Tensions of Empire: Colonial Cultures in a Bourgeois World* (Berkeley: University of California Press, 1998), 263–86.

3. "Aus Windhoek," *Deutsch-Südwestafrikanische Zeitung* (hereafter *DSWAZ*) 8, no. 6 (7 February 1906).

4. Carl Becker, "Das Gemeindewahlrecht und die Ehe Weißer mit Eingeborenen," *DSWAZ* 11, no. 55 (10 July 1909).

5. "Aus Windhoek," *DSWAZ* 8, no. 6 (7 February 1906).

6. "Die Zahl der Mischlinge," *Südwest* 2, no. 27 (4 April 1911). Emphasis in original.

7. German Federal Archives in Koblenz, Namibia Collection, Medizinangelegenheiten, Gesundheitspolizei. (H.II.H.1. Bd. 1–2). Maßregeln gegen geschlechtliche Ausschweifung, (5244.G.IV.d.2, Bl. 85).

8. "Aus Keetmanshoop—Ein Sittlichkeitsverbrechen," *Lüderitzbuchter Zeitung* (*LZ* hereafter) 4, 19 (11 May 1912); "Aus Windhuk," *LZ* 4, 31 (3 August 1912).

9. See Krista O'Donnell, "Poisonous Women: Sexual Danger, Illicit Violence, and Domestic Work in German Southern Africa, 1904–1915," *Journal of Women's Hisory* 11, no. 3 (Autumn 1999): 31–54; Pam Scully, "Rape, Race and Colonial Culture: The Politics of Sexual Identity in Nineteenth-Century Cape Colony," *American Historical Review* 100, no. 2 (1995): 335–59.

10. Heide Fehrenbach, "Rehabilitating Father*land*: Race and German Remasculization," *Signs* 24, no. 1 (1998): 107–28, esp. 110–13.

11. German Federal Archives in Berlin, Reichs-Kolonialamt (Collection of the Imperial Colonial Office, hereafter RKA), Akte 5423, Bl. 169, Seitz, Windhoek, March 1911.

12. "Die Versorgung der Mischlingskinder," *Kolonie und Heimat* (hereafter *KH*) 4, no. 35 (1911/2), Nachrichtenbeilage.

13. Fehrenbach, "Rehabilitating Father*land*"; Robert G. Moeller, *Protecting Motherhood: Women and the Family in the Politics of Postwar West Germany* (Berkeley: University of California Press, 1993).

14. Helmut Bley, *Kolonialherrschaft und Sozialstruktur in Deutsch-Südwestafrika* (Hamburg: Leibnitz Verlag, 1968), trans. Hugh Ridley, *South-West Africa under German Rule, 1894–1914* (Evanston, Ill.: Northwestern University Press, 1971); Tessa Cleaver and Marion Wallace, *Namibia: Women in War* (London: Zed Books, 1990).

15. Gesine Krüger, *Kriegsbewältigung und Geschichtsbewußtsein: Realität, Deutung und Verarbeitung des deutschen Kolonialkriegs in Namibia 1904 bis 1907* (Göttingen: Vandenhoeck & Ruprecht, 1999), 155–82.

16. RKA, Akte 5423, Bl. 158–9, Dr. Spieker, Central-Ausschuß für die Innere Mission der deutschen evangelischen Kirche, Berlin-Dahlem, to Colonial Secretary Lindequist, Berlin, 28 March 1911; "Die Versorgung der Mischlingskinder"; "Die südwestafrikanischen Bastards. Betrachtungen der Rassenfrage," *KH* 4, no. 13 (1911/2).

17. "Die Versorgung der Mischlingskinder."

18. Daniel Walther, "Creating Germans Abroad: White Education in German Southwest Africa," *German Studies Review* 24, no. 2 (2001): 325–52; Cynthia Cohen, "'The Natives Must First Become Good Workmen': Formal Educational Provision in German South West Africa and East Africa Compared," *Journal of Southern African Studies* 19, no. 1 (1993): 115–34. RKA 5423, Bl. 149, Abschrift, Verordnung des Kaiserlichen Governeurs von Deutsch-Südwest Afrika betreffend die Mischlingsbevölkerung and Bl. 146–8, Governor Seitz, Windhoek, to the RKA, Berlin, 24 February 1911.

19. German Federal Archives in Koblenz, Namibia Collection, Personenstandssachen: Mischehen, 666.F.IV.r.1, Bd.1, Bl. 109, Auszug aus Protokoll über die geheime Sitzung des Landesrats am 18 Mai 1911. In 1912 RKA advisors recommended waiting a year or two before implementing the fine. Bl. 126–7, Lange, Berlin, to Governor Seitz, 4 March 1912.

20. RKA, 5423, Bl. 149ff: "The birth of a child, whose father is non-indigenous and whose mother is an indigenous person, must be registered within two months at the district (or regional) office of the place of birth. The announcement must contain the place, day and time of birth, sex of the child, the given name of the child, the first and family name, tribal affiliation, status or profession, place of residence and passport number of the mother." The order contained no provision for identifying the father of the child, but further asserted the police right to order the separation of a mixed-race couple or an employment relationship in which the father of the mixed-race child is the mother's employer.

21. Namibia Collection: Personenstandssachen: Mischehen, 666.F.IV.r.1, Bd.1, Bl. 105–7, Auszug aus Protokoll über die geheime Sitzung des Landrats am 18 Mai 1911 indicates that members of the colonial council fully expected such a provision to be forthcoming.

22. "Zum Rassenmischmasch," *Südwest* 3, no. 69 (27 August 1912). Anonymous letter to the editor.

23. Namibia Collection: Personenstandssachen: Mischehen 666.F.IV.r.2., Bd. 2, Bl. 105 ruling quoted by Bezirksamtmann Weber, Swakopmund, 12 December 1912.

24. Namibia Collection: Personenstandssachen: Mischehen, 666.F.IV.r.2., Bd. 2, Bl. 105 ruling quoted by Bezirksamtmann Weber, Swakopmund, 12 December 1912.

25. See also "Gegen die Mischehen," *Swakopmunder Zeitung* 1, no. 64 (20 June 1912), which remarked, "Und diesen ganzen Unrat will man durch Gestattung der Ehe zwischen Weißen und Eingeborenen sozusagen legitmieren, womöglich sogar rein deutschen Kindern auf dem Wege der Schulkameradschaft zuführen? Unglaublich."

26. "Aus dem Schutzgebiet—Der Omaruruer Fall," *Südwest* 3, no. 38 (10 May 1912); "Zum Omaruruer Fall," *DSWAZ* 14, no. 13 (12 February 1912); "Der Omaruruer Verbrecher benädigt," *Südwest* 3, no. 53 (2 July 1912). "Ein scheussliches Verbrechen," *Südwest* 3, no. 10 (2 February 1912) refers to two other cases in Windhoek. "Zum Omaruruer Fall," *Südwest* 3, no. 57 (11 July 1912) reports a second serving boy in the same household was arrested.

27. "Ein 'mene tekel,' " *DSWAZ* 14, no. 10 (2 February 1912). Subsequently retracted in "Zum Omaruruer Fall," *DSWAZ* 14, no. 12 (9 February 1912).

28. "Größere Schutz für unsere Minderjährigen!" *Swakopmunder Zeitung* 1, no. 23 (21 February 1912).

29. "Mischlingswesen in Deutsch-Südwestafrika," *Staatsbürger Zeitung* (14 September 1912) clipping in Namibia Collection, Personenstandssachen: Mischehen, 666.F.IV.r.2., Bd. 2, Bl. 193.

30. "Der Rassenmischmasch und seine Folgen," *Südwest* 3, no. 63 (6 August 1912).

31. Namibia Collection: Personenstandssachen: Mischehen, 666.F.IV.r.2., Bd. 2, Bl. 192 (21 December 1912).

32. "Eingesandt," *Swakopmunder Zeitung* 1, no. 50 (18 May 1912). Underlined text spaced apart in newspaper report.

33. Charles van Onselen, "Witches of Suburbia: Domestic Service on the Witwatersrand, 1890–1914," in *New Ninevah*, vol. 2 of *Studies in the Social and Economic History of the Witwatersrand, 1886–1914* (Johannesburg: Ravan Press, 1982), 49–60; Elizabeth Schmidt, "Race, Sex, and Domestic Labor: The Question of African Female Servants in Southern Rhodesia, 1900–1939," in *African Encounters with Domesticity*, ed. Karen Tranberg Hansen, (New Brunswick: Rutgers University Press), 233–34.

34. Birgitta Schmidt-Lauder, *"Die verkehrte Hautfarbe": Ethnizität deutscher Namibier als Alltagspraxis* (Berlin and Hamburg: Dietrich Reimer Verlag, 1998), 392.

3

CONVERGING SPECTERS OF AN OTHER WITHIN

RACE AND GENDER IN PRE-1945 AFRO-GERMAN HISTORY[1]

Tina M. Campt

In his early, seminal volume on the figure of the Black in German culture, *On Blackness Without Blacks*, Sander Gilman argued that the uniqueness of the German conception of Blackness lay in its paradoxical development in the virtual absence of a Black presence. Gilman maintained that in Germany, the image of Blackness developed independently of an "external reality," composed rather of "elements taken from external traditions and altered to fit certain needs of a radically different culture." He described this image as "an accretion of borrowings which were altered and shaped to create patterns into which these projections were cast." According to Gilman, this "mirage of Blackness" defined German responses to Blacks when the latter were eventually confronted "in reality."[2] Yet as more recent analyses of German colonial history and the history of Blacks in Germany have demonstrated, German conceptions of Blackness and Black Germans in particular have been shaped in profound ways by a series of encounters with Blacks both domestically and in its former colonial territories.[3] As part of this emerging body of literature, this essay attempts to add an important historical dimension to our understanding of contemporary articulations of Black German identity and subjectivity through an examination of some of the early discourses of Blackness enunciated in Germany society. These discourses would have a lingering influence on later attempts by the Black German community to construct the terms of their identities as Black people as the implicit and explicit negation against which they were often forced to define themselves.

In the early twentieth century, the status of Germany's mixed-race Black citizens was contested and constructed in public and political discourse as a threat to the survival of the German nation. By extension, the imagined danger posed by this specter was expressed in Germany as a sense of racial endangerment seen to have dire consequences for the future of the white race. Like many nationalist discourses, it too invoked the need for a defensive mobilization and unification against an internal enemy constituted along complexly gendered lines of racial difference. My analysis explores how Germany's response to its Afro-German population in the first quarter of the twentieth century constituted this group as a dangerous specter. Focusing on two of the most important historical events in the formation of the public discourse on Afro-Germans, it engages how the threat posed by this specter was mobilized with particularly volatile effects. I examine how the threat of miscegenation was articulated through a discourse of racial endangerment in the German colonies in the debates on the status of racially mixed-marriages and the Afro-German progeny of these relationships. I then link this discourse with its later resonances in the 1919–22 campaign protesting the use of French African troops in the occupation of the Rhineland. The following pages unpack the ways in which racialized discourses of purity and pollution constructed Black Germans as a threat to the German body politic, and trace the trajectory of what I term, "echoing specters of racial mixture"— for the specter of racial mixture associated with the Afro-German population can be seen to have "echoed" or recurred repeatedly in German history.[4]

As one of the key events in the history of the Black German community, the use of African colonial troops by the French in the occupation of the Rhineland between 1917 and 1919 was important not only as a site of confrontation between myth and reality or what Gilman describes as "the first major confrontation between the German image of Blackness and the reality of the Black."[5] It is also both a historiographical and discursive location that witnessed the emergence of a "figure" of the Black which synthesized and rearticulated many of the images of Blacks and Blackness that had developed in the preceding centuries. The "Rhineland Bastard," a term coined during the 1919–22 newspaper campaign against the occupation, is a trope that came to embody the children fathered by French African colonial soldiers. These mixed-race children were seen as a complex representation of the manifold tensions of the occupation. The Rhineland campaign plays a pivotal role in the history of the Black German community because it articulated the central elements of a specter of imagined danger of racial mixture that can be found in German public discourse both before and after World War I. Indeed, the discourse on Blacks and Black Germans enunciated during this campaign represents an important turning point, when public discussions of the implications of a Black population shifted from a focus on external concerns (i.e., issues of social administration and the regulation of contact among Germans and Blacks abroad) to internal ones (specifically, the presence of and confrontation with a Black population on German soil.)

Unlike the stereotypes that preceded it, the Rhineland Bastard is the first representation of a *domestic*, German-born Black "native." Contrary to Gilman's "mirage of Blackness," this trope emerged simultaneously with the people it represented and eventually would eclipse as a particularly imposing threat posed from *within* the boundaries of the German nation. Notwithstanding the ideological shift initiated by this newer incarnation of the German image of the Black, the significance of the discursive link between the Rhineland Bastard and the prewar constructions of race, Blackness, and racial mixture that historically preceded it should not be underestimated. It is these discourses that in many ways enabled this figure's emergence. The trope of the Rhineland Bastard resonates and at the same time rearticulates both essentialist scientific constructions of race and racial mixture and colonial conceptions of the social and political consequences of racial mixture that were historically seen to pose such a dire threat. Reading the discourse of this campaign in relation to its historical antecedent, the 1912 Reichstag debates on mixed marriages in the German colonies, reveals important resonances between these two events as sites where the danger posed by racial mixture became the focus of political agitation.

Examining the ways in which these early discourses constituted Afro-Germans as a threat to the German nation helps us to understand how and why these discursive constructions provided fertile soil for the actions and ideologies of subsequent regimes. When National Socialism overturned the young Weimar Republic, the public discourse that had constituted the Black children of the Rhineland as a racialized threat to the purity of the German national body made them an available target for persecution in the Third Reich. Indeed much of the groundwork had been laid as early as 1927, when the first official calls were made for the sterilization of the Black children of the occupation.[6] Because of their illegitimate status, their existence had been documented through their registration with social welfare organizations, which legally served as guardians for children born out of wedlock. The registration of these children later proved both convenient and invaluable to the Gestapo in their secret program to sterilize the Black children of the Rhineland. In the end, 385 of an estimated six hundred to eight hundred mixed-race children were sterilized.[7]

Rather than structuring this essay as a linear, chronological narrative, my analysis takes the form of a backward glance at the historical events it presents. It takes this approach in order to emphasize that despite the importance of the connections between these discourses, the links between the historical periods examined here should not be viewed as cumulative or inevitable in their relation. Nor should the developments documented with regard to the public discourse and response to Black Germans be read as necessarily culminating in the sterilization of Black Germans by the Nazis. On the contrary, my aim is to paint a far more complex picture. Resisting a convenient or predictable teleology of Nazi persecution, I focus instead on a more nuanced notion of historical "echoes" and "specters." For what is most remarkable about the relationship between discussions about and discourse on Black Germans in the colonies following World War I and in the Third Reich are the discursive "echoes" that recurred in each context. These echoes of a dangerous specter posed by a Black German population link the very different historical events of each of these periods and demonstrate the resilience of the perceived threat of racial mixture throughout. At the same time, it shows how the discourse of nation was and remains an inherently gendered and racialized discourse that relies on gender and race to incite and sustain its efficacy. Overdetermining the links between these events and epochs would be a mistake that denies and occludes the complicated ways that race and gender have worked together historically with powerful social and political effects. This essay attempts to move in a different direction by connecting and historicizing the discourses that incited and enabled these historical events, not necessarily the events themselves. In this way, by placing the history of Black Germans in the Third Reich in the context of Germany's colonial legacy and the scientific discourses of race that played such a significant role therein, I mean to underline continuities in how Black Germans were constituted as particular kinds of raced subjects. More importantly, this analytic structure highlights important continuities in the stakes and salience of a conception of national purity as racial purity.

In the campaign protesting the use of Black occupation troops, at least four powerful discourses converged to create this early and perhaps most enduring image of a Black German population. The first of these was a scientific discourse of race as a biologically immutable category of human difference. The authority of this essentialist notion of race lies in its value as a means to differentiate among individuals and the social and political implications these distinctions were imputed to have. What was seen as the significant genetic consequences of racial mixture postulated in the work of geneticists and eugenicists at the turn of the century constitutes a second, particularly potent discourse in these debates. The threat racial mixture was seen to pose within these essential discourses of race was artic-ulated as a form of endangerment and violation of the boundaries that constituted German national identity. In Imperial Germany, these discourses came together with a third, equally compelling colonial discourse on racial mixture, specifically the legacy of prewar debates on mixed marriage in the German colonies. Together, they had a significant impact in shaping German responses to the presence of a Black population in their midst before, during and after World War I. Finally, German military defeat and a pervasive resulting sense of national humiliation combined with these discourses of race in the Rhineland protest campaign to transform German defeat into a larger narrative of German victimhood. In this narrative, Germany was only the first and most innocent victim of a racial conspir-acy/pollution that would ultimately unite it in victimhood with its former enemies—in the process, recasting defeat as heroic martyrdom. It was through these discourses that German responses to Blacks and Afro-Germans were articulated, and in their terms that Black Germans came to take on meaning.

In each of these discourses we find historical echoes and resonances of a recurring "specter" which in each context figured racial mixture as an imagined threat to the German nation, to German identity, and by impli-cation, to the purity and survival of the white race. In the first case, the specter was a genetic one that transmitted the negative traits of an "infe-rior race" to contaminate and degrade the genetic pool of the pure and thus superior white race. In the second case, it was the specter of a mixed-race colonial citizen who through his claim to the rights of legitimate political subjecthood posed a threat to the German body politic through the prospect of racial parity symbolized by a mixed-race, Black-German citizen. In the postwar occupation, this specter returned in the form of the Rhineland Bastard as a threat to both the purity of the German nation and its postcolonial balance of power in the former colonies—a threat posed from within the boundaries of the Reich itself. Eventually, in the Third Reich the echoes of this imagined danger would come together with the vision of a National Socialist racial state. The sterilization of members of this group of Afro-German children ultimately became the most concrete response to their embodiment of the fantastic threat to the purity of the Aryan race.

Resonances of Discourses Past—Essential Discourses of Racial Mixture

On 23 April 1920, responding to an article by Edmund Dene Morel in *The Daily Herald*, six Reichstag delegates petitioned the German government for an inquiry into the rapes and assaults allegedly committed by Black soldiers on civilians in the occupied territory. The language of their charges linked alleged rape incidents to the trampling (*zertreten*) of German national honor and dignity and further of the purity of the white race. In this way, what were initially formulated as racial objections to a Black military presence in the Rhineland were refounded on the basis of the purported sexual misconduct perpetrated by these soldiers, in addition to the most serious consequence associated with this uncontained sexual menace: miscegenation. This coupling of Black sexuality with the threat of interracial sex and miscegenation was a primary element around which the discourse of the campaign against the postwar Black occupation troops was structured.

Yet the images of Blacks and Africans used in this period to represent the threat posed by Black occupation troops in the Rhineland campaign and out of which the trope of the Rhineland Bastard would eventually emerge cannot be said to have originated in the Weimar Republic. In fact, they had a much longer history that considerably predates the contentious debates and diplomatic rhetoric of the post-World War I period. These representations are, first and foremost, products of a post-Enlightenment, scientific discourse on race, which defined race as essence, locating its origins and meaning in nature and biology. Indeed, the notion of race as a biological human trait has been the focus of scientific research for centuries. Yet the aim of this research has never been limited to the strictly "scientific" goal of understanding the biological basis of race. More often, and perhaps more importantly, it has also sought to explain the meaning of race for society as a whole, and its implications for human interaction in particular.

Racial mixture played an important role in scientific efforts of the late nineteenth and early twentieth century to define and interpret the significance of race and racial difference. For the innate or inherited differences thought to exist between the races did not in and of themselves necessarily present any problems that could not be remedied through the legislation of interracial social contact. More significantly, racial mixture represented the most problematic outcome of the genetic implications of racial difference, in that it posed the question of what "racial traits" would be passed on to mixed-race children, and what long-term implications these individuals and their offspring would have for the future of the race. Hence, at the turn of the century, racial mixture became an important site for scientific inquiries into racial difference, for it was here that scientific laws of heredity (specifically, the applied and adapted theories of Mendel and Darwin, and concrete proof of the pessimistic prognoses of the racial theories of Gobineau)[8] could be put to the test. Paradoxically, people of mixed-racial heritage came to be seen as both absolute proof of the untenability of racial theories of heredity, as well as their absolute truth.

Although racial mixture had popularly been seen as a social problem for some time, scientific studies of individuals of mixed-racial heritage began shortly before the war to formulate a somewhat different objective. These investigations of racial mixture explicitly aimed at clarifying how physical, psychological and intellectual traits were transmitted genetically among humans. At the same time, their explorations were also intended as scientific investigations of social problems.[9] Most of these studies were conducted in the European colonial territories. The question they sought to answer was to what extent human social and cultural development would be influenced by the resulting biological or genetic effects of racial mixture believed to accompany modern colonialism, migration, and acculturation. The argument explored by these studies was that racial intermixture had not only *physical effects* but more important, had an impact on both the *intellectual capacity* and *psychological constitution* of racial groups. In spite of the fact that these studies did not necessarily assume that racial mixture negatively affected the larger population, many posited social and psychological deficits among mixed-race people to be the result of the genetic inadequacy of racial mixture. Echoing the arguments of Gobineau, the predominant view among geneticists at the turn of the century and shortly thereafter was that in the majority of cases, racial interbreeding resulted in the "pauperization" of the genetic traits of the "superior" white race.

The earliest, and by all accounts, most influential study of racial mixture was conducted in 1908 by the German scientist Eugen Fischer in what was at that time the German colony of Southwest Africa (currently Namibia) in a town called Rehoboth. Fischer studied a population of mixed-race people then known as the "Rehoboth Bastards." These were the descendants of white European Boers of Dutch descent and Black women who migrated from the Cape in the late nineteenth century. Fischer proclaimed his study to be a groundbreaking scientific investigation. He asserted that prior to his own research, anthropologists had focused primarily on the "purest" strains of racial groups, whereas little was know about racially mixed groups. Yet it was from these groups that Fischer claimed science could learn the most as it was here that effects of the genetic transmission of racial differences appeared most dramatically and could best be traced.[10]

Fischer's study of the Rehoboth made use of the dominant method-ological approach to investigating racial difference of the time, interpreting a series of anthropological measurements and categorizations of their phys-ical attributes and reconstructing family genealogies. His conclusions were that Mendelian rules of heredity were in fact applicable to humans and that in this population, there was no evidence of the dominance of one race over the other. He rejected the assertion of sterility or reduced fertility, or a higher incidence of illness among this population, thus also rejecting the assertion of "biological inferiority" of mixed-race people. Yet in a chapter on "the psychology of the Rehoboth" (a chapter that lacked any empirical basis), Fischer also remarked on the mental aptitude of the group. Relying on no scientific data whatever, Fischer asserted that the intelligence of many of these individuals is equal to that of their white counterparts among the Boers. Nevertheless, he made the dubious assertion that "culturally" the psy-chological and intellectual aptitude of these individuals was inferior to that of "pure whites," and for this reason declared any evidence of the equality of whites and mixed-race people based on individual cases to be irrelevant. Fisher went on to argue that these German colonial "bastards," like all others, were inferior to whites and because of this, they were in need of "constant supervision."[11]

In both the racial discourse of the Rhineland newspaper campaign and in scientific studies of the genetic implications of race, individuals of mixed race have a special status, for the issue of racial mixture is of par-ticular significance in this context. Here it is important to emphasize that as a marker of difference between individuals, racial difference becomes an issue of contention only with regard to the interaction between individuals of different races (as opposed to mixed-race individuals). In this logic (as scientists like Eugen Fischer and Charles Davenport attempted to prove) racial mixture was the ultimate test of racial difference in that it is here that the consequences of racial distinctions would supposedly become apparent. It is for this reason that racial mixture is often constructed as a threat, as the site of the inherent conflict of difference that underlies racial distinctions. Hence, racial mixture has often functioned as a driving force (either implicit or explicit) in discussions of racial difference. As a vehicle with the potential to catalyze such discussions in volatile ways, the combination of essential conceptions of racial mixture with a discourse of racial endangerment offers a powerful tool of political mobilization with often unpredictable results.

Nation Time/Body Politics—Racing the German National Body

One of the first important sites of public articulation for Germany's response to its Black German population was the public debate in Imperial Germany on the status of Black individuals born of unions between Germans and Africans in Germany's colonial territories. In this and the larger issue of interracial marriage in the colonies scientific notions of race as essence converged with a colonial discourse on racial mixture. In the course of these debates we see the formulation of some of the key features of what became a recurring public discourse on Afro-Germans. Scientific conceptions of the negative genetic consequences of racial mixture were already an element of nineteenth-century German colonial policies on the issue of "*Rassenmischehe*" or racially mixed marriages between white colonial settlers and indigenous colonial peoples. Only six years before the Rhineland occupation, the Reichstag debates on racially mixed marriages prefigured many of the same arguments and fears voiced later in the newspaper protest campaign.[12]

Although interracial marriage was not illegal under German Imperial law, colonial officials began refusing to register interracial unions in the colonies in 1890. In 1905 Governor von Lindequist issued the first such measure in the form of a decree banning interracial marriages in German South West Africa. His explicit rationale cited what he saw as the dangerous effect of racial mixture on the purity of the white race. As he stated, "such unions do not preserve, but rather diminish (deteriorate) the race. As a rule the offspring are physically and emotional weak and unite in themselves the negative traits of both parents." Lindequist's administrative order was followed by similar decrees banning mixed marriages in the German colonies of East Africa in 1906 and Samoa in 1912. The bans were not officially codified as laws sanctioned by the Reichstag, but only decrees issued by colonial governors and a colonial secretary. In response to the 1912 Samoan decree a protest ensued in the Reichstag, prompting delegates to debate the legality of these colonial decrees in light of their conflict with imperial law. But the objections raised in protest of the bans did not focus in any fundamental way on juridical arguments on the question of the precedence of imperial over colonial legislation. Rather, numerous explicitly moral arguments were made both for and against the bans, all of which presented marriages between German colonists and nonwhite colonial natives as a threat to sexual morality and existing racial hierarchies of difference.

Despite the virulence of this debate, most historians and even those involved in the debates at the time concede that the bans themselves could never effectively have been enforced. Individuals wishing to marry in contravention to these colonial restrictions needed only to travel to any of the neighboring colonial territories or return to Europe to wed, after which their marital status must legally be honored upon their return. But as Lora Wildenthal astutely argues, by restricting the rights of German men to marry and pass on the rights of German citizenship to their wives and children on racial grounds, the bans were an attempt to assert race as a legal category in defining citizenship.[13] Clearly the central issue behind the decrees was that of the citizenship of both indigenous colonial spouses and, more importantly, the mixed-race children of these unions. What was thought to hang in the balance of the legality of mixed marriages was the status of Blacks as German citizens and a future Black German population with a legitimate claim as German political subjects. Two deputies to colonial governors in Southwest Africa gave the following justification for the bans.

> The native woman, the mixed-blood children produced by both [her and her German husband] and their offspring [become] German citizens and are thereby subject to the laws valid for the Germans here. The male mixed-bloods will be liable for military service, capable of holding public offices, and will partake of the right to vote to be established sometime in the future, as well as other rights tied to citizenship. These consequences are of a high degree of seriousness.[. . .] Not only is the preservation of the purity of the German race and of German civilization here very substantially impaired because of them, but also the white man's position of power is altogether endangered.[14]

This group of mixed-race Germans became a source of alarm in that their presence triggered expressions of racial endangerment that tapped into both scientific discourses on the hereditary consequences of racial mixture and popular beliefs in their negative impact on the race, and thus raised the question of the implications for the future of the German (and/or white) race. The legalization of unions between white German colonists and nonwhite indigenous colonials was deemed problematic in that it undermined racial assumptions of purity with regard to citizenship, which until then had served as one of the clearest and most fundamental boundaries delineating German national identity. Granting nonwhite colonial spouses and their mixed-race children the status of German symbolically represented an entry into the German national body, which threatened to dissolve the boundaries of racial difference around and in relation to which Germanness was intrinsically constituted. Through the invocation of an imagined specter of racial contamination associated with the negative consequences of racial mixture the issue of mixed marriages evolved into an even more volatile issue. More than a "problem," it was seen as a *threat* both to the fragile colonial balance of power, as well as having detrimental implications for domestic politics within the Reich.

The official Reichstag discussion of colonial mixed marriages began in May 1912, when Colonial Secretary Solf was one of the first speakers arguing in favor of parliamentary support of the colonial bans. Using the violent backlash against emancipated Blacks in the United States as a cautionary example of racial parity gone awry (American antimiscegenation laws had served as a model in the conception of the mixed-marriage bans), Solf appealed to the emotions of the representatives, urging them to allow themselves be led by their "instincts." As a strategic attempt to mobilize and exploit the emotional potential of this issue, Solf repeatedly invoked the figure of a racially mixed child as a specter that threatened the purity and sanctity of any German family. "You send your sons to the colonies: do you want them to return with woolly-haired [Black] grandchildren?" He continued to raise the stakes on this issue, emphasizing the particular danger racial mixture posed to (white) German women. Here the German national body is a raced body made vulnerable through the female body as the conduit of racial pollution.

> Do you want these girls [those sent by the Colonial Society (*deutsche Kolonialgesellschaft*)] to return with Hereros, Hottentots and bastards? [. . .] Consider these facts, consider them according to your instincts as Germans and as white men! The entire German nation will thank you, if you consider nothing else than this: we are Germans, we are white and we want to stay white.[. . .] Do you want to our race to be bastardized?[15]

The combination of scientific and colonial discourses of racial purity that converged on the issue of mixed marriages was also constructed around a gendered and sexualized discourse that, as Wildenthal contends, "counterposed men's rights to German racial purity."[16] Foreshadowing what would later recur in the protest campaign against the Black occupation troops, racial mixture was an imagined danger that mobilized racial and sexual fears in the form of *racial parity*—a specter whose power lay in the threat it posed to white men's position of power. Here gender played an integral role on both sides of the debate, where women were engaged as both primary and secondary victims of this threat. On the one hand, opponents and supporters of the bans relied on gendered arguments for the protection of native women. Whereas Representative Ledebour, for example, argued that the bans allowed for the protection of indigenous women from the exploitation of white settler men in search of cheap housekeepers, cooks and concubines, the colonial secretary, Solf, also argued that because of the shortage of native women, they should be protected from white male colonists' attempts to take them away from their men. On the other hand, opponents of the ban offered a complexly gendered argument that combined a defense of male marital and sexual privilege with a vision of the civilizing mission of a (superior) white German colonialist as a *Kulturträger* (bearer of culture) among Black inferiors. For example, liberal parliamentarian Freiherr von Richthofen emphasized that the objective of German colonial politics was to bring a "higher culture" to the natives "in order to educate ["civilize"] them to a higher sensibility" (*[um] sie zu einer höheren Lebensauffassung erziehen zu können*). Toward this end, both "appropriate bearers of culture" (*geignete Kulturträger*) and the proper distance between him and his "civilizing object" (*Erziehungsobjekt*)[17] were necessary. Here German women were constructed as a necessary bulwark ensuring this distance and the maintenance of this important cultural—read racial—boundary.

Furthermore, German women saw themselves as important protectors of the purity of German nation/ "race."[18] Their self-proclaimed mission in the colonies was based in part on a notion of white female bodies as barriers to the potential pollution of the German race via miscegenation. Indeed, the availability of white female bodies offered what was seen as an important alternative to the dangerous temptations of nonwhite, indigenous female sexuality. Indigenous women's bodies were figured as vessels and conduits for transporting pollution and contamination into the German national body. It was the sexual lures they presented to German male colonists that were seen to produce the mixed-race progeny that destabilized the equation of Germanness with whiteness and violated the imaginary boundary separating the German national body—a body constituted as pure and white—from the Others from which it attempted to distinguish itself.

Contrary to the vehement opposition and reservations voiced against the ban on both sides of the discussion, the result of these heated debates was the passage of a resolution affirming the legality of colonial mixed marriages, along with a second resolution aimed at strengthening the influence of the Reichstag in colonial legislative affairs. In spite of the fact that the legality of mixed marriages was upheld, racial mixture continued to be viewed with ambivalence and foreboding. Indeed, when confronted with the consequences of mixed marriages in the flesh, the response of German colonial officials was an equally ambivalent reaction to the threat of racial parity these individuals were seen to embody.

Throughout these discussions essential, biological notions of racial difference, superiority, and hierarchy enunciate a scientific discourse of race that pervades these debates. Though often articulated in the language of "culture" and "civilization," the discussion nevertheless belies the logic of racial purity that was used as a compelling political tool. Here references to "culture" and "civilization" referred to what were viewed as essential differences and immutable traits attributed to skin color. This elision marks an important tension in these discourses of race and racial difference, one that dissolves the boundaries between groups of individuals and raises the question of which distinctions between them are considered learned or innate. Yet regardless of what these distinctions are attributed to, they are purported to *matter* nonetheless, with extremely serious implications for those seen to trespass the boundaries of such differentiation, as in the case of racial mixture.

Imagined Danger Realized: Racial Parity, Victimhood, and Racialized Body Politics

As Wildenthal's study has shown, the cases of disputed citizenship in the colonies pursued during and after this debate demonstrate that the debate was not resolved with the parliamentary resolutions taken in 1912.[19] Rather, they emphasize the resilience of the gendered and sexualized threat that racial mixture was seen to pose to the German body politic—a specter that would recur shortly thereafter in an even more virulent form. The fears of racial parity articulated in these discussions did indeed return with a vengeance following the war, and in many ways even came to be realized in the scenario presented by African occupation troops and their Black German children.

> What offends European sensibility in the use of Black troops is not their Blackness but rather the fact that savages are being used to oversee a cultured people. Whether these savages are totally Black or dark brown or yellow makes no difference. The prestige of the European culture is in danger. That is what is at stake. And precisely those peoples, those such as England and France who are dependent upon the dominance they exercise over colored peoples, should consider that with the degradation of Germany in the eyes of the colored, they degrade the white race and with this, endanger their own prestige.[. . .] Thus the fact remains unchanged that a cultured people like the French allow another cultured European people to be overseen by savages. Whether these savages are slightly more Black or brown or yellow is of no matter. They must feel themselves to be policing a people of the white race. This is what outrages the German people. At the same time, it is the dangerous thing for the white race in general.[20]

The language of this quotation echoes resoundingly with the fears expressed in the Reichstag debates of the threat posed by Blacks and their mixed-race offspring. Taking up the issue of the racial/cultural hierarchies raised in these debates, the above article refers to the *Demütigung* (humiliation) Germany was seen to face through the imposition of primitives on a *Kulturvolk*. The dichotomy implicitly set up within this discourse opposed Germany as a white, civilized *Kulturvolk* to Blacks as an uncivilized or primitive *Naturvolk* characterized by savagery, unbridled passions, appetites, and instincts. As earlier, what was seen to be at stake in the interracial contact that transpired through the use of Black troops in the postwar occupation was the violation of the boundary that implicitly divides the *Kulturträger* (bearer of culture) from his *Erziehungsobjekt* (his so-called civilizing object)—a boundary that forms one of the ideological cornerstones of the colonial hierarchy. The use of Black troops as a force of occupation in Germany in this way both reversed this relation and transgressed this sacred boundary, while at the same time, the language used to articulate this threat naturalized "culture" as an essential attribute, access to which is necessarily mediated by race.

The significance of the presence of these "primitives" in Europe was that this contact would have *essential, genetic* implications for the white race. Germans could not simply "unlearn" civility and culture. Rather, the prospect of miscegenation was tantamount to the ruin of the race, for the consequence of miscegenation was the pollution of white German genetic

stock. Here the German nation is constructed as a body vulnerable to contamination through the introduction of Black troops within its national
boundaries. This violation of its boundaries posed a fundamental danger
to its existence, for the German body seems only able to exist in a pure
form. Violation/ contamination by the Black thus represents its essential
negation. In this way, the humiliation decried in this and numerous other
articles in the campaign articulates an injury inflicted upon a wounded
German national body. It is an injury that stands at the beginning of a
larger continuum. As a racial injury inflicted by the victorious powers on
a vanquished German state, it is only the first step in a process of postwar
victimization.

The article cited above is one example of the accusation frequently
leveled against the victorious powers of their participation in the *Schändung*
(desecration) of the white race. This charge aimed not only at compromis-
ing France and Britain's position as victorious powers, but also at discrediting their status as colonial powers inasmuch as this status is predicated on
the racial hierarchy that such *Rassenschande* (racial desecration) would
destroy. The discrediting of France and Britain as colonial powers in turn
legitimated Germany's own status through its defense of the racial hierarchy
on which it was based—this time, and most dangerously, within Europe
itself. The language quoted above is a typical example of a strategic deployment of skin color as essentialized "culture," a conflation that occurs frequently in the articles of the campaign. In the article, as in numerous others
published during this campaign, skin color is rhetorically rejected as playing
a role in the protests against the Black troops, while at the same time, race/
racial inferiority (Blacks as a savage race) is emphasized as the primary
danger presented by the use of these troops in the occupation. Skin color is
equated with culture, thus eliding racial difference and level of "civilization."

The articles in the newspaper campaign against the Black troops
illustrate that Germany's defeat in World War I was experienced not only
with a sense of loss and humiliation, it was also articulated as a threat.
Here, as was the case less than a decade earlier in the mixed marriage
debates, the threat, which served as the implicit and explicit subtext of this
campaign, was the perceived threat of racial parity. Racial parity was the
danger perceived to result from Germany's loss of the war, and with which
Germans were confronted in several areas including the military and, to a
certain extent, within German society itself. In the military, the use of
Black colonial troops by other European countries ostensibly set Blacks on
an equal level with whites. Although Germany did not use colonial troops
during the war, it had in fact considered this as an option. France's use of

Blacks alongside white troops in the occupation forces presented Germany with a superficial form of racial parity that it had never before encountered, either in the colonies, in the military, or in German society as a whole.

> The main danger in the use of colored troops in the heart of Europe lies far more in the systematic awakening and cultivation of their sense of power over the white race.[. . .] The French have provided amply for the military training of the Blacks through their use of them in the war and as occupation forces. But, drunk with their victory, the French military still refuse to see the terrible danger. Not long ago Senegalese negroes were exuberantly celebrated shortly before their transfer to Paris as the "Heroes of Dirmuiden, the Marne, the Dardanelles and other places where one [had to hang on] {word unreadable in the original} at all costs." . . . It is in this way that the feeling of power of the colored race against the whites is only strengthened by the French military.[21]

Perhaps more significantly, racial parity was also perceived as a threat to German society itself. Again, the threat of racial parity was articulated as a gendered, sexual threat to the German body politic. Unlike in the mixed marriage debate where white women figured as necessary barriers to interracial sexual pollution/contamination, in the Rhineland campaign, the white female body became a dangerously porous conduit of the violation of this boundary. In several articles the white German woman was presented as the channel of this threat, portrayed as both a whore and a victim and, as such, as both an active and passive conduit of Black male sexuality. The latter, in turn, was demonized as, among other things, infectious, instinctual, uncivilized, and most notably, insatiable and uncontrollable. At the same time, Black men were also seen as irresistible seducers of white women, who were supposedly unable to resist their exotic colonial desire for Black male sexuality. The access of Blacks to white female bodies via the use of Black troops in the occupation represented another form of racial parity; that is, a sexual equality between Black and white men in relation to (or, perhaps, in the possession of) white women. This, in turn, was articulated in the campaign against the Black troops as a threat to the German man.

> The white woman has always had a visibly privileged position among Europeans. For this reason the negro has also shown her for the most part, absolute respect and submissive obedience. But the white woman was alsosomething different to him; something beyond the term "Weib." She was something unreachable to him; something he certainly only seldom

consciously desired.[. . .] Now the Negro, who inhabits Africa and parts of the rest of the world in countless millions and generally stands on a lower rung of the evolutionary ladder, is not only being brought to Europe, not only being used in battle in a white country; he is also systematically being trained to desire that which was formerly unreachable for him—the white woman! He is being urged and driven to besmirch defenseless women and girls with his tuberculous and syphilitic stench, wrench them into his stinking apish arms and abuse them in the most unthinkable ways! He is being taught that [. . .] he can do anything his animal instincts even remotely demand, without the slightest restraint, he even finds support for this from the "victors."[22]

In this excerpt, the white female body again forms the conduit of the racial pollution that endangers the German body politic. It is unbridled Black male sexuality—essential in its insatiability, and yet socially malleable in its ability to discern between appropriate and inappropriate objects of desire—that is the perpetrator of this act of national pollution. The violation of this most fundamental of boundaries presented this sexualized form of racial parity as perhaps the most intolerable threat to the German nation, making it a rallying point for the German people and eventually other whites. Ultimately racial parity posed the most significant danger to white German men in the threat it presented to their masculinity. This is also true of the military, where *Wehrhaftigkeit*, the ability to perform military service and protect one's country and property, has long been regarded as a primary masculine attribute. Here racial parity threatened the emasculation of the white German male. In the logic of national body politics, it appears that this masculine potency could only be maintained through inequality.

But the "Black Horror" is—how long must one scream it into the ears of a deaf world—not only a disgrace for Germany. It is much more. It represents the desecration of white culture in general. At the same time, it means the beginning of the end of the supremacy of the white man.[23]

The discourse on the Black troops in the 1919–23 newspaper campaign can in many ways be read as an attempt to recover Gemany's prewar "Great Power" status. This involved the displacement and/or projection of the fears aroused by the changes occurring in postwar German society onto another surface. The Black occupation troops were one such surface, and the threat of racial parity served as a catalyst in this process. However, the ultimate result of the displacement of German national anxieties onto the Black troops was the *racialization* of the postwar situation: German society attempted to regain its prewar status by affirming its racial superiority to Blacks and specifically the Black troops. This was achieved through the extension or generalization of the problem of a Black presence in Germany, and the exaggeration of the perceived threat of racial parity into a crisis, which threatened all Europeans and the white race in general. This process of racialization is also part of a dynamic that strategically transformed the presence of a Black force of occupation in Germany into the fiction of an all-encompassing racial threat to civilization. Here, the merging of fiction and reality was intended to have strategic political consequences—namely, the potential and much hoped for revision of the postwar settlement along racial lines. The most dubious effect of this process was the way in which this racialized discourse succeeded in presenting the Black troops as a common "enemy" of all white nations, against whom they should unite and overcome their differences. The extension of the threat posed by the Black troops to this more encompassing formulation created a point of identification between Germany and its former European adversaries via the threat to racial purity, that is, "whiteness." This, in turn, led to a defensive closing of ranks among whites against an alleged threat to the white race.

> Only too late will they realize that they have conjured up a catastrophe for the whole of Europe through the use of colored troops in the Rhineland. All hope rests on the remaining European states and America. Hopefully the feeling of solidarity among the white race will break out in time to effectively meet the rising African threat.[24]

In addition to creating a racially inferior "Black enemy," the discourse of the newspaper campaign simultaneously constructed a position of racial superiority for the white German counterpart to this figure, a scenario that might be described as follows: the racially inferior Black enemy poses a threat that must be controlled and contained. The racially superior white German champions this moral campaign of containment. The effect of this is the reestablishment of the old colonial hierarchy at the ideological level. Through a racialized discourse in which the use of Black troops in the postwar occupation was constructed as a dangerous attack on the established racial order, Germany is constituted as the victim of a racial conspiracy. Its defense of the racial hierarchy in the discourse of the campaign effectively makes it the last protector of the white race. In this way, its victimization is recast as a heroic sacrifice (or martyrdom) for the race.

In this trajectory, the Afro-German children of the Black occupation troops were the realization of the fears expressed in the propaganda campaign, as the concrete embodiment of racial parity and postwar German defeat and humiliation. As in the *Mischehe* debates, these children were used provocatively as a shock tactic aimed at evoking outrage and repulsion and creating a sense of endangerment caused by Black troops in Europe. The message behind this strategy was that the use of Black troops would have long-term repercussions for Germany, or more explicitly, for the "German race." Here the public statements of one of the most prominent speakers involved in the campaign, Ray Beveridge, are of particular significance.[25]

One highly publicized example of Beveridge's rhetoric is her much-publicized speech given at a protest rally in Munich on 22 February 1921. At the rally, Beveridge presented two "little martyrs" of the occupation to the audience: an undernourished and underdeveloped white German child, said to be the victim of the Allied "hunger blockade," and a Black German child, described as one of the "living and unfortunate witnesses to the Black disgrace and white shame" (*lebendigen und unglücklichen Zeugen Schwarzer Schmach und weißer Schande*). Beveridge's speech, which was published repeatedly in newspapers throughout Germany, quite literally cast these "little Bastards" as symbols of German defeat and the impending threat to the purity of the German race, in that the former (the white child) was a symbol of defeat, whereas the latter (the Black German child) was a symbol of both defeat and the imagined threat to racial purity. As part of the deployment of the Rhineland Bastard, the children of Black soldiers were also depicted as the carriers of the infectious diseases of their fathers, in particular sexually transmitted diseases. Sexuality played a crucial role in the campaign against the Black troops, as it was the representation of the Black soldiers as a *sexual* threat that provoked the most vehement popular reaction. Interracial sex was seen as a mode of contamination that represented the ultimate rape of the German body—a body both raced as white and gendered as a virginal female whose purity is lost through the violation of the Black. Here, racial discourses were permeated by and combined with discourses of gender and sexuality. Whenever the issue of race was raised, it was immediately and invariably posed in relation to a sexual threat; for example, essential notions of biological difference and stereotyped ideas of the exaggerated sexual passions of Blacks combined with the threat of the sexual transmission of infectious diseases. This in turn was exacerbated by the excessive sexual appetites of Blacks and their supposed lack of capacity to control them, as well as the powerful allure they were also thought to have for white women.

The Black German children of these soldiers were seen as a lasting legacy of the occupation, while their mixed racial heritage and illegitimate birth posed both a moral and biological threat to the chastity and purity of the German "race." The danger they posed surpassed that of the Black troops, for as German citizens whose presence in the country was in no way temporary, the children presented a more far-reaching threat. In the articles written in this period, this danger is formulated as *Mulattisierung* (mulattoization) of the German race—a warning that, should this situation be allowed to continue, "one need not wonder if, in a few years, there are more half-breeds than whites walking around, if sacred German motherhood has become a myth and the German woman, a Black whore." [26]

That passage offers a vivid example of how scientific discourses on race permeated the 1919–22 newspaper campaign. Read together with the article excerpts cited above, the Rhineland protest campaign demonstrates a powerful convergence of scientific and colonial discourses on race and racial mixture with a postwar discourse of German victimhood. Ray Beveridge's comments in particular synthesize some of the most important resonances between the discourse of the campaign and the earlier debates of racial mixture and mixed marriages: among others, the deployment of gender (via the threat to women of Black sexuality and women's supposed role in the campaign against the use of the Black occupation troops); the deployment of race and sexuality (through the construction of Black men as uncivilized savages, infectious and sexually depraved); and, in the case of the postwar protests, the deployment of the figure of the Rhineland Bastard as a threat to the purity of the "German race."

Conclusion

As a recurring specter of racial mixture, the images of Blacks and Afro-Germans constructed in the post-World War I campaign against the Black troops resonate and at the same time rearticulate both essentialist scientific discourses of race and racial mixture and colonial conceptions of the social and political consequences that racial mixture was seen to pose to the German nation. The concept of the nation that structured and sustained each of these discourses was one that, in many ways, took the body as its model—a model in which bodily boundaries and their defense against violation and contamination functioned as the bedrock of social order and cohesion.

In the early discourses that interpellated Black Germans in German society, the raced bodies of these individuals were viewed as having dire consequences for the German nation through the threat they were thought to pose to German identity. This essay has sought to examine some of the implications of the repeated instances in Germany during the first part of this century when race was conceived as essence and German national and cultural identity were articulated as having an essential racial substance. In the discourses of race that came together in each of these historical contexts, both Black people and the German nation were naturalized as bodies whose substance was endowed with specific forms of meaning that were seen as one basis for regulating social interaction in German society. On the one hand, Germanness was equated with purity and superiority, while racial mixture represented dangerous forms of impurity, pollution, and inferiority. The mixed-marriages debates in the colonies and the discussions of how to deal with the Black German children of the postwar occupation were concrete attempts to legislate and negotiate this assumed substance and the implications its meaning was perceived to have for the German nation. On the other hand, this racialized national discourse was simultaneously a gendered one whose mobilizing effects were catalyzed by its invocation of a sexualized danger to the purity of the nation. For the threat of racial endangerment inherently (en)gendered the German nation as a vulnerable female body open to the seduction of violation by the Black and thus in dire need of protection.

In the discourse that emerged from the 1912 *Mischehe* debate and in the postwar protests against Black occupation troops, Black Germans represented a deeply threatening specter of racial mixture that endangered German national identity through the perils of racial parity. Unlike the prewar debates, the discourse of the newspaper protest campaign portrayed this specter as a racial injury inflicted on Germany by the victorious allies. This injury functioned as the source of Germany's victimization and at the same time elevated its status as such through a heroic glorification of victimhood as racial martyrdom. Like other equally compelling discursive configurations of enemies and victims in German history, the post-World War I discourse of victimhood functioned as what Omer Bartov has described as a "national adhesive."[27] For the presence of a Black German population was similarly used with strategic intent in opposition to the Versailles settlement. Here, too, metaphors of victimhood and endangerment served as a form of national adhesive that offered a source of unity and identification in this period of postwar national crisis.

Notes

All translations from the original German, unless otherwise noted, are by the author.

1. This essay was first published in slightly different form in *Callaloo* 2 (2003) and is reprinted here with kind permission. It is based in part on research funded by grants from the American Association of University Women, the Social Science Research Council, the Volkswagen Foundation and the German Academic Exchange Service (DAAD). It builds on and greatly expands arguments initially presented in one section of my article (co-authored with Pascal Grosse and Yara-Colette Lemke Muniz de Faria), "Blacks, Germans and the Politics of Imperialist Imagination, 1920–1960," in *The Imperialist Imagination: German Colonialism and Its Legacy*, ed. Sara Lennox, Sara Friedrichsmeyer and Susanne Zantop (Ann Arbor: University of Michigan Press, 1998), 205–29. I am indebted to the Resident Fellows Program of Center for German and European Studies at Georgetown University, in particular Roger Chickering and Jeffery Peck, whose generous support and intellectual exchange allowed me the opportunity to undertake the substantial revisions that resulted in the production of this essay. For a more extensive discussion of the issues raised in it, see chapter one of my book, *Other Germans: Black Germans and the Politics of Race, Gender and Memory in the Third Reich* (Ann Arbor: University of Michigan Press, 2004), 25–62.

2. Sander Gilman, *On Blackness Without Blacks* (Boston: G.K. Hall Publishers, 1982), xi. See also Gilman's later writings on Blacks in German culture in: *Difference and Pathology* (Ithaca, NY: Cornell University Press, 1985) and "Black Bodies, White Bodies: Toward and Iconography of Female Sexuality in Late Nineteenth-Century Art," in *Race Writing and Difference*, ed. Henry Louis Gates Jr. (Chicago: University of Chicago Press, 1986), 223–61.

3. See most notably the essays published in Lennox, *Imperialist Imagination*.

4. My discussion of specters of racial danger in this essay in some ways might be read as a (somewhat oblique) historical counterpoint to the fascinating arguments of Avery Gordon in her highly acclaimed monograph, *Ghostly Matters: Haunting and the Sociological Imagination* (Minneapolis: University of Minnesota Press, 1997). However, the specificity of my own analytic project and disciplinary vantage point precludes direct comparison with or an extensive discussion of her extremely compelling points here.

5. Gilman, *On Blackness Without Blacks*, xii.

6. In 1927, a local official in the Pfalz, Hans Jolas, wrote to the Bavarian Minister of Health, Sperr, regarding what he described as the growing concern in the province about the danger posed by the presence of these Black German children who would soon be coming of age. He asked the minister to investigate what measures might be taken to secure and protect the purity of the race in the region from this emerging threat. Jolas suggested sterilization as a possible solution to this problem, though he acknowledged that such measures were illegal according to existing law. Jolas's request was denied by the Bavarian ministry. In his response, Sperr emphasized the fact that the ministry recognized the "serious racial danger" presented by the procreative potential of these Black German children. Yet he affirmed that there was to date no legal basis on which to carry out such sterilizations. As German citizens (German citizenship followed along maternal lines of parentage) the children could also not be deported—a possibility also discussed within the ministry. Moreover, such an undertaking would be hindered by the fact that few mothers would agree to it. A further consideration was its potentially negative effects on domestic and foreign policy. Yet what is most salient about these discussions is the fact that, as was also

the case earlier in the colonies as well as later in the Third Reich, these discussions revolved around the protection of the purity of the race from the dangers of "colored blood." See Reiner Pommerin, *"Sterilisierung der Rheinlandbastarde": Das Schicksal einer farbigen deutschen Minderheit, 1918–1937* (Düsseldorf: Droste, 1979), 30.

7. Gisela Bock, *Zwangsterilisation im Nationalsozialismus* (Opladen: Westdeutscher Verlag, 1986), 354. See also Pommerin, *"Sterilisierung,"* and Georg Lilienthal, "'Rheinlandbastarde,' Rassenhygiene und das Problem der rassenideologischen Kontinuität," *Medizinhistorisches Journal* 15 (1980): 426–36.

8. Here I must acknowledge a cogent point suggested to me by Michelle Maria Wright. Although Gobineau's *Essai sur l'inégalité des races humaines* (Essay on the inequality of the human races), the first secular argument for racial hierarchization, became a popular reference for a wide variety of late-nineteenth-century and twentieth-century white supremacist movements, the *Essai* is far from consistent in its argument. While Gobineau's thesis asserts on the one hand that civilizations collapse because of miscegenation when inferior blood pollutes that of the superior race, elsewhere in the *Essai* he argues that a civilization cannot become a great artistic culture, nor its people adequately vigorous, *without* intermixture, specifically mixing with Blacks. This is less surprising if one considers, as Michael Biddiss has noted, that the ultimate goal of the *Essai* was to prove that French civilization would collapse if power were not returned to the aristocracy whom, he maintained, were racially distinct from the middle class and peasant class. At one point in the *Essai*, Gobineau angrily reminds his readers that he is well aware that an African chieftain is easily superior to the French peasant or even the French bourgeoisie. See Arthur Comte de Gobineau, *Essai sur l'inégalité des races humaines*, 2nd ed. (Paris: Firmin-Didot, 1884) and Michael Biddiss, *Father of Racist Ideology: The Social and Political Thought of Count Gobineau* (London: Weidenfeld & Nicolson, 1970).

9. For a more extensive discussion of these and other studies of racial mixture, see Tina Campt and Pascal Grosse, "Mischlingskinder in Nachkriegsdeutschland: Zum Verhältnis von Psychologie, Anthropologie und Gesellschaftspolitik nach 1945," in *Psychologie und Geschichte* 6 (1994): 48–78, and Grosse, "Kolonialismus und das Problem der 'Rassenmischung' in Deutschland: Zur Geschichte der anthropologischen Psychology 1920–1940," in Siegfried Jäger et al. (eds.), *Psychology im soziokulturellen Wandel– Kontinuitäten und Diskontinuitäten* (Frankfurt a. M.: Peter Lang, 1995), 75–85.

10. Campt and Grosse, "Mischlingskinder in Nachkriegsdeutschland," 48–78, and Grosse, "Kolonialismus und das Problem der 'Rassenmischung' in Deutschland," 75–85.

11. On the other side of the Atlantic, a second study of racial mixture was conducted during World War I by one of the United States' leading eugenic scientist, Charles Benedict Davenport. Davenport's primary concern was in the potentially negative result of racial mixture. Concurring with Fischer's study, Davenport asserted that the most important effect of these "mixtures" was not physical, but rather *psychological.* Published in 1917, the study used the same methodology as Fischer's: anthropometric measurements and family genealogies. Davenport's study provided scientifically sophisticated arguments for much older claims about the psyche of the mulatto. He argued that mulattoes combined "an ambition and push [. . .] with intellectual inadequacy which makes the unhappy hybrid dissatisfied with his lot and a nuisance to others." Ambition was an attribute assumed to have come from the white parent and inadequacy from the Black. Davenport concluded that miscegenation necessarily meant disharmony and that a "hybridized" people were inevitably badly put together, dissatisfied, and ineffective. As cited in William Tucker,

The Science and Politics of Racial Research (Urbana and Chicago: University of Illinois Press, 1994). At least nine subsequent studies on racial mixture were conducted between 1921 and 1927 by German, American, Norwegian, Dutch and Chinese scientists. See also Campt and Grosse, "Mischlingskinder," 51–58, and Annegret Ehmann, "From Colonial Racism to Nazi Population Policy: The Role of the So-Called Mischlinge," in *The Holocaust and History: The Known, the Unknown, the Disputed and the Reexamined*, ed. Michael Berenbaum and Abraham J. Peck (Bloomington: Indiana University Press in association with the US Holocaust Memorial Museum, 1998), 188–221.

12. For an extensive discussion of the racial and gendered politics of the mixed marriages debates see Pascal Grosse, *Kolonialismus, Eugenik und bürgerliche Gesellschaft in Deutschland 18501918* (Frankfurt: Campus, 2000), 145–92, and Lora Wildenthal, *German Women for Empire, 1884–1945* (Durham: Duke University Press, 2001), 79–130.

13. Wildenthal emphasizes that each of these bans was unique among the existing European colonial regimes. More importantly, as she demonstrates, the bans mark the first attempt to introduce explicitly racial definitions into German citizenship law. As she convincingly demonstrates in her article, the National Socialists were the first to successfully codify race formally into law, for until that time, neither the 1913 law, nor its predecessor, the Reich citizenship law of 1870, contained any explicit formulation of racial categories in their interpretation. Lora Wildenthal, "Race, Gender and Citizenship in the German Colonial Empire," in *Tensions of Empire: Colonial Cultures in a Bourgeois World*, ed. Frederick Cooper and Ann Laura Stoler (Berkeley: University of California Press, 1997), 267. See also Wildenthal, *German Women*, 85.

14. As cited in Wildenthal, "Race, Gender and Citizenship," 267.

15. As cited in Cornelia Essner, "Zwischen Vernunft und Gefühl. Die Reichstagsdebatten von 1912 um koloniale 'Rassenmischehe' und 'Sexualität'," in *Zeitschrift für Geschichtswissenschaft* 6 (1997): 509.

16. Wildenthal, "Race, Gender and Citizenship," 264.

17. Essner, "Zwischen Vernunft und Gefühl," 507.

18. Wildenthal, *German Women*, offers a comprehensive and detailed analysis of the manifold forms through which German women utilized and engaged the discourse of womanhood in strategic ways to achieve a number of different feminist and political ends.

19. See Wildenthal, "Race, Gender and Citizenship," 267–81, and *German Women*, 79–130.

20. "Die Farbigen Truppen im Rheinland," *Die Leibziger T.* [title unreadable in original] 26 May 1921. All of the newspaper articles cited in this chapter were taken from the Bundesarchiv Potsdam, Germany, Records of the *Reichskommissar für die besetzten rheinischen Gebiete, Abteilung I/1755, signature no. 1602.* These files contain clippings on the Black occupation troops from German newspapers 1920 to 1922.

21. "'Die Geister, die ich rief . . .': Die Gefahr der farbigen Besatzungstruppen für Europa," *Die Weser Zeitung*, 23 July 1921.

22. "Die Schwarze Schmach," *Hamburger Nachrichten*, 30 July 1921.

23. "Völker Europas . . .!" *Grenzland Korrespondent*, 24 April 1922.

24. Ibid.

25. Ray Beveridge was one of the most outspoken figures involved in the Rhineland campaign, second perhaps only to E. D. Morel and Henry Distler, editor of the *Berliner Zeitung.* During the campaign, Beveridge gave numerous speeches protesting the "Horror on the Rhine." It is unclear, however, whether she was a German or U.S. citizen. She had

apparently worked for the German embassy in Washington and claimed to be an American, yet she is also said to have held a German passport.

26. *Fränkische Kurier Nürnberg*, 24 November 1920.

27. See Omer Bartov's masterful interpretation of the power of the discourse of victims and enemies in the constitution of German national identity in "Defining Enemies, Making Victims: Germans, Jews, and the Holocaust," *The American Historical Review* 103, no. 3 (1998): 771–816. Although his analysis focuses specifically on anti-Semitism and the role of Jews as scapegoats in Germany, Bartov's explications of how the construction and glorification of victimhood and its inextricable link to locating enemies both from without and within have functioned as a "national adhesive" in the history of Germany since World War I is illuminating in the broader context of understanding how these constructions function similarly with regard to the concept of race more generally.

PART II

Cultural Representations and Self-Representations of Afro-Germans

4

LOUIS BRODY AND THE BLACK PRESENCE IN GERMAN FILM BEFORE 1945[1]

Tobias Nagl

The history of people of African descent has profoundly influenced German film. Although blacks have been forced to remain invisible in German society for a long time, they have been highly present on the big screen. However, this visibility contributed in no small part to their loss of individuality: if they appeared in film black actors were always forced to represent a longstanding stereotypical image. Their history in film is one of white fantasies and projections: page boys, bartenders, butlers, musicians, sailors, dancers, bell boys, porters, chauffeurs, and "wild" native people. These have always been the recurring stereotypes that blacks had to fulfill. These images proclaimed not only white superiority, but often also envy and contempt. At the same time these pictures are also historical documents of the everyday reality as well as the presence of blacks in Germany. Because of the prevailing racism in the majority of the population, strategies of economic exclusion and the controlling racial policies during the Nazi period, the majority of blacks in Berlin before 1945 worked at least temporarily as "artists" in the entertainment industry or other areas where they were on display. The predominance of male roles in film reflects the gender-specific mobility within the colonial migration. It is difficult to ascertain today what role the movies played for black Germans, whether as actors or as audience members, and it is too late to reconstruct films' function as part of their subjective experience. In addition, there are few

109

remaining sources concerning the specific interaction between the film industry and nonwhite actors; those that exist are rarely free of racism. Nonetheless it is beyond doubt that nonwhite actors played a significant role in the consciousness of white German film audiences. In contrast to the U.S., Great Britain, and France, this consciousness did not have a corresponding counterpart in reality. Only a few specific names of film extras or individual actors appear in the censorship files, reviews, or other historical sources. Thus, the production of stereotypical images was perpetuated by the refusal to grant individual identities in the form of names.

"An unprecedented authenticity"

It is all the more remarkable that the film journal *Film-Kurier* published an overtly racist column in the early 1920s, in which the author Martin Proskauer tells the story of "Mr. Negro Mpumpu." The column in the journal's art section was labeled as a "farce" and deserves to be quoted extensively.

> When Mr. and Mrs. Kikibumbo (baobab tree no. 2, immediately left at the Ugandan jungle) had a son, Father Kikibumbo took the infant to the village magician in order to have the little one's future told. The old magician fumbled with his human bone amulets and predicted a great luminous future for the nigger baby Kikibumbo Jr. in the land of the white-faced devils. [. . .] He was called Mpumpu, which translates as "the one with the great future."

Several colonialist clichés such as inner-African slavery, alcoholism, laziness, and criminal conduct follow. After various travel episodes, Mpumpu, with his tropical saucer-like eyes, finally arrives in Berlin as the pimp of "Red Anna and blond Mitzi," and Proskauer gets to his point concerning blacks in German films.

> A film director searched for twenty Negroes, who were to provide unprecedented authenticity as dark honorable men. Searching on Friedrichstrasse, the director bumped into Mpumpu. Now the latter's fortune was made. From now on he starred in films almost daily. Mpumpu didn't have to do much of anything, simply stand around in beautiful, golden-laced clothes, walk once through bright sunlight (the luminous future—the prophesy!), and wait some more. [. . .] But Mpumpu's career improved even more. Once in a while he played supporting roles, had calling cards printed, wore stiff collars, red neckties, and light yellow shoes. He was soon known as the

dashing Mpumpu. Now he wouldn't act for less than 200 Marks a day, overtime extra (outside shots only for an additional charge because the air could damage his complexion.)

One day a lady fell in love with his screen image. The widow Dietsch, owner of a butcher shop (referred to respectfully among colleagues as the eighty-Taler-horse) saw him in the film palace, fell in love with his noble, manly looks (for further explanation of such emotions see the collected works of Mrs. Courts-Mahler), searched for his address, looked him up, and married him on the spot. Mpumpu was an angel of a man, treated his wife tenderly, was faithful to her, and waited until he finally had discovered the hiding place of the day's profits. It was in the second pillow in Mrs. Mpumpu's bed. The next night he stepped up to her bedside, lovingly regarded her charming features, placed his hand around her neck to prevent the sleeper from shaking, and slipped the right hand into pillow no. 2. Then disappeared into the night, as dark as his skin color. When Mrs. Dietsch (formerly Mrs. Mpumpu) left the hospital, Mr. Mpumpu had long returned to his tropical homeland.

He went straight [. . .] into the jungle of Rwanda and founded a large film business with the hard-earned money, the Central Africa Jungle Film Company (MUFA for short). Unfortunately the cinemas did not flourish. The Negroes didn't go because they did not understand the inter-titles, the orangutans did not go to the movies out of principle, and the mandrills, worried about their colorful behinds, feared the hard seats. In short, nobody went to the movies, and Mpumpu went bankrupt: in Negro talk, he flopped. That is the story of Mr. Mpumpu's fortune and fall.[2]

Proskauer's writing provides many clues regarding the construction of race in the film culture of the early 1920s, in particular the idea that the filmed black body represented the promise of "authenticity" for white audiences. Black extras were thus not so much "acting" but embodying "nature" in a reproduced authenticity that the new film medium celebrated. Cinema itself, the *Lichtbild*, was used as a cultural tool against this "dark nature" just as the black male body and its inherent sexual threat required containment with all available rhetorical means. Ernst Bloch wrote in a 1930 film review: "The telescope on Africa was set up by whites, but it also shows through Africa the cannibalistic hot desires of the whites." This review may have been the first to analyze the imaginary function of blackness for spectators in Weimar cinema.[3] But Proskauer's story also reveals a degree of individuation that is highly unusual for the discourse of the time: his fictional character of Mpumpu is depicted as a person, with an income and calling cards. It is unclear whether this fictional character combines the features of several actual people or whether it is based on a single real person. In any case, members of the black community in Berlin apparently used the Bantu term "Mpumpu" jokingly when greeting each other until the 1950s.[4]

Although we can identify several black Germans in the films of the Weimar Republic—Anjo Diek, Theophilius Wonja Michael, Volde Tadek, Victor Bell, Peter Makembe, and the child actor Willy (Mac) Allan—it is likely that Proskauer was referring to the actor, musician, dancer, wrestler, and singer known by the stage-name Louis (also Lewis or Lovis) Brody (1892–1951). Only a few other nonwhite actors, such as the Asians Henry Sze and Nien-Sön Ling or the "Creole" Madge Jackson,[5] achieved similarly prominent status, which was reflected in Brody's depiction on artist's postcards, and his mention in film reviews, film credits, and press releases. Brody is the only one among these actors who is mentioned in *Glenzdorfs Internationales Film-Lexikon* (Glenzdorf's International Film Encyclopedia) of 1960. His brief entry reads: "actor (Negro)." Brody's more than fifty film roles provide one of the most important reflections of the image of blacks in German popular culture, which is characterized by an almost "Manichean opposition" vis-à-vis the white film characters, leaving hardly any room between the alternatives foe or slave.[6] By reconstructing Brody's biography we can, to reverse Sander Gilman's well known phrase "blackness *with* blacks," thus symbolically give a name and agency back to all those who were little more than a decorative element in the history of German film.[7]

"Killed by a gigantic Negro"

(Ludwig) M'bebe Mpessa was born on 15 July 1892 in Duala, Cameroon, and arrived under unknown circumstances in Germany. In 1915, at the age of twenty-three, he acted in Joe May's *Joe Deebs* mystery series in the episode *Das Gesetz der Mine* (The Law of the Mine.) A contemporary reviewer reports about this film, which is lost today, that:

> one of the protagonists stuck his head out of the rolling car window and was killed by a gigantic Negro, who in turn was motivated by revenge. The murdered man had been an inspector in the diamond mine and had ordered that the father of the Negro, who had swallowed diamonds, *be cut open while alive* according to the law of the mine to remove the precious stones.[8]

Brody was to play many such threateningly demonic parts. They all follow the iconography of the black executioner that can be traced back through Franz von Stuck's symbolist Salomé depiction to medieval Christian paintings,[9] likewise in Robert Wiene's expressionist film *Genuine* (1920), where the "competent ensemble" is "completed by the Negro Lewis Brody."[10] The film tells the story of the vampire Genuine (Fern Andra) in the tradition of the horror-romance spiked with fin-de siècle exoticism. Genuine is being guarded as a "slave" in the house of a peculiar man by the "gigantic Negro," Louis Brody. When the barber's apprentice, Florian, falls in love with her, he "tames the vengeful feelings of the Negro with a mysterious ring."

> [But Genuine] cannot live without blood. She demands Florian's death. She has stolen the ring of power from him. The Negro obeys. But he has a white heart in his black bosom, pushes Florian into freedom, [. . .] opens his own vein, and offers his blood to Genuine. [. . .] But her ecstasy has vanished, she flings the cup away in horror.[11]

Here the racialist imagination of the early German cinema is acted out almost programmatically through a web of projections and condensations in the figure of Brody's character. It is constituted by a series of elements such as the sensationalistic sexualized thrill of the encounter between the white woman and the gigantic black man, which is heightened by medical discourses of the time describing both as "nature." Other components include the white slavery trope, the "black danger," which must be domesticated along the lines of foe-slave ("white heart,") in order to reemphasize white dominance with a blood sacrifice, and finally the obsessive metaphysics of the idea of "pure blood," which under the threat of horrible punishment may not be mixed with racially inferior blood.[12] Brody's character then offers a second and last sacrifice. The village mob enters the enchanted house, and "the Negro falls under the strikes of the scythes."[13]

Similar again is Brody's part in the Venetian episode of Fritz Lang's allegorized "ballad film" *Der müde Tod* (1921) in which he plays the executioner of the lover (Walter Janssen). The heroine (Lil Dagover), in a tragic error, had given the order to murder him herself. Lang manages to reinforce the association of blackness with death through an early film trick. Bernhard Goetzke, who plays the lead in the film, portrays death. Through a fade-in, Lang lets the "Moor" (inter-title) dissolve after his murderous act into the archaic grim reaper (Goetzke). Brody thus incorporates death. The Cameroonian Brody was introduced as a Malaysian character in the films *Der Dolchen des Malayen* (1919) and *Genuine*. In Joe May's monumental eight part series *Die Herrin der Welt* (1919/20) he even appears as Chinese, not at all unusual for the orientalist obsession of early Weimar cinema. The studio sets of India or Asia

Figure 4.1. Film still from *Genuine* (directed by Robert Wiene, 1920) featuring Louis Brody and Hans Heinz von Twardowsky (kneeling).
Permission granted by Stiftung Deutsche Kinemathek/Berlin.

were populated by African extras dressed in Arabian "Moor" costumes, as was the case for *Das indische Grabmal* (1921), in which Louis Brody stars as well or in *Die Jagd nach dem Tode* (1920). Designed for spectatorial pleasures, these monumental settings are reminiscent in their opulence of images of the medieval encounter between Europeans and Africans in a fantastic Orient.

Der bekannte Negerdarsteller

Louis Brody

der in verschiedenen großen Weltfilms, so zum Beispiel in dem
May-Film „HERRIN DER WELT" 4. Teil, König Makombe
als Zauberer, sowie in dem jetzt im Ufa-Palast laufenden
Gloriafilm „DIE VERSCHWÖRUNG ZU GENUA" als
:~: Mulay Hassan mit anerkannt großem Erfolge spielte :~:

Berlin W35, Kurfürstenstraße 40

Fernsprecher: Amt Kurfürst Nr. 2730

Figure 4.2. Advertisement for the actor Louis Brody in the film magazine *Der Film* no 11, (1921).
Permission granted by Jügen Keiper, Deutsches Institut für Filmkunde, Frankfurt.

At the same time there is a tendency in the narratives to layer different forms of ethnic and racial difference into *one* singular image of the exoticized "Other" in order to express a position of ethnocentric dominance, which rejects difference as a pluralistic, heterogeneous, and nonhierarchical category and corresponds to contemporary white fears of a "colored danger."[14]

Figure 4.3. Advertisement for the actor Louis Brody in the film magazine *Der Film* no 8, (1922).
Permission granted by Jügen Keiper, Deutsches Institut für Filmkunde, Frankfurt.

The shooting of May's adventure film *Die Herrin der Welt*, which takes place on several continents, was covered by the press with such great sensationalism that it seemed like cinema's revenge for the Versailles treaty. The press repeatedly described the large number of nonwhite extras on the set, turning the film shoot into a spectacle similar to the *Völkerschauen*, a popular exhibition of native peoples at world fairs or in zoos: "72 Chinese men and women who were imported from Scandinavia, Norway, and Switzerland live in Chinatown, and in the barracks *that are located behind the barbed wire* (emphasis added) live Negroes of all tribes, several hundred, who also populate the African kraal."[15] Unlike most of the extras, Brody was playing important supporting roles, often several in the same film. In the first part "Die Freundin des gelben Mannes" he guards the heroine Mia May, who had been abducted into a Chinese brothel. Only Brody's costume might be called "Chinese" at best. In part five, "Der Schatz von Ophir," he provides comic relief as the good-natured and completely domesticated leader of an enslaved African tribe, which is liberated by the white heroes thanks to their superior technology. This was a part that Nazi cinema would cast him in repeatedly. In part six, "Die Frau mit den Milliarden," he flees with his liberators in an airplane from Ophir, the former German East Africa. He is offered a meal on the flight but cannot eat it because he is unable to use a fork and knife. The camera lingers painfully long on this demeaning spectacle for maximum impact. Brody continued to be cast as the "exotic face" for multiple parts in the same film even in the talkies of the 1930s and 1940s. We may assume that audiences could not recall his striking features from one film to the next and were not confused by his portrayal of many different characters as the various parts of *Die Herrin der Welt* were launched in weekly intervals.

Brody's own thoughts on such roles cannot be reconstructed today. It is likely that he regarded them as strictly business. But a campaign by Chinese students in Berlin against anti-Asian representations in the serial and similar exotic adventure films shows that such images were controversial from the very beginning. Later, the students wrote what might be the first antiracist film review:

> Life in China is portrayed in a distorted way in the film. The depiction of the peoples' weaknesses and vices is exaggerated. It is neither humanitarian nor in solidarity to evoke feelings of contempt towards an entire race in the masses of viewers. Only few Chinese are sinners such as they are commonly depicted in the film. There is no trace of the ancient age of our civilization and culture [. . .] or of our noble customs.[16]

Because of their complaint to the Imperial Ministry for Import and Export, some scenes of the episode *Die Freundin des gelben Mannes* had to be changed. This and several other students' campaigns were successful because they managed to involve the Chinese ambassador and thus elevate the matter to a diplomatic level. Due to the small number of nonwhite immigrants in the Weimar Republic and the prevalence of racial ideologies, disputes over the representation of race could only be staged politically as conflicts between nation-states. Because of their precarious legal status and the colonial rule in their countries of origin, such a strategy was not an option for the Africans from the former German colonies.[17]

Racism, Colonialism, Modernism

There is little information on the circumstances of Brody's life in those early years. His name appears relatively infrequently in the files of the Imperial Colonial Office as compared to other colonial migrants. This might indicate that Brody was able to provide for himself with fairly little involvement by the authorities. At the end of World War I, he lived at Berlin's Kurfürstenstrasse No. 40 and was a member of the African Aid Association (Afrikanischer Hilfsverein) founded in 1918 in Hamburg to assist Africans in their dealings with the authorities and employers. Other members included Bonifazius Foli, the entrepreneur Ernst Wilhelm Anumu, the ship clerk Joe Metziger, and the merchant Peter Mukuri Makembe.[18] Based on the shared diaspora experience, the association's statute allowed "any member of our black race and any colored person" to become a member. The diaspora experience during the war was marked not only by the racism of the early colonial period but by the reinforced and radicalized debates about the expansion of colonial laws regarding "racial purity" to pertain to colonial migration into German cities. These debates were fed by a new radicalized mass nationalism. Heinrich Class, for example, wrote for the Pan German Association in 1917:

> The soil of the Reich shall be kept clean: therefore we will not tolerate any colored people here, even if they come from our own colonies. If they are absolutely indispensable for our foreign fleet, we will tolerate them in our harbors; but they will be strictly confined to certain areas, which they may not leave. *Otherwise no colored person is to show his face on German soil.* The silly custom of employing black, brown, and yellow porters for advertisement must end. [. . .] We shall shake ourselves free of these strange *fashions* and consider how undignified it is to imitate the nonsense and the tastelessness of foreigners.[19]

Representing the African Aid Association, Brody wrote to the press in 1921 to protest diplomatically against the so-called "Black Shame"

(*Schwarze Schmach*) campaign by appealing to the patriotism of white Germans. This campaign had been launched by the entire political spectrum to the right of communists and socialists against the French occupation of the Rhineland by North African troops. Under the title "The German Negro and the Black Shame," he wrote:

> Blacks who came from the former German colonies and now live in Germany suffer greatly because of the accounts regarding the "Black Shame" that are being published in certain papers. Germans do not seem to consider that they once owned colonies and that as of today no decision has been reached about the fate of the natives from those former German colonies; will they become members of the *entente* or will they remain Germans? The natives of the occupied colonies are politically speaking considered to be Germans; for this reason the natives' return to their home countries from Germany is very difficult. We kindly ask Germans to consider that we have to suffer just like they do and please not to treat us with disrespect. We want to point out especially that we are not a wild race without morals, as is currently maintained everywhere in Germany. Furthermore we have to remind Germans that Lettow-Vorbeck did not fight the war alone in Africa but that many natives fought alongside the Germans and risked their lives for the German flag. Blacks who live in Berlin and in the unoccupied territories of Germany are not the same blacks and yellows of the occupied territory. We ask Germans therefore to be considerate against these blacks and not to agitate against them because of the news regarding the "Black Shame." This appeal is occasioned by the following incident: 14 days ago one of our compatriots was attacked by pedestrians and seriously beaten because he was taken for a black person from the occupied territory.[20]

While most black extras were routinely booked anonymously through the film agency at Friedrichstrasse (*Filmbörse*), the "well-known Negro actor" "Lovis" or "Lewis" Brody ran a few ads in various film magazines in 1921 and 1922, in which he points to his exotic roles in theater and film including *Die Herrin der Welt*, *Die Verschwörung zu Genua*, and his "major parts" in the Austrian productions *Knock-Out* and *Homo Sun*.[21] The illustrations show him either with a hat, dressed in a suit, in Arabic-style "Moor" costumes, or as the signature of one portrait drawing indicates, as a Malaysian. His contact address and phone number are listed as 20 Kurfürstenstrasse. In the summer of 1925 the extra Wilhelm Mumumé, who had been arrested on charges of making opportunistic "German-nationalist" comments in the Rhineland, mentions Brody's address as 66 Steglitzer Strasse in his petition to the former governor of Cameroon, Seitz; in the fall, a list of unemployed Cameroonians that was composed by Mumuné and forwarded to the Foreign Ministry by Seitz indicates that Brody was living at 3/I Magdeburger Platz. An attached handwritten note gives his profession as "musician."²² At the end of 1926 Brody was one of seventeen Africans to sign a power of attorney allowing Privy Councilor Dr. Mansfeld of the German Society for the Study of Natives to "represent us in all legal matters of social and economic interest before the German government."²³ It appears that Brody never required any such assistance in the following years. His name does not appear in any official files until the 1930s.

In 1926 Brody could be seen in the "colonial movie" *Ich hatt' einen Kameraden—Ein Drama aus den Heldentagen*, which premiered during the "colonial week" organized by a colonial association, the *Koloniale Reichsarbeitsgemeinschaft/Korag* in Hamburg. This propaganda event was accompanied by an unprecedented press coverage and opened with a "festive parade" that, in an imperial gesture, featured not only a "group of Massai" provided by the Hagenbeck company, but also a major contribution by colonialist supporters: a not insignificant number of them had painted their faces black in order to portray life in the colonies. The pitiful nature of such postcolonial nostalgia was noted even by the usually pro-colonial middle-class press: "The masquerade of boys and girls in black leotards and the heavy black and brown face painting should have been supervised by an artist," judged the *Hamburger Anzeiger*.²⁴

To round out the visual offerings during colonial week, a "Tarzan" circus show was organized ("Of greatest interest for all supporters of the colonial enterprise! The novel from the deepest Africa [. . .] in the glorious stage show by the Circus Busch") as well as screenings of "cultural films" such as *Verlorenes Land* and *Tierfang in Abessinien*. One, *Ich hatt' einen Kameraden*, shows Brody with the white actress Andja Zimova, who plays an African woman in blackface and features the musical accompaniment of the *Deutschlandlied*. Zimova greeted the guests at opening night in the Nazi film theater *Passage* with a dance number. The film itself recapitulates the outbreak of World War I in German East Africa with chauvinistic-colonial overtones and forms an ideological link in its contrasting depiction of a white and a black woman between the racist colonialist mentality and *völkisch*-nationalistic male fantasies. Klaus Theleweit's notion of whiteness, which he extracted from the idealized, de-sexualized images of women in *Freikorps* literature, receives an entirely unmetaphorical, racialized meaning here.²⁵ Brody plays the lowlife counterpart of the "military men" (*Schutztruppler*) and Zimova's thwarted lover. His part, although entirely negatively characterized, still signifies the collective memory of the long history of Southwest African resistance against the German colonialists. He faces the imperialists with the words: "The day will come when he will not hold his head high, the white man!" and is thrown subsequently to "real" alligators.

Figure 4.4. "Der Schauspieler Lewis Brody" (portrait of the actor Lewis Brody).
Photo by Yva Else Neulaender-Simon (1900–1942), in *Das Deutsche Lichtbild-Jahresschau* (1930), 75.
Permission granted by Das Verborgene Museum—Dokumentation der Kunst von Frauen e.V.

A few photographs and autograph cards provide some information about Brody's life in the late 1920s. The Jewish avant-garde photographer Yva (Else Neulaender-Simon, 1900–42), who was murdered in a concentration camp, took several pictures of him. One postcard produced in her studio depicts him as a dandy with hat and cane. In a 1926 double page insert entitled "Revue, Revue" in *Das Magazin*, Brody is shown as a tuxedo-clad tenor saxophonist side by side with the revue dancer Inez G. Emphasizing the modernist enthusiasm for jazz is the photo *Charleston* with Brody in the same pose. As one exhibition catalogue put it: "Like the girls the saxophone was a stereotypical signifier of the eroticized and dynamic 1920s."[26] But not just the saxophone fulfilled this function: Yva portrayed "the actor Lewis Brody" again in 1927 with a naked torso, photographed from below using clearly erotic lighting (fig. 4.4). Only Brody's sad-serious gaze towards the left corner of the frame resists his photographic stylization into a phallic image. Towards the late 1920s Brody occasionally uses the stage name "Brody-Alcolson" for his theater engagements, paying homage to the Jewish American actor Al Jolson who introduced sound in movies with a famous blackface performance of "You ain't heard nothing yet" in the film *The Jazz Singer* (1927).[27] Another artist's postcard shows Brody in black tie with the white dancer Lucy Day; his own claim to have studied voice in Italy has not yet been confirmed. Among his friends and acquaintances were names of now long-forgotten black musicians and athletes such as William Thomson, "Negro Champion, St. Thomas, Danish West Indies," the black drag queen "Mannelusiano," or the dance pair "Rastus & Banks," all of whom performed in Berlin.

But the political conflicts of the late 1920s did not pass Brody and other African migrants by unnoticed. In 1927 the German section of the League against Imperialism and Colonial Oppression (*Liga gegen Imperialismus und koloniale Unterdrückung*), which was founded at the World Congress in Brussels, began its work. Two years later the second Congress met in Frankfurt. In the same year a section of the League for the Defense of the Negro Race (*Liga zur Verteidigung der Negerrasse*) was founded under the leadership of Victor Bell, the former spokesman of the informal Association of Black Film Workers (*Filmbörsen-Neger*). When the Cameroonian Joseph Bilé appeared as a speaker at a socialist students' meeting against the colonial and revisionist Association for Germandom Abroad (*Verein für Deutschtum im Ausland*) side by side with Professor Alfons Goldschmidt, who had been active in the Scottsboro campaign, warning bells began to sound in the Foreign Ministry and the German Colonial Society (*Deutsche Kolonialgesellschaft, DKG*). DKG president Seitz stated: "I am convinced that the natives still residing in Germany will all become communists under the prevailing economic conditions. I have requested years ago that all Africans be returned to their homeland and I hereby repeat this request."[28] Brody, too, was targeted by surveillance. After a conversation with the journalist Geyer, an employee of the Foreign Ministry notes: "It was interesting to me [. . .] that the natives are now preparing a revue in which only colored performers and one or two whites will appear. A certain Brodi [*sic*], apparently a West African native, whom Geyer describes as very intelligent, wrote the texts and poetry for this revue. I do not know Brodi. I also can't imagine how the natives are planning to produce this revue."[29] It is not known whether this show ever came to pass.

A cinematic articulation of the "race-question" from a communist position occurred only in Victor Trivas' *Niemandsland* (1931), starring the African-American dancer Louis Douglas, who had also choreographed Josephine Baker.[30] Brody's appearance in the romantic film *Nie wieder Liebe* (1931) with Willy Fritsch and Lilian Harvey, on the other hand, reflects the modernist discourse about the black body as a visual icon of a technical and cultural Americanism. In a technically exhilarating montage sequence, which like Yva's photographs seeks to capture the "tempo" and speed of the metropolis, Brody appears in a sailor's suit with an unknown black actress amidst a group of young lovers. Perhaps the first film to recognize positively the role of black Germans was Kurt Gerron's *Der weisse Dämon* (1932), in which Brody plays a part that is the furthest removed from the usual stereotypical roles. As a pageboy in a Parisian hotel, Brody tells the perplexed German film star Hans Albers, who addresses him in various languages, including an "African" one: "I am a native Hamburger!" Albers responds: "Gee whiz, *hummelhummel*! You're my compatriot, why didn't you say so!" Brody retorts nonchalantly in Hamburg dialect: "Well, I didn't know what language it was. French and English and then at the end something totally incomprehensible!"

Surviving in the Dream Factory

The Nazi seizure of power immediately worsened the situation for blacks in Germany. An internal note in the Foreign Ministry stated in 1934: "The general mood in the population concerning the question of race has the effect of frequent insults and discriminations against Negroes. No employers dare to hire Negroes in the current climate, thus leaving them stranded without the possibility of earning an income here."[31] Formerly isolated attacks against blacks increased,[32] and the new climate was noticeable in film policies as well. "In the more serious genres we need the simple-heroic plots connected to blood and soil (*Blut und Boden*) and featuring solid German characters. [. . .]. In the lighter genres we look for relaxing and refreshing stories but no rhumba-dancing Negroes."[33] Although the 1939 ordinance that forbade black artists to appear in public was meant to include film as well, it seems that no serious attempt was made to comply with the law.[34] Until the end of the war the film industry offered one of the most important employment opportunities for blacks under the Nazi regime.[35]

Indeed, Brody's career did not suffer a significant interruption because of the Nazi takeover. Between 1933 and 1945 he starred in twenty-three films. He was subletting a room from his white partner—"a certain Mrs. Dehmel"—at 232 Kaiser Friedrichstrasse. His name appears in a letter sent by the Foreign Ministry to the Ministry of the Interior in 1935 regarding the "damaging effects of the racial policies on natives from the former colonies, who reside in Germany" in connection with this address, and the note "three illegitimate children." Six months earlier, he is listed in a letter from the Foreign Ministry to the Office for Colonial Policy of the Nazi Party (NSDAP) that requested support for Africans seeking employment. Together with Victor Bell and Benedikt Gambe, Brody is included on an attached list with the standard remark that he "wishes to continue working in his artistic field."[36] It seems that he was not looking for work for long. Several autograph cards dedicated to Brody indicate that he was working increasingly as a wrestler in the 1930s. In 1935 he wrestled in Berlin, Stettin, and Magdeburg, in 1936 again in Magdeburg and in the winter quarters of Circus Krone in Munich, as well as in Berlin's sports palace against the local hero "*Zehe*" ("Toe"). In 1938 Brody, known as a "beaming ladies' man," was celebrated as a singer in Riga and a wrestler in Danzig. On 9 March 1938 he married Erika Diek, a black woman from Danzig, who moved in with him and Mrs. Dehmel. Economically speaking this *ménage a trois* was faring far above average as all three had an income. Brody even considered opening a business. In the course of the increasing racist surveillance of blacks in Germany, Brody's name showed up once more in a letter by the Office for Racial Policies of the NSDAP, listed among "Negroes and Mulattoes registered on our index of colored individuals."[37] Shortly thereafter he is recommended as an "artist and wrestler" for the colonial and revisionist "Africa Show" that had been initiated in 1937 to employ, control, and isolate Africans from the former colonies who resided in Germany.[38] The main goal and problem of this pursuit was the prevention of contacts with the white German population. It is not known whether Brody indeed participated in the shows. At any rate, his name does not appear in the programs that still exist today.

Brody is listed in the "appendix of exotic individuals" of the 1938/39 film workers' almanac together with thirty-seven other "Mongols, Malaysians, Negroes, Mulattoes etc." as a "foreigner in the sense of the film-quota ordinance." The almanac explained that "exotic individuals are not considered members of the Reich's film association (*Reichsfilmkammer*) [. . .] but are only listed here as well as in the register of Berlin's employment agency for film workers (*Vermittlungabteilung Film-Bühne des Arbeitsamtes Berlin*). The appendix of exotic individuals is added only for comprehensive purposes."[39] In reality the employment agency had difficulty in fulfilling its task in Goebbels' centralized dream factory. It struggled especially to provide enough nonwhite extras for larger film productions. Dr. Röber of the *Reichsfilmkammer* wrote to the film and theater section of Berlin's employment office in 1941: "It is well known that the employment office has registered only the names of a limited number of Africans [. . .] so that adequate placement can sometimes be difficult, especially when the number of required Africans is increased and not communicated to the agency in time. Therefore even POWs had to be used lately."[40] Six months earlier von Lindequist, president of the German Society for the Study of Natives (*Deutsche Gesellschaft für Eingeborenenkunde*) had protested to the supreme command of the army and the propaganda ministry against the forced recruitment of black French soldiers and demanded a halt to the "abuse of POWs for private, capitalist interests" and the resulting "salary gouging for black professional film extras."[41] But this intervention remained as unsuccessful as Bonifazius Follis's petition to the film company Tobis. The Propaganda Ministry argued in its reply letter to von Lindequist:

> The demand for crowds of exotic individuals as extras in large-scale productions such as *Carl Peters* and *Ohm Krüger* could only be satisfied by the use of colored French POWs. The Reich's Propaganda Ministry has therefore naturally supported the film productions' request for colored POWs with the responsible army officials. It is incorrect that this has caused an economically detrimental effect for the colonial blacks residing in Germany. [. . .] Moreover, the [film company] Bavaria has complained about quarrels and difficulties with the local colored extras throughout the entire shooting period and accused them of making unreasonable demands and endangering the workplace morale. In any case it is not up to you to decide whether the use of colored POWs in German film productions is necessary or appropriate. [. . .] I thus consider the matter closed.[42]

Meanwhile, the POWs used for the production of *Carl Peters* were in such poor physical shape that the participating Afro-German extras organized a collection among themselves and donated clothing and tobacco worth 108 Reichsmarks.[43]

However, in most cases the white art dealer Hans von Hellfeld, who had ties to the black community and owned a vast collection of African art, managed the procurement and supervision of nonwhite extras for the studios. Hellfeld had been a merchant in China from 1910 to 1919 and returned there again after his forced repatriation in 1927. He edited the English-language art journal *China Arts & Handicraft*. After recovering from heroin addiction and undergoing psychiatric treatment in Beijing,[44] the now impoverished Hellfeld was returned to Berlin in 1932 by the German embassy in China. There he became an "artistic adviser and consultant" for Germany's largest film studio UFA in the following year. But because the Third Reich prohibited managerial "procurement activities," Hellfeld, who was rumored to have had an illegitimate child with the black German Soja Akwa, found himself continuously in conflict with the respective authorities: *Reichsfilmkammer*, the employment agency, the German labor service, the Foreign Ministry. In 1940 the German Society for the Study of Natives complained to the *Reichsfilmkammer*:

> Hans von Hellfeld, otherwise unknown to us, collects 10% of the colored extras' salary as commission. This leads to undesirably diminished earnings, which are miserable to begin with, so that our office might be forced to support those blacks in difficult economic circumstances. There is absolutely no need for Mr. von Hellfeld's services because any office can receive from us at any time the addresses of all Negroes residing in Berlin, if the number of required exotic extras exceeds those already registered with the film employment agency.[45]

The charges against Hellfeld also seem supported by a letter of complaint from the Korean Chang Yuon Ling and a few other East Asian actors to the *Reichsfachschaft Film*. Hellfeld is charged with having received up to forty *Reichsmark* per person for the productions *Ich liebe alle Frauen* and *Der Kaiser von Kalifornien* while paying out only twenty Reichsmarks to the extras.[46] This individualized labor struggle lasted several weeks. Hellfeld defended himself with the countercharge that Chang had skillfully "pushed me out of the business after I made promising connections by emphasizing mysterious connections to the Chinese embassy, which was apparently negatively disposed towards me. I was therefore forced to rely on welfare because that conniving scoundrel foreigner deprived me of my livelihood."[47] Hellfeld fled to Prague after his apartment was bombed out. Nothing more is known of him.

Louis Brody appears to have maintained a unique position within this practice of hiring and firing by telephone. Because he was an actor for important supporting parts, especially speaking parts, written contracts with him still exist. His pay was three or four times as high as that of other black Germans. For his portrayal of a "Negro Chief" in the colonial film *Carl Peters*, Brody received one hundred Reichsmarks per day; only the language coach Mohammed Husen, who was later murdered in the concentration camp Sachsenhausen, came close to this salary by earning seventy-five Reichsmarks for his role as a "Negro Chief and coach for Swahili."[48] Most black extras did not only derive welcome wage-earning possibilities for many months from such film productions or gain recognition with acquaintances, neighbors, and employers, but also found a rare opportunity during these times of forced expatriation, sterilizations, racial laws, and deportation into concentration camps to meet other black Germans in a context that was relatively free from discrimination.[49] Unlike these extras, Brody's name appears from time to time in the credits or press releases and sometimes the acting abilities "of the well-known Negro actor Louis Brody" even find honorable mention in film reviews: "Leading the primitives of the jungle quite expressively is Louis Brody."[50] However, this popularity only reached so far, as an Askari still photo of Brody from the movie *Die Reiter von Deutsch-Ostafrika* (1934) demonstrated. The film still was used in a photo collage for *Das Volksbuch unserer Kolonien* (1938) without upsetting the historical or documentary claim of the illustration.[51]

Brody's parts in the 1930s and 1940s were mostly free of Weimar films' ambivalence regarding the black body, which functioned in Nazi cinema only as the guarantor of a rather abstract worldliness. Genre films such as *Der unmögliche Herr Pitt* (1937/38), *La Habanera* (1937), *Dr. Crippen an Bord* (1943), *Kautschuk* (1938), *In geheimer Mission* (1938) *Wasser für Canitoga* (1938/39) and even the anti-Semitic propaganda production *Jud Süß* (1940) leave no doubt about his subaltern, undemonized position. His roles in these films are bar keepers, "Moors," servants, porters, or sailors who obey with a crisp *Jawohl!*, dance a little, possibly lie, or get themselves involved in a wrestling fight. Brody's multifaceted talents and his excellent language skills kept him employed until the end of the war and thus possibly alive.[52] His best-known roles took place in Nazi colonial films such as *Carl Peters* (1941), *Ohm Krüger* (1941), *Vom Schicksal verweht* (1941/42), *Germanin* (1942/43), and *Quax in Fahrt* (1943/44). They all show Brody stereotypically as a "chief" in native attire. Whenever the colonial practice, even as an imagined one, was potentially traumatized by "those terrifying stereotypes of savagery, cannibalism, lust and anarchy, [. . .] scenes of fear and desire," Nazi cinema had the tendency to depict a completely domesticated African image that prevented this threat from developing.[53]

Figure 4.5. Film still from *Ohm Krüger* (directed by Hans Steinhoff, 1941) featuring Louis Brody and Emil Jannings.
Permission granted by Stiftung Deutsche Kinemathek/Berlin.

Figure 4.6. Advertisement, "Mohamed Husen und Louis Brody" in *Künstleralmanach für Bühne und Film* (1941), 277, private collection.

This is one of the major differences from British or American productions of the same period. In *Vom Schicksal verweht* Brody plays a "voodoo priest," whose power is only narrated but not shown and who is overtaken by a simple trick. In *Ohm Krüger* (fig. 4.5), Brody is easily persuaded by the fatherly advice of Emil Jannings, and all obstinacy is overcome. In a key scene from *Germanin*, he confesses nostalgically to the German tropical doctor about the time of German colonization in a moment when he feels free from the surveillance of the British overseers. Although these films show a consistently anti-British position, they indeed participated in the imperialist division of the world that was fought out in Europe. The films' ultimate lack of interest in the dramatic potential of Brody's characters illustrates the thesis that German colonialism was oriented less towards concepts of *race* than of *space*.[54] In an attempt to denounce the Weimar *Systemzeit* this obsession, which Hans Grimm's novel *Volk ohne Raum* (1926) had elevated into a nationalistic catch-phrase, reversed itself into its paranoid opposite, namely the idea that Germany herself had become a colony of the Western powers, the "Jewish world conspiracy" and the black French colonial troops during the Rhineland occupation. The semi-documentary film *Blutsbrüderschaft* (1939/40) traces the Nazi movement's development and illustrates this train of thought by establishing retrospectively the importance of the "Black Shame" campaign as a focal point for various nationalistic forces. It thereby draws a heroic connection between the *Freikorps* in 1918, the "national uprising" in 1933, and the beginning of World War II.[55] Brody sings a German jazz tune in the style of that period in this film. The montage of his scene emphasizes its propagandistic purpose: it follows directly after documentary footage of black *tireilleurs sénegalais* who march into the Rhineland and was thus intended to underscore the "degenerative" influence of blacks on Weimar culture.

Nowhere are the politics of whiteness in the German cinema of the 1930s and 1940s, as well as Brody's status within the Nazi studio system, more obvious than in the Agfa Color stock "test film" *Groteske* (1941), produced for internal use by UFA. The film presents an interesting German variation on Richard Dyer's lucid description of how classic Hollywood cinema tended to privilege white skin as the norm in the development of illumination and coloring standards.[56] *Groteske* connects film color and skin color in a racist joke ("washing the Moor white"): in order to demonstrate the improved filming abilities of the Agfa Color technology the test film chose a film studio set and a beauty parlor as two exaggeratedly colorful, almost campy settings of traditionally great importance for the construction of body images. Louis Brody appears in both. On the fictional movie set he is dressed in an elegant double-breasted suit and presents himself to the production manager, who rejects him with the words: "Don't you understand, I can't use you. I need white men!" He is then referred to the "Cassandra Institute," whose manager had boasted over the phone: "But listen, that's nothing unusual. We're all white, nothing easier than white." Brody proceeds to the beauty parlor, which in the meantime had been used as a stage for effeminately hysterical comedy by a series of white actors. Facing the proprietor, Brody points to his white vest and demands "White, white like this, can you make a white man out of me?" "White is the color of innocence," responds the proprietor, "and in any case our specialty. It wouldn't be the first time that I've white-washed somebody [*jemandem etwas weiss gemacht habe*]." After this wordplay Brody is brought into a cabin, and the treatment begins. A machine with a disproportionately large, metal dragonhead exhales steam in order to emphasize the technical "production process" of creating whiteness, and then the preserved film fragment ends.

Whatever might have been the film's ending, it is clear that the black presence cannot be eradicated from the history of German cinema. Brody experienced the collapse of the Nazi regime in Berlin, secretly listening to "enemy radio" under his bedspread. After the war his acting career continued with parts in such East German (DEFA) films as *Der Läufer von Marathon, Sonja—Nächtlich am Nil* und *Die letzte Heuer*. Abandoned by both his women, he finally moved into a small apartment on Naunystrasse and worked as a circus artist and musician—for example, in 1947 as a solo singer in Leipzig's *Kabarett Perner*, and for a month with the revue group *Südseezauber* in the Circus Barley. Brody also sang and played drums with the "Mac Allen Band" in the black-owned bar *Pinguin—Berlins einzige Negerbar* (Penguin—Berlin's only Negro bar) on Bülowstrasse. The jazz band was led by the former Weimar cinema child actor Willy (Mac) Allen and also included Gottlieb Kala Kinger, Kwassi Bruce, the Brazilian Nelly Pirado, and Volde Tadek.[57] In 1950 Brody traveled with this band for a number of concerts to the North Sea island of Westerland. On 11 February 1951 Brody died a natural death in Berlin and was buried by his friends in the Berlin-Hohenschönhausen cemetery. He never had a German passport. His gravesite no longer exists. And of course, no street is named after him.

Translated by Reinhild Steingröver

Notes

All translations from the original German are by Reinhild Steingröver.

1. An earlier version of this essay was published as a biographical entry in *CineGraph—Lexikon zum deutschsprachigen Film*, 35, Lieferung (München: Edition Text und Kritik, 2002).

2. *Film-Kurier* 164 (28 July 1920).

3. Ernst Bloch, "Trader Horn in Afrika" (1930), in *Literarische Aufsätze* (Frankfurt/ M.: Suhrkamp, 1985), 480.

4. Personal communication by Herbert Reiprich, 13 February 2003.

5. According to an advertisement for John Hagenbeck's film *Darwin*, in *Der Film* 38 (1919). Nothing is known so far about Jackson's origins and biography.

6. Abdul R. JanMohamed, "The Economy of Manichean Allegory: The Function of Racial Difference in Colonialist Literature," in Henry Louis Gates, Jr. (ed.), *"Race," Writing, and Difference* (Chicago: University of Chicago Press, 1986), 78–106.

7. See also my, " '. . . und lass mich Filmen und Tanzen bloß um mein Brot zu verdienen': Schwarze Komparsen und Kinoöffentlichkeit in der Weimarer Republik," in Marianne Bechhaus-Gerst (ed.), *AfrikanerInnen in Deutschland und schwarze Deutsche—Geschichte und Gegenwart* (New York: Peter Lang, 2003).

8. *Der Kinematograph*, 441, 9 June 1915. Italics in original.

9. Jean Devisse, *The Image of the Black in Western Art*, vol. 2, part 1 (Lausanne: Office du Livre, 1979), 63–75.

10. *Film-Kurier*, 3 September 1920.

11. Ibid.

12. That categories of "race" and "blood" play an important role in the discourse of Weimar cinema can be seen in a review of Fritz Lang's lost film *Halbblut* (half-caste). The review states succinctly: "A half-caste inherits the weaknesses of both races and these have to appear sooner or later. That's the topic of the drama. [. . .]", *Der Film* 16, 19 April 1919".

13. *Film-Kurier*, 3 September 1920.

14. Ella Shohat and Robert Stam, *Unthinking Eurocentrism: Multiculturalism and the Media*, (New York: Routledge, 1994). The nationalistic popular literature of the inter-war years is full of such anxieties. In Hans Dominik's novel *Die Spur des Dschingis-Khan* (1922/23), Chinese rioters cause racial unrest in the U.S. and in Africa. Such politically unambiguous plots were not common in early Weimar cinema but they do exist, for example *Schiffe und Menschen* (1920) or *Die Trommeln Asiens* (1921).

15. *Die illustrierte Filmwoche*, 7/39, 1919.

16. *Licht-Bild-Bühne*, 1 May 1921. See also Tobias Nagl, " 'Kaiser Wilhelms Minen': Kolonialismus, 'Rasse' und Gender in Joe Mays exotischem Abenteuer-Serial *Die Herrin der Welt* (1919/20)," in Knut Hickethier (ed.), *Das Genre als Abenteuer: Der Abenteurfilm*, (Münster: LIT, forthcoming 2004).

17. See Katharina Oguntoye, *Eine Afro-Deutsche Geschichte. Zur Lebenssituation von Afrikanern und Afro-Deutschen in Deutschland von 1884 bis 1950*, (Berlin: Hoho-Verlag Hoffmann, 1997).

18. Statute of the afrikanischer Hilfsverein, Hamburger Staatsarchiv, SA 2819/331-1. See also Leroy T. Hopkins, Jr., "Race, Nationality and Culture: The African Diaspora in Germany," in his *Who is a German? Historical and Modern Perspectives on Africans in Germany*, vol. 5, (Washington, D.C.: American Institute for Contemporary German Studies, 1999), 1–32, as well as Peter Martin, "Der Afrikanische Hilfsverein von 1918" (unpublished manuscript).

19. Heinrich Class, *Zum deutschen Kriegsziel*, (München: Lehmanns, 1917), 71ff.

20. *B.Z. am Mittag*, 24 May 1921.

21. See *Der Film* 11 (1921), *Der Film* 8 (1922), *Der Film* 34 (1922). Octav von Klodmicki's *Homo-Sum* was advertised as an "anthropological, monumental film." It was produced with the "scientific advice" of O. Hauser and A. Heilborn. Hauser wrote the

nationalistic and anthropological treatise *Rassebilder* (race images, 1925), which contains the chapter "From the African to the White." As with the Hagenbeck production *Darwin*, the lost film is likely to have propagated a Eurocentric paradigm of evolution that associates blackness with primitivism. One ad for the film proclaimed, "Thus lives till today unconsciously/ the animal within each human" (*So lebt bis heute unbewußt/Das Tier in jedes Menschen Brust*), and it showed two cave men with clubs while two modern men were dueling in the background. The production year for this film is sometimes given as 1919, despite Brody's ad. *Der Film* 29 (1919).

22. Letter from Wilhelm Munumé to Seitz, 26 June 1925, Bundesarchiv (BA hereafter) R 1001/1077a, Bl. 91–95; letter from Seitz to the Foreign Ministry (Auswärtige Amt), 14 October 1925, Bl. 87–89.

23. Power of Attorney, 6 November 1926, BA R 1001/1077a, Bl. 82. The document was indeed signed only by Munumé alone. The authorship of the other Africans has to be doubted because Munumé was known to act as an informer for the German government. For the history and racial goals of the Society for the Study of Natives (*Deutschen Gesellschaft für Eingeborenenkunde*) see Heiko Möhle, "Betreuung, Erfassung, Kontrolle—Die Deutsche Gesellschaft für Eingeborenenkunde," in Ulrich van der Heyden and Joachim Zeller (eds.), *Kolonialmetropole Berlin. Eine Spurensuche* (Berlin: Quintessenz, 2002), 243–51.

24. *Hamburger Anzeiger*, 2 August 1926.

25. Klaus Theweleit, *Männerphantasien*, 2 vols. (Frankfurt/M.: Roter Stern, 1977/78).

26. Marion Beckers and Elisabeth Moorgat, *Yva—Photographien 1924–1938* (Tübingen: Wasmuth, 2001), 45.

27. Al Jolson's minstrel appearances later became the target of Nazi propaganda against the "cultural plague" of Americanism. See: "Geschmacklosigkeit oder Rassevergessen?" in *Neues Volk–Blätter des Rassenpolitischen Amtes der NSDAP* 7 (22–27 July 1936). Research on the function and the conditions of blackface in German popular culture is still lacking. For important thoughts on ethnic performance *after* 1945 see: Katrin Sieg, "Ethnic Drag and National Identity: Multicultural Crises, Crossings, and Interventions," in Sara Lennox, Sara Friedrichsmeyer, Susanne Zantop (eds.), *The Imperialist Imagination: German Colonialism and Its Legacy* (Ann Arbor: University of Michigan Press, 1998), 295–320.

28. Letter from Seitz to the Foreign Ministry (*Auswärtiges Amt*), 17 December 1929, BA R 1001/4457/7, Bl. 228.

29. Note from Eltester, Foreign Ministry (*Auswärtiges Amt*), 8 January 1930, BA R 1001/6761, Bl. 122ff.

30. See Tobias Nagl "'Afrika spricht!' Modernismus, Jazz und 'Rasse' im Kino der Weimarer Republik," in Andrea Pollach, Isabella Reicher und Tanja Widman (eds.), *Singen und Tanzen im Film* (Wien: Zsolny, 2003), 171–86.

31. Note by Brückner, Foreign Ministry (*Auswärtiges Amt*), 7 November 1934, BA R 1001/7562, Bl. 88.

32. See the following articles regarding Joseph Bilé, who went into French exile, and his campaign against the Nazi regime: "Africans Feel Lash Of Adolph Hitler," *The Philadelphia Tribune*, 18 October 1934; "Africans in Germany living in Terror, French Report," *Norfolk Journal and Guide*, 20 October 1934; "African Student Tells of Hitler Tortures in Germany," *The Chicago Defender*, 18 May 1935. See also "Fascist Terror Against Negroes In Germany," *The Negro Worker* 3 (April–May 1933): 1–3.

33. Eduard Schläfer-Wolfram, "Der Film im neuen Deutschland," in *N.S.-Frauenwarte* 1934/35, 335.

34. As late as 1940 a handwritten internal note from an employee of the Foreign Ministry states: "Such a directive has not yet been received [. . .]," Aufzeichnung Bielefeld, Auswärtiges Amt, 9 July 1940, BA R 1001/6383, Bl. 372.

35. John Welch, "I lived 12 Years under Hitler," *Pittsburgh Courier*, 6 May 1944. Welch reports here about meeting Bonifazius Foli and some other black extras. On the history of black extras in the Third Reich see also my " 'Sieh mal den schwarzen Mann!': Komparsen afrikanischer Herkunft im deutschsprachigen Kino vor 1945," in Peter Martin and Christine Alonzo (eds.), *Zwischen Stechschritt und Charleston. Schwarze im Nationalsozialismus* (Hamburg: Dölling & Galitz, 2004), 69–90.

36. Letter by Brückner, *Auswärtiges Amt* to the *Kolonialpolitisches Amt der NSDAP*, 29 March 1935, BA R 1001/7562, Bl. 104–6 and letter by Gunzert, *Auswärtiges Amt*, to the *Reichs- und Preußisches Ministerium des Innern*, 18 December 1935, Bl. 114–17. Brückner's letter includes a design for an I.D. card for musicians and artists from the former protectorates that was supposed to certify the protection of the NSDAP.

37. Letter from the *Rassenpolitisches Amt der NSDAP* to the *Auswärtiges Amt*, 18 October 1938, BA R 1001/6383, Bl. 268.

38. Letter from Lindequist, *Deutsche Gesellschaft für Eingeborenenkunde*, to the *Auswärtiges Amt*, 13 January 1939, BA R 1001/6383, Bl. 299. For information on the "Afrika-Schau" see Marianne Bechhaus-Gerst, "Afrikaner in Deutschland 1933–1945," in *1999* 4 (1997): 10–28; Elisa Forgey, " 'Die große Negertrommel der kolonialen Werbung': Die deutsche Afrika-Schau 1935–43," in *Werkstatt Geschichte* 9 (1994): 24–33; Tina Campt, Pascal Grosse, Yara-Colette Lemke-Muniz de Faria (eds.), "Blacks, Germans, and the Politics of Imperial Imagination," in Lennox et al., *Imperialist Imagination*, 205–29.

39. Almanach der Reichsfilmschaffenden 1938/39, o.A., p. 196.

40. Letter from Dr. Röber, *Reichsfilmkammer*, to the *Arbeitsamt Berlin*, 26 May 1941, BA (formerly Berlin Document Center), "Hans von Hellfeld," RKK, Akte Nr. 2600, Box 82, File 05.

41. Letter from Lindequist, *Deutsche Gesellschaft für Eingeborenenkunde*, to the *Oberkommando der Wehrmacht*, 6 November 1940, Bl. 432–34.

42. Letter from Gutterer, *Reichsministerium für Volksaufklärung und Propaganda*, to the *Deutsche Gesellschaft für Eingeborenenkunde*, 9 December 1940, BA R 1001/6383, Bl. 444ff.

43. Letter from Dustert to the *Deutsche Gesellschaft für Eingeborenenkunde*, 23 October 1940, R 1001/6383, Bl. 425.

44. See the medical evaluations of the German hospital, Beijing, 26 January 1932, *Auswärtiges Amt/Politisches Archiv* R 85833.

45. Letter from *Deutsche Gesellschaft für Eingeborenenkunde* to the *Reichsfilmkammer*, 16 June 1940, BA (formerly Document Center), "Hans von Hellfeld," RKK, Akte Nr. 2600, Box 82, File 05.

46. Letter from Tschang Yuon Ling to the *Reichsfachschaft Film*, 5 March 1937, ibid.

47. Letter from Hans von Hellfeld to Prof. Dr. Lehnich, *Reichsfilmkammer*, 3 March 1937, ibid.

48. Contracts from 23 August 1940 and from 3 August 1940. BA R 109I, Akte Nr. 2139. By way of comparison: top earnings in the early forties constitued a monthly pay of up to 200 RM.

49. Katharina Oguntoye, May Opitz und Dagmar Schultz (eds.), *Farbe bekennen— Afrodeutsche Frauen auf den Spuren ihrer Geschichte* (Frankfurt/M.: Fischer 1992), 77ff.

50. Quoted from an undated film review in a daily paper for *Vom Schicksal verweht* by Dr. Erich Krafft, private collection of Harry Heps.

51. Paul Kuntze, *Das Volksbuch unserer Kolonien* (Leipzig: Dollheimer, 1938), figure 29.

52. Nazi officials ruthlessly pursued other Africans and Afro-Germans living in "racial shame," such as the Hamburg case of Jonas Alexander Ndoki, who was sentenced by the local court in 1942 to death by beheading.

53. Homi Bhabha, *The Location of Culture* (New York: Routledge 1994), 72. See also: Sabine Hake, "Mapping the Native Body: On Africa and the Colonial Film in the Third Reich," in Lennox et al., *Imperialist Imagination*, 163–88.

54. Russel A. Berman, *Enlightenment or Empire: Colonial Discourse in German Culture* (Lincoln: University of Nebraska Press, 1998).

55. Regarding this pattern in Nazi documentary film see Tobias Nagl, " 'Von Fremder Rasse durchsetzt'. Anti-schwarzer Rassismus im Kulturfilm des Nationalsozialismus," in DFG-Projekt *Geschichte und Ästhetik des dokumentarischen Films in Deutschland 1895–1945*, vol. 3 (forthcoming).

56. Richard Dyer, *White* (New York: Routledge, 1997), 82–144.

57. For more information on the "Pinguin"-bar see "Kala Kinger, Kronprinz von Dibamba. Oberkellner in der Pinguin-Bar," in *Der Abend*, 22 October 1949. For more information on Willy (Mac) Allen as a musician, see Rainer E. Lotz, *Black People: Entertainers of African Descent in Europe, and Germany* (Bonn: Birgit Lotz, 1997), 283–96, who cites a different composition of the band.

Thanks for their support and valuable hints to the following individuals: Beryl Adomako, Herbert Reiprich, Herta and Manga Ngando, Katharina Oguntoye, Fatima El-Tayeb, Peter Martin, Marie Nejar, Martin Baer, Ursula Trüper, Dominik Nagl, Kanak Attak, Metropolis-Kino/Hamburg, Eiszeit-Kino/Berlin, CineGraph e.V., Harry Heps, Rea Brändle, Christian Stuck, Stiftung Deutsche Kinemathek/Berlin (Frau Lorenz, Herr Theis), Lars Amenda, Friedrich-Wilhelm-Murnau-Stiftung (Frau Weiß), Bundesarchiv/Filmarchiv (Frau Schütz, Evelyn Hampicke), George Eastman House, Library of Congress/Washington, Universitätsvermögen der Universität Hamburg, Rosa Luxemburg Stiftung and the staff of the Schomburg Center for Research in Black Culture, the Staatsarchiv Hamburg, the Bundesarchiv Berlin, the Politischen Archivs of the Auswärtiges Amts, the Haus des Dokumentarfilms/Stuttgart and the Deutsches Institut für Filmkunde/Frankfurt.

5

NARRATING "RACE" IN 1950s' WEST GERMANY

THE PHENOMENON OF THE *TOXI* FILMS[1]

Heide Fehrenbach

In the spring of 1952, West German moviegoers flocked to the feature film *Toxi* (R. A. Stemmle), the fictional story of a black German girl, making it one of the top ten box-office hits of the year. The film was notable on a number of counts. First, it was the first feature-length film to explore the subject of black "occupation children" born to white German women and fathered by occupation soldiers of color in postwar Germany. Released to coincide with the start of the school year for the oldest of the postwar black German children, the film had the explicit purpose of cultivating, in addition to profit, "social understanding" for the children as they made the difficult transition from the privacy of home to the public arena of school and classroom. Second, it was one of the few postwar films—and to my knowledge the only one in the early 1950s—to explicitly thematize the "race problem" (*Rassenproblem*) in Germany and call it by its name.[2] Finally, the film initiated the popularity and brief acting career of Elfie Fiegert, who played the title character of *Toxi* and later reprised the role of black occupation child (this time as Moni) in the 1955 West German film *Der dunkle Stern* (The Dark Star, Hermann Kugelstadt). I argue in this essay that the thematic treatment of *Toxi* yields insight into the precise ways that "race" was renarrativized after 1945 as a social category and national marker. Critical attention to Elfie Fiegert's brief career and the so-called sequel to *Toxi* provide a context in which to assess the contours and evolution of racial ideology in Adenauer's Germany.

By the time of the film's release in early 1952, black German children numbered over three thousand in West Germany, and despite their small numbers had already become its premiere minority group, to judge from the continual coverage of the children in the print media. In scores of articles in newspapers, popular magazines, and scholarly journals, the children were described as posing a significant social "problem" for postwar Germany and were either pitied or pilloried due to the racial and national heritage of their fathers and the perceived provocative and censorious behavior of their mothers, who fraternized with the nonwhite soldiers of enemy armies.[3] Through the 1950s, the children were treated as marked by their white mothers' moral failings and their black fathers' racial ancestry by German commentators of all political and ideological stripes. This strategic (if common Euro-American) practice established the children's fundamental, essentialized difference from white children, along with the social need for German contemporaries to seek solutions to this "problem" of difference. And although the children's fathers represented a wide range of nationalities and ethnicities (coming, for example, from such diverse places as French Indochina, Morocco, Senegal, Chicago, Alabama, or Puerto Rico), the children were consistently assigned a homogenous racialized group identity that assumed their affinity for things African, or more typically, African American, regardless of the specific national affiliation or ethnic heritage of their individual fathers of color.[4] As a result, interracial children were never viewed as unproblematically German in a social or cultural sense, although their legal status as German citizens was inarguable, since they took their mothers' nationality due to their out-of-wedlock births.[5]

Within a year of the founding of the Federal Republic, an official census had been taken to count the number of occupation children in Germany. Children of color (the so-called *"farbige Mischlingskinder"* or *"farbige Besatzungskinder"*) commanded special attention from the authorities, and their numbers were segregated from the white cohort through separate tabulations.[6] Since the late 1940s, West German officials at the federal, state, and local levels had been interested in encouraging adoption of occupation children abroad, particularly to the United States. The authorities' efforts focused most closely on interracial children, and through the mid-1950s, one of the most popular "solutions" advocated for the "problem" of black occupation children was emigration via intercountry adoption.[7]

This social policy was consistent with the liberal discourse of race that was emerging in post-fascist, post-occupation Germany.[8] The film *Toxi* is significant because it helped both to constitute this liberal discourse of race and to popularize it for the West German public at large. Attention to the narrative strategies of *Toxi* and its cinematic "sequels" reveals some of the precise ways that race was revalued after 1945 and indicates the centrality of race in the reconstitution of postwar German mythologies of national belonging.

Toxi's Liberal Discourse of Race

I begin with a brief description of the film's storyline. *Toxi* opens in the evening with a street shot of a handsome single-family home. The main action is the return from work of Dr. Theodor Jenrich at the end of the day. Entering the home, he finds the household in the throes of hectic preparations for a birthday celebration for Grandma Rose, Theodor's mother-in-law. It quickly unfolds that Theodor, his wife, and two young daughters share the house with Theodor's parents-in-law, Grandfather and Grandmother Rose, and their grown daughter, Herta. This German home, it seems, has two patriarchs, and much of the domestic drama of the film centers on the battle between their diverging views on race and social responsibility.

This battle is first unleashed and articulated when Toxi, a black German child, arrives unexpectedly on the doorstep of the white German family. Toxi's African American father is absent, and her mother is dead, which leaves only an ailing maternal grandmother who is unable to care for the child and deposits her at the door of the middle-class home. Toxi's arrival disrupts Grandma Rose's birthday party, causing consternation and establishing the central conflict in dramatic drawing-room scene that will be played out in the film.

After Theodor and Grandpa discover a suitcase left outside the house with Toxi's belongings, the assembled conclude that they are confronted with a case of child abandonment and call the police. In the meantime, Herta and her beau, Robert, tend to Toxi and feed her leftover dinner before the child is questioned by the police. As the police officer prepares to depart, Theodor questions why he is not taking Toxi with him. His protest initiates an exchange that exposes the adult characters' racial attitudes and sketches the topography of the possible dramatic solutions to the problem of race that the film invokes.

As Toxi is led off to bed by Grandma Rose, Theodor expresses his strong disapproval that Toxi is staying overnight in the house.

Grandpa Rose: You'd rather we put her out on the street, suitcase and all?
Theodor: If you want the child to stay in the house tonight, fine, it's your house. . . . But I forbid her to be with my children in the morning.

Herta's fiancé, Robert, objects to Theodor's attitude, but Theodor is adamant and counters that the child could have a communicable disease. When a guest who is a doctor leaves the room to examine the Toxi, Theodor continues, "But even if the child is healthy, I don't want her with our children." As Robert criticizes Theodor's focus on skin color, and Grandpa Rose agrees, Theodor gets to the heart of the matter:

Theodor: I can't speak to you about this problem. This Negro child [*Negerkind*]. . .
Robert: . . . is also just a person [*Mensch*].
Theodor: Right, but nevertheless there are differences.
Robert: I don't see any differences, perhaps because I'm not a philistine [*Spiessbürger*].
Grandpa: Don't make such a big deal of this. I don't see any problem either. One child more in the family is only a problem if there is no food. Otherwise there is no problem.
Theodor: I mean the race problem.

Silence, exchange of meaningful looks. Closeup shots of Theodor and Grandpa together in one frame, Herta and Robert in another, then back to Theodor and Grandpa, as Grandpa recovers: "Of course, that still exists. But I think we've learned to see with different eyes." Theodor's wife tries to interject, but is cut off.

Theodore: You know that our opinions differ on certain points.
Grandpa: Yes, I know and I don't take offense at you for it. But you must break the habit of approaching all people and things with prejudice.
Herta: You have your opinion and we have ours, as every person does. But you have to recognize that the child can't be blamed; such a child is innocent.
Male guest: In any case, the child will leave the house tomorrow.
His wife: No, tomorrow is Sunday!
Male guest: Ok, then the day after.

His wife:	I know what Herr Doktor Jenrich means. It's a child of shame.
Male guest:	Anna! Please be quiet. [Closeup of Theodor and Grandpa.]
Theodor:	You spoke of prejudice. I find it a matter of sensibility [*Gefühlssachen*].
Grandpa:	Sensibility!? A small black child comes to us, helpless. Who knows what has been done to the child. And your first emotion is "racial difference!" Now listen . . .
Robert:	Herr Doktor, I've only just met you today, but . . .
Herta:	Please be quiet!
Robert:	If I'm not permitted to speak I'd rather leave. [Leaves, slamming the door].
Grandpa:	It appears he wasn't properly raised.
[Robert returns]:	I'm sorry, the door slipped. [Leaves again, this time the front door slams off camera. Herta starts to exit room].
Grandpa:	Please stay here, Herta. Don't run after him.
Herta:	But I may be allowed to go upstairs. Excuse me. [Camera follows Herta into front hall, where Doctor emerges, pronouncing Toxi healthy. Guests depart.]

As this scene illustrates, and the film bears out, the family's response to Toxi and her black skin divides along generational lines. She is treated sympathetically by the family's young adults, Herta and her fiancé, Robert. While Herta's and Robert's formative years technically would not have postdated the Third Reich (they appear to be in their early twenties in the film), they—along with Theodor's younger daughters, who later befriend Toxi—are meant to represent the "new" postwar generation, graced by late birth and therefore unmarred by the racist ideology of the Nazi past. Grandpa Rose, in contrast, is clearly of a generation whose coming of age predated the Third Reich. This grace of early birth, the film seems to suggest, inoculated him against the disease of racism that ravaged his son-in-law's generation, freeing him to see in Toxi "only a child" and not a problem. Thus in this scene, the film defines the postwar *Rassenproblem* as Theodor's inability to dispense with racial classifications and hierarchies when encountering individuals or social situations. Grandpa, in effect, articulates the problem by suggesting that, rather than "learn[ing] to see with new eyes," Theodor continues in the habit of confronting the world through the prejudices he continues to carry with him like so much outdated baggage. It is precisely this act of locating the problem of race in the skewed perspective of the *white* beholder (rather than the body, culture or intellect of a black individual or group) that constitutes the liberal kernel of this film's own ideology of race.

Nonetheless, there are some notable amendments to this liberalizing discourse of race in the film. As noted above, the film identifies the residue of racist perspective and practice as adhering most stubbornly to the middle-aged ranks that came of political age under Hitler. While the film avoids explicitly demonizing Theodor as a Nazi holdover—opting instead for a softer, less controversial approach to characterization to avoid alienating its postwar German viewers—the generational topography produced by the film anchors racist ideology firmly and exclusively in the Nazi past (rather than a longer German history) and in the belief system of its adult generation (rather than Germans in general). The problem is thereby minimized and made manageable: broad-minded Germans need only help reeducate the tainted cohort of the Nazi years.

Thus far I have argued that *Toxi* is unambiguously liberal in the way it articulates the problem of race early in the film, but I am sorry to have to report that this dramatic scene of articulation also represents the culmination of the film's liberal perspective. In fact, the liberal perspective is unsettled—and the dialogue on race terminated—as the scene breaks down due to Robert's impassioned exit, quickly followed by that of Herta and the rest of the group. This scene and its disruption point to the perceived dangers of race in postwar Germany, for it indicates Germans' inability to confront the issue of racial prejudice—even within that most intimate social grouping, the family—without the threat of social dissolution. This becomes clear as we move from a consideration of the problem posed by the film to the solutions it proposes, for it is here that we run smack into the limits of postwar racial liberalism in 1950s West Germany.

Before I launch into a critical discussion of the full range of the film's solutions for Toxi, I would like to take a quick look at what first seems the likely solution, but one quickly betrayed as a fleeting utopian moment in the film.[9] Toxi has been taken to stay in an orphanage (*Kinderheim*) following the weekend she made her appearance at the Rose/Jenrich home. To fulfill his promise to her, Grandpa Rose arrives at the orphanage for a visit, where he sees a clean, orderly home for mostly black (and a sprinkling of white) German children. As Toxi greets Grandpa and leads him into the room, the children begin to sing in unison: "I would like so much to go home/I would like to see my homeland again/I can't find my way on my own/Who will love me and take me along?"[10] This song of homelessness—which not incidentally generalized Afro-German children as unloved orphans—is reprised throughout the movie at critical points and comes to serve as Toxi's theme song.

Soon Grandpa Rose's visit comes to an end, and Toxi is permitted to accompany him to the outside gate. Grandpa, clearly moved by the sight of the roomful of unwanted children and concern for Toxi, uncomfortably comments on the time and begins to say goodbye to her. But then he says, "Wait, I'll bring you back," takes Toxi's hand, and proceeds to walk her back in the direction of the orphanage. This begins the filmic moment (lasting fewer than thirty seconds) of promise and possibility. The camera pulls in for a close-up of Grandpa's face as they walk, which observes Toxi with affection and enjoyment; a reverse shot shows her smiling back at him, innocent and undemanding. Again, a reverse shot follows to Grandpa, and back to Toxi. It is during these brief fleeting seconds that we see Toxi and Grandpa interact as individuals outside of a racialized perspective, as individuals who share a human connection, a compatibility that renders race irrelevant. Within a few minutes, we realize that he had decided not to "bring her back" to the children's home, but to his family's home. Racial integration—even in the most intimate sphere of the family—appears imminent.

However, this moment is over just after it begins, and the scene concludes with the camera settling on a less fortunate black German girl, nose pressed against the window glass, apparently observing the happy scene from inside the orphanage. This concluding shot reminds us of the children left behind and, not incidentally, begins to transform the race problem within the film. It is no longer a narrow issue of white racism but has been broadened to include the social alienation and loneliness experienced by forsaken, institutionalized children. One might suppose that attention to the plight of black German children might have had a salubrious social effect, but there is little evidence that that was the case. Rather, it diffused (one is tempted to write *de*fused) the issue of white responsibility, since the camera lens shifts focus from the social fact of white racism to that of the putatively unwanted black children yearning in vain for love, family, and home in the Federal Republic.[11] Later in the action, moreover, the film closes off the possibility of Grandpa becoming the solution for Toxi and children like her. The utopian moment of mutual enjoyment gets subverted, as we will see.

The second solution proposed by the film is—predictably enough, following the generational analysis of the film—adoption by the young couple, Robert and Herta. In reaction to Theodor's continued insistence that Toxi leave his home, Robert and Herta decide to marry quickly and raise the child. This decision follows an earlier scene in which Herta and Toxi visit Robert at his studio and Robert photographs the child after handing her a chocolate bar to nibble. When Herta asks what he's doing, Robert, who is in advertising, answers simply, "poster." The scene in which

Robert and Herta agree to care for Toxi opens with a shot of the advertising poster he has made, which features a coal-black caricature of a girl with white saucer-shaped eyes and protruding lips. Robert clearly required no photo of Toxi to draw this image that, rather than betray a likeness of the child, draws liberally on familiar tropes of racist black stereotype. He marvels at his work, declaring that the company "will have to reorganize production around it." In fact, shots of the poster and his response to it serve to frame the short scene in which the couple decide to adopt the child. After appearing to admire the poster, Herta leaves rather abruptly following Robert's prideful display. As the camera follows them to the door, the poster of Toxi moves out of the frame and the backdrop to the action is dominated by another advertising poster of a sheep inscribed with the word "Dura-wool" (*Durawolle*). The imagery is subtle, but can be taken as a critical comment on Robert's willingness to commercially exploit and objectify Toxi in a way that established a representational equivalence between (black) child and (white) sheep. As Herta moves towards the door to leave, and the scene concludes, the couple's embrace is filmed through a divider in the room that resembles a wire fence. Both the "Dura-wool" poster and the fencing visually indicate the inability of even this younger generation to break out of the constraints of enduring cultural norms and values since Robert—at some less-than-conscious level—appears as conditioned by racial stereotypes and careerist ambitions as Theodor. This scene, in fact, is the first and last in which Robert and Herta are proposed as surrogate parents to Toxi. The film abandons the theme of their marriage and adoption altogether although they continue to appear as a couple. Thus solution number two is quietly killed as an option.

The third possible solution the film proposes revolves around Theodor's character. Throughout much of the film, Theodor protests Toxi's presence as an economic burden and epidemiological hazard and prohibits his young daughters from playing with her. That command is quickly subverted by the curious girls, but he continues to devote his energies to having Toxi removed from the family home when he's not busy pursuing business investments. The dramatic culmination comes when Grandpa suffers a heart attack after a heated show-down with Theodor, which allows Theodor the opportunity to act. Early the next morning, while the household sleeps, Theodor awakens Toxi and readies her for a drive to the orphanage. On the way, however, his car breaks down. While the car is repaired, the two become better acquainted over breakfast. In a comedy of errors, Toxi gets lost. Theodor gets worried and searches frantically for the child, and in the process gains a healthy dose of both paternal and social responsibility.

Figure 5.1. Film still from *Toxi* (directed by R. A. Stemmle, 1952). Robert proudly admires his advertising poster of Toxi, which draws on the visual lexicon of black stereotype, while Herta looks on. This scene signals the end of the couples' aspirations to adopt the child in the film. Photo courtesy of Deutsche Kinemathek, Berlin.

Following a telephone lead, Theodor and the police rescue the hapless Toxi just before she is spirited away in a gypsy caravan by a disreputable family of street performers who have realized her economic value as a curiosity for their panhandling. The rescue scene concludes with a medium close-up of a relieved Theodor warmly hugging a grateful Toxi, as an instrumental reprise of Toxi's theme song swells on the soundtrack. Thus Theodor's conversion story and Toxi's search for home appear to reach a happy, shared conclusion.

Blood Is Thicker Than Good Intentions: The Failure of Integration

In the film's narrative, the German father is successfully weaned from his recidivist racial prejudices of yesteryear, and Toxi finds herself in the embrace of white father and family. However, the filmmakers do not leave it at that. One of the most striking things about the film is that it refuses to end on the high celebratory note of this first, transformative ending. Rather, the first ending turns out to be a false one, and the drama continues. Toxi is returned to the family home and readily included in the family's preparations for the Christmas holidays. The long final scene that concludes the film begins with the apparent effacement of race as Theodor's white birth child plays one King of the Magi in blackface in the family Christmas drama, while Toxi performs in whiteface.

Yet rather than undermine the significance of race and the salience of the color line, the painted faces initiate a scene that reasserts both, vigorously reestablishing racial boundaries and race-based definitions of German identity by insisting on the power of blood and heredity. In the second—and final—happy ending, Toxi's African American father arrives unexpectedly at the family's door that Christmas Eve to collect his child and take her "home" to the United States. This overdetermined sentimental finale was foreshadowed in the Christmas drama, in which Toxi, while performing as a King of the Magi, abruptly steps out of character to reprise her theme song. The camera moves in for a tight close up of Toxi, establishing a psychological moment that betrays her ongoing yearning for a home and sense of belonging that she has not yet found. Within minutes that search is over, and the film concludes with Toxi's introduction to her African American father. The last sequence of shots in the film, in which the camera pulls in for increasingly tighter close-ups of the reunion and filial embrace, visually disengages the pair from the German domestic scene and releases a carefully choreographed crescendo of emotion that

Figure 5.2. Film Still from *Toxi* (directed by R. A. Stemmle, 1952). Toxi and Theodor's daughters in their Christmas eve pageant. Toxi (left) plays one King of the Magi in whiteface, while Theodor's white daughters perform in blackface.
Photo courtesy of Deutsche Kinemathek, Berlin.

anticipates and justifies Toxi's imminent emigration. As a result, the German family—and German identity—is first healed through inclusion of the racialized other, then restored to whiteness by her *elective* exit.

This second ending reveals that the film, all along, has been advocating the principle of tolerance rather than integration. In fact, it seems to suggest that racial integration would have destructive social and psychological consequences for (white) family and (black) child alike. This suggestion is dramatized toward the end of the film in a confrontation between Theodor and Grandpa, two scenes before Theodor loses Toxi on the drive to the orphanage. In the scene, Theodor again demands that Toxi be removed from the house, but this time threatens that if she is not, he and his family will leave instead. The threat triggers a violent reaction from Grandpa, who condemns Theodor's "heartless principles" and declares that he never wants to see his son-in-law and daughter again. With this, Grandpa appears to have a heart attack and collapses. While Grandma rushes to his aid, Theodor mutters to his wife that Grandpa's "love for this exotic [*fremdartigen*] child is not normal." After Grandpa is seen by the doctor and his condition stabilizes, Grandma Rose, who has been sympathetic to Toxi all along, tells Grandpa that he "cannot allow his grandchildren to leave the house on Toxi's account." Strikingly, neither Grandpa nor the film argue with this. Delivered by Grandma with calm demeanor, her counsel is treated as indisputable assertion and common sense. It is precisely this "common sense" response that begins to defuse the ideological rift between Grandpa and Theodor and shift the terms of the conflict. For Grandma's response implicitly questions whether Grandpa has the right to assert equivalence between Toxi and his own white grandchildren, whether Grandpa is right to stubbornly elevate Toxi and the principle of racial integration over their own progeny and loyalty to bloodline. Confronted in this manner, and assured by the doctor that Toxi will thrive in the healthy, stable environment of the orphanage, Grandpa immediately relents and agrees to have Toxi returned there. But do it quickly, he orders, "I can't look her in the face." Commitment to intact family trumps commitment to intact principle. And so Theodor wins the battle, if only to be converted from his most overtly racist ways a bit later in the film, and the scene ends without seriously challenging the reasonableness or racial assumptions of Theodor's demand.[12]

In fact, the film establishes a symmetry that works to reinforce and ultimately *reify* the black-white binary, since it insists that the pull of race is as strong among black as among white characters. Despite Toxi's being welcomed into the family at the end, we hear a reprise of her theme song,

"I would like so much to go home/ I would like to see my homeland again," at the very moment her father enters the family home. This refrain is intended to serve as a window into her emotional and psychological state, to signal a condition of incompleteness. As a result, heredity and belonging is envisioned as inherently racialized, and racial segregation is depicted as unconscious *natural* mandate.[13]

Toxi's Plight

"I guess that's the dream most of us black children had," commented a black German woman I know after she viewed the film.[14]

Thus far, my discussion has focused on the way the film's treatment of the *Rassenproblem* helped construct a normative national identity predicated on whiteness in postwar West Germany. Yet my friend's comment indicates that certain aspects of the film resonated with her experiences and fantasies growing up in the Federal Republic of the 1950s. Initially I was surprised by her response, perhaps because my analysis focused so single-mindedly on reading the film as text in order to determine the racial ideology it articulated for the white German audiences it addressed. My friend, however, viewed the film in terms of its "accuracy"—judging it by how well it conformed to, or diverged from, her personal experiences and social treatment. In fact, the film cultivates an aura of sociological accuracy in order to make its case for racial tolerance but also, ultimately, for segregation through expatriation. And it does this precisely in the ways it chronicles and dramatizes the "plight" of Toxi—and by extension, that of any and every black German child of the era—as one of abandonment, social isolation and marginalization, and cultural stereotyping.[15]

Toxi is deposited on the doorstep of the Rose/Jenrich home by her grandmother early in the film. Aside from a couple of shots of child and grandmother outside the home, which convey little about Toxi or her emotional state (except to establish the characters' liminal qualities in terms of race and class), the film introduces meager biographical details of the child only during interrogations by the white police officer and family members. Within the film, neither the child nor her plight exists apart from them. Any psychological or emotional depth she has as a character is revealed in interaction with white family members or white society. The film accords her little independent subjectivity; rather, her character functions as a kind of cipher onto which white Germans project their racial attitudes and fears.

I have discussed the film's depiction of racial attitudes in terms of their generational taxonomy above. Now I want to consider briefly the way the film articulates white fears regarding racial difference and its social consequences. Significantly, these fears were displaced from their white source to Toxi's fate: they are represented as threatening her emotional and physical health and cinematically dramatized as potential dangers, not explicitly to white German society, but to Toxi herself. So, for example, while Toxi is depicted as receiving the compassion and concern of most family members in the Rose/Jenrich household, barring Theodor and perhaps his wife (who is interrupted as she tries to speak her mind on the issue), Toxi's brief forays into public in the beginning of the film show the opposite: hostile glances, contempt from the friends of Jenrich daughters, treatment as a curiosity. The film suggests that while black German children may be able to find the necessary "*Nestwärme*" (warmth of home) in the private sphere of home, their experience in public is fraught with dangers. But even here, the film's depiction of home is ambivalent and ultimately problematic for Toxi—for the child is bounced among an ailing white grandmother who cannot care for her, a home inhabited by a surrogate white family riven by conflict over her, and an institutional home peopled by abandoned children like herself. None, then, are presented as optimal solutions or as places where Toxi unambiguously *belongs*.

Although *Toxi* is fundamentally a domestic drama, with most of the film's action occurring within the confines of the family home, there is one noteworthy scene in which Toxi wanders the city alone after being separated from Theodor. Intercut with shots of Theodor's frantic search, this sequence provides hints about the dangers confronting Toxi, which are not, for the most part, immediate dangers, but rather incipient ones. Toxi wanders the city nearly free from racist remarks (except when a man dubs her a "little black beast" in a clearly disreputable part of town), but she is also nearly free from social interaction. We see her nose pressed against store windows: the first shot shows her hungering for food. In a second shot, a night scene, she inspects the showcase of a lingerie store, with the camera positioned from within looking out through the window at her. Toxi is shown peering in, occupying barely a quarter of the frame to the far left, while two pairs of white opaque mannequin legs displaying women's stockings dominate the rest of the frame and tower over Toxi. Her placement at the edge of the frame, with the window acting as a barrier cutting her off from the symbols of white female sexuality, is telling. It depicts her as an observer, suggesting her outsider status and the unattainability of German norms of femininity, desirability, and reproduction which are coded as exclusively white. That shot fades to a tilted-angle shot of Toxi on some stairs, indicating her dislocation. We hear the sounds of a toy piano, and she is drawn to its player, a boy panhandling. A gathering crowd of white adults assume Toxi is part of the show and readily hand her loose change. When the boy senses the police, he folds up his piano and runs with Toxi back to his caravan home and unsavory parents. When they register Toxi's commercial value as curiosity—their son has brought home more money than usual, which he attributes to Toxi's presence—they resolve to take her with them, without consulting the girl, when they depart later that night, thus initiating the rescue scene with Theodor and the police.

In sum, this extended scene indicates that the filmmakers could only imagine a future of social isolation, commercial exploitation, and economic marginality for Toxi and children like her. In the lingerie window shot, the film obliquely raises the question of what would happen when Toxi reached sexual maturity. The panhandling scene and intended abduction, along with Robert's earlier advertising poster of Toxi's stereotyped caricature, suggest that she would always be treated as an exotic object of curiosity, that exploitation was inevitable. It also, however, signals her anticipated social and economic status in West Germany if left to her own devices: not the lofty ranks of the respectable bourgeoisie that Theodor and family inhabited, but the more lowly ranks of "gypsy" street performers or ailing indigent grandmothers.

This cultural conceit, which preached racial tolerance but insisted on maintaining racial difference and gauging relative worth, was pervasive in the liberalizing discourse of 1950s West Germany and, I would argue, accounts at least in part for the alignment of *Toxi's* fictional ending and my friend's desire to be united with her unknown father. As it was not culturally permissible for my friend to be classified according to her white maternity, her social experience taught her not to self-identify that way. Rather, she fantasized about embracing her black paternity in order to escape the subordinate social status assigned her as racialized other. The desire may have been motivated in part by geneological pull, but it was certainly also a self-preserving strategy to foster a personal sense of dignity and worth by shaking off a destructive, socially ascribed identity of immutable difference.

Toxi's Trajectories

Although *Toxi* is a highly ambivalent text that forsakes the principle of racial integration in favor of racial tolerance—and ultimately exhibits more concern about rehabilitating the German patriarchal family through the maintenance of racial boundaries—it nonetheless represented a banner moment in the cultural expression of postwar racial liberalism in West German popular cinema of the 1950s. Plainly stated, it was downhill from here. This becomes evident when one examines the next film Elfie Fiegert appeared in, *Der dunkle Stern*, released in 1955.

Der dunkle Stern has been dubbed inaccurately a "sequel" (*Fortsetzung*) to *Toxi* in the film's promotional materials and press reviews from the 1950s—and even by an archivist at the federal film archive in Berlin when I was doing research there a few years back. The film, however, is not a sequel in any meaningful sense of the word. Although its script, like *Toxi*'s, was authored by Maria Osten-Sacken, and both films featured Elfie Fiegert in the role of a black occupation child, the second film represented neither a continuation of the story nor its fictional characters. Any continuity between the films has to do with the ways the second film selectively amplified some of the themes of the first within its new fictional constellation. And this selective amplification, I would argue, resulted in a retreat from the expressly (if inadequately) liberal commitments of its predecessor. Specifically, a reading of *Der dunkle Stern* reveals a noticeable narrowing of the definition of tolerance; a marked unwillingness even to entertain the possibility of racial integration, if only for most of the duration of the film, as in *Toxi*; and an overwhelming obsession—from the film's very beginning—both to locate a suitable place for the black German child outside the white German nation and to reconcile the child intellectually and emotionally to the wisdom, and indeed compassion, of this choice.[16]

The film opens in an "idyllic village" in the mountains of Upper Bavaria in winter. Moni, the black German child played by Elfie Fiegert, lives in a small cottage with her foster mother, Frau Lechner, loves rural life, skis to school in winter, and is well-regarded by the villagers, none of whom remind her of the "the blemish of her heredity [*Makel der Herkunft*]."[17] One day in school, Moni's teacher, Fräulein Rieger, asks the children what they want to be when they grow up. Few of the children have well-formed answers, but Moni replies with passion, "I'd like to have a farm [*Hof*]! I'd like to be a peasant-farmer [*Bäuerin*]!" The children quickly taunt her, "A black peasant! . . . Even the chickens would laugh! There's no such thing!"[18] Moni's aspirations, and not the other children's responses, stimulate Fräulein Rieger to take action on Moni's behalf. Convinced that Moni's dreams cannot be realized, Fräulein Rieger consults the village veterinarian, who puts her in touch with an agent for the circus where he once worked. In short order, the Italian circus artist Casseno shows up at the village to collect Moni, who will live and work with him and his family. Frau Lechner agrees to the plan since she has been notified that she will lose her rental cottage soon and cannot continue to care for the child. Moni, meanwhile, is told that the arrangement is temporary and embarks on the adventure, but quickly develops a case of homesickness for the Bavarian mountains. Once at the circus, she is readily befriended by the circus performers. She helps a traumatized young woman get over her fear of the trapeze after witnessing her mother's fatal fall from the ropes. She becomes surrogate sibling and caretaker to a blind orphaned boy-clown, and after a stint serving as a human target for Casseno's knife-throwing, ultimately discovers her own stereotypical "natural talent" as a clown and trapeze artist, as well as her popularity with audiences. By the end of the film, as the circus director announces that they will be embarking on an international tour through South America, and after a brief reunion with Fräulein Rieger, Moni finally surrenders her dream of returning to her mountain village and accepts the circus as her new *Heimat* (home).

The film's treatment of racial difference is so outrageous by our contemporary standards that it begs the question of how this was justified and rendered acceptable within the context of the film's fictional space. The answer, I would argue, resides in the way that the film's narrative was organized around the cultural logic and postwar mythology of *Heimat*.

Der dunkle Stern opens by invoking the visual conventions of *Heimat* and *Heimatfilme*, with shots of the natural majesty of the Bavarian Alps and nostalgic scenes of rural village life. Postwar *Heimatfilme*, the most prolific and popular film genre in West Germany between 1950 and 1956, sought to locate an "authentic" Germany—unmarred by passing political regimes—in the values and practices of hearth, village, and church. At the same time, however, they also recognized recent traumas unleashed by the war and frequently peddled new norms of moral German masculinity and femininity to postwar German audiences. In short, *Heimatfilme* appealed to their audiences because, unlike Hollywood imports, their orientation was fundamentally *national*; they addressed their audience first and foremost as Germans. *Heimatfilme* released through the mid-1950s tended to acknowledge and engage critical issues of the day, such as the benefits and boundaries of national belonging, the desire for national rehabilitation, and the need to adjust to new postwar realities—albeit in ways that emphasized the reassuring stability and longevity of the German *Heimat*, which was accorded an existence independent of the more volatile, transitory, and politicized German *Vaterland*.[19]

Heimat, then, was ideologically encoded as something fixed and eternal, Christian and white. Its evocation of natural beauty, community, and security could stimulate longing in the child, Moni, but by definition it was not something that could readily assimilate *her*. This is made apparent in the school essay Moni writes on the topic "What I want to be when I grow up," which Fräulein Rieger reads aloud to her veterinarian friend," and in the exchange between the two that follows:

> I want to be a farmer. Just like I said today at school when everyone laughed. But that's the most wonderful thing there is in the world. It's lovely to walk through the grain fields when the stalks are high. It's lovely to lead the cows to pasture. They have large and small bells hanging around their necks that jingle and ring all together—its wonderful, just like in church. It's lovely to be in the fields early in the morning when the sun rises, and to spend the whole day working together with the farmhands [*Knechten*] and milkmaids [*Mägden*]. But my favorite time is the harvest festival when everyone is happy and dances and sings. I would like to marry a hardworking farmer, have a farm, and many children.

"And she'll get him!" responds the vet, impressed by the author's conviction and unaware that the author is Moni.

"She will not get him," counters Fräulein Rieger. "Or do you really think that some farm boy will lead Moni to the altar?"

The veterinarian considers a moment, "Yes, well, what with our tiny village here! As long as she's a child it's still all right. But as soon as she turns seventeen or eighteen, she'll be run out of town like a unwanted dog!"[20]

The scene conforms, at least initially, to the conventions of *Heimatfilme* in Moni's veneration of the natural beauties of the rural landscape and the cyclical yet steadfast quality of agrarian life which, even in their most mundane details (bells on cow's necks), are infused with Christian imagery— or at least aurality, in the form of church bells. Moni has demonstrated through her essay both her love of *Heimat* and her intimate cultural familiarity with its iconography. Yet this mastery is rapidly revealed to be transgressive. She may fervently *desire* it—along with marriage and children within the *Heimat*—but her love must remain unrequited since *Heimat* by definition is constant, unchanging, and therefore unable to accommodate "difference." This is made manifest in an earlier scene, when Moni tells her foster mother of the schoolchildren's taunts. "Black peasant!" her mother questions, "Where did they get that?" As Moni explains how she responded to the teacher's question at school, her mother effectively dismisses the child's aspirations as inappropriate, admonishing her, "Well, it really would have been best if you hadn't said that." Thus the film, through its responsible adults, consistently declares Moni's heartfelt desire an impossible and, more significantly, a *forbidden* one. The dramatic action of *Der dunkle Stern* pivots and is predicated upon an unquestioned affirmation of the exclusionary ideology—and racial immutability—of *Heimat*, that dominant cultural category of 1950s West Germany.[21]

A related point is that the putatively apolitical concept of *Heimat* (precisely because it was invested with the function of encapsulating an authentic, unchanging German nation untouched by transitory murderous politics of National Socialism) *enabled* filmmakers and other cultural producers to envision and enforce a fundamentally racialized definition of the German nation without having it appear to be an overtly political or even racist move. *Heimat*, after all, resided in locality, home, family, emotions; as such, it was understood to stand apart from politics. It was rooted not only in the soil, but in the very viscera of Germans. This sense of intimate connection is what gave it its strength and staying power as a cultural concept. This is also what accounts for the fact that most Germans "knew" that their *Heimat* was traditionally, historically, irrevocably white.

Placing the issue of racial difference within the context of *Heimat*, then, nullifies integration as a possibility precisely because of the hundred-year history of the concept. The film *Toxi* could entertain the issue of integration, at least temporarily, because the drama played out in the urbanized context of modern postwar family life in which the need for reconstruction and rehabilitation was at least recognized. *Der dunkle Stern*, by opening in the Upper Bavarian *Heimat*, set as its stage the supposedly timeless German community, that bedrock of German identity that could tolerate no reform without jeopardizing its imagined essence. As a result, the question of integrating Moni could not be raised, for racial integration would alter the very nature of that timeless "essence." *Heimat*, then, continued to be a fundamentally racialized concept.[22] So in spite of the fact that it was presented as an innocuous cultural building block of German (and not incidentally also gender) identity after 1945, *Heimat* played an important role in *reconstituting* racially exclusive notions of national belonging after National Socialism.[23]

And so at the end of *Der dunkle Stern*, Moni is exiled to the circus, that "colorful world" of diverse ethnicities where she "must—no! wants to—to find a new *Heimat*," and is booked to depart for a year-long tour of the great cities of South America: from Rio to Buenos Aires to Montevideo.[24] Coincidentally, or not, perhaps, Elfie Fiegert next lands on the screen in *Das Haus in Montevideo* (The House in Montevideo, 1963). By now a young woman, Fiegert plays a bit part as the exotic attendant in a hypersexualized fantasy villa owned by lead character Herr Professor Doktor Nägele's recently deceased sister, who left Germany years before under a cloud of shame due to an out-of-wedlock pregnancy and subsequently made a fortune, which the white German patriarch has now come to claim on behalf of his teenage daughter. The film treats the sexual impropriety with a light touch, engages in double entendre, and finally teaches the Herr Professor to be less judgmental and morally rigid. As such, the film evinces a more general transition in mores occurring in popular commercial feature films by the early 1960s. For the purposes of this essay, however, the important points are three. First, the onset of puberty demoted Elfie Fiegert from leading roles to bit speaking parts. Second, it altered the roles into which she was typecast from black occupation child to exoticized, sexualized beauty. And third, it changed the location of her character from Germany to abroad—a transition that was already underway in *Der dunkle Stern*. She no longer played the exotic German girl, but rather the exotic foreign one. And most importantly, perhaps, no explanation or apologies were deemed necessary for this ascription. The retreat from the liberal discourse of race—at least as it concerned the intersection of blackness and Germanness—was complete.

Despite this evolving disassociation of Elfie Fiegert's characters from Germany, Fiegert continued to be referred to—and refer to herself—as "Toxi" or even "Toxi Fiegert."[25] In part, of course, this was a marketing ploy that attempted to capitalize on her early success and popularity in her original role as black occupation child. Even so, it is telling. Because even before the film's release and box office success, the historical Elfie Fiegert was literally reinscribed as her fictional counterpart: while the names of all other actors are provided in the film credits and publicity materials, "Toxi" is listed as played by "Toxi." As a result of the repeated identification of actress with character (in a stream of personal appearances, interviews, and press releases), the story of Toxi became the story of all West German "colored" occupation children, and the name "Toxi" entered the German language as a generic term for Afro-German children. And the term stuck. The print media, over the course of the next decades, would continue to invoke the name "Toxi" when titling articles discussing black Germans and their social condition.[26]

Elfie Fiegert, too, took the stage name "Toxi," it seems, and by the early 1960s, as she continued to have trouble getting parts, expressed her intention to have her name legally changed to "Toxi." This insistent identification with character can be attributed to her attempt to build a professional career by reminding the industry of both her early professional success and the critical recognition she received in the role. Yet she also seems to have experienced a certain wistfulness about playing Toxi: positive attention from public and press, media events fêting her as a budding and adorable star, and, one would suppose, the professional career these seemed to portend. By the time she reached her teens, Elfie Fiegert, like her characters, had become trapped by a socially ascribed identity of immutable difference. Industry interest in her had dried up; the promise of her early career had dwindled into a couple of bit parts; and her part-time agent was encouraging her to reorient her career aspirations downward—to the secretarial job she held in Munich. "There is just no demand in Germany for an actress like you," her agent put it bluntly. By the turn of the 1960s, Elfie Fiegert—and indeed the earlier sustained public attention to the "fate of the postwar colored occupation child" had been rudely pushed from the limelight.

The trajectory of Elfie Fiegert's career—as well as the narrative structures of *Toxi* and *Der dunkle Stern*—are part of the as yet unwritten history of the cultural devolution of Nazi-era racial ideologies. The 1950s was an extended moment when the issue of race and its postwar meanings were explicitly addressed and performed for West Germans. But this was accomplished by shifting the location of race from Jewishness to blackness in order to distance it from the Holocaust and Germans' crimes against humanity (which, after all, were still on trial in these postwar decades). This displacement rendered the issue one of juvenile stewardship and German control, and thus facilitated the articulation of a liberalized discourse of race as proof of West Germany's successful racial reeducation and rehabilitation. Yet the focus on blackness also allowed white Germans (like their white American contemporaries) to draw the line at interracial sex and reproduction. By the time that black German children reached puberty, these earlier discussions were muted, and "race" was on its way to becoming a taboo topic.

This resulted in a silencing of public discussions regarding the role of race in German society and identity. What is more, it authorized a cultural atmosphere of racial exclusivity in defining the nation. That is, while contemporary Germans since the 1960s have recognized an increasing ethnic diversity within their borders as demographic fact, they have interpreted this as resulting from an influx in *foreign* laborers and asylum-seekers, attracted by Germany's strong economy and social welfare provisions. However, membership in the nation was culturally imagined (and until a few years ago, to a large extent legally prescribed) as the more exclusive domain of homogenous whiteness. This has left little space—social or psychological—for German citizens of color who, to borrow from W. E. B. DuBois, daily feel the "doubleness" of their lives as blacks and

Germans in a hostile, or at best, indifferent society that is their own. The silence that overtook issues of race in West Germany muted discussions of the relationship between blacks and Germanness for nearly two decades. The silence has now been broken, but a serious and sustained dialogue between black Germans and white has yet to occur.

Notes

1. The research for this essay, and the larger project from which it derives, has been generously funded by grants from the National Endowment for the Humanities, the Deutscher Akademischer Austauschdienst, and the American Council of Learned Societies, as well as Northern Illinois University, Emory University, and Colgate University. My thanks to Bob Moeller for his helpful comments.

All translations from the original German are mine.

2. On the representation of Jews in postwar German cinema, see Frank Stern, "Film in the 1950s: Passing Images of Guilt and Responsibility," in *The Miracle Years: A Cultural History of West Germany, 1949–1968*, ed. Hanna Schissler (Princeton: Princeton University Press, 2000), 266–80; Robert R. Schandley, *Rubble Films: German Cinema in the Shadow of the Third Reich* (Philadelphia: Temple University Press, 2001), 77–115.

3. Among the more serious studies were: World Brotherhood, Gesellschaft für christlich-jüdische Zusammenarbeit, *Protokoll der Arbeitstagung über das Schicksal der farbigen Mischlingskinder in Deutschland* (Wiesbaden, 15–16 August 1952); Walter Kirchner, "Eine anthropologische Studie an Mulattenkindern in Berlin unter Berücksichtigung der sozialen Verhältnisse" (Ph. D. diss., Freie Universität Berlin, 1952); Hans Pfaffenberger, "Farbige Kinder im Heim—ein Prüfstein," *Unsere Jugend* 5, no. 12 (1953); Luise Frankenstein, *Soldatenkinder: Die unehelichen Kinder ausländischer Soldaten mit besonderer Berücksichtigung der Mischlinge* (Munich: W. Steinebach, 1954); Hermann Ebeling, "Zum Problem der deutschen Mischlingskinder," *Bild und Erziehung* 7, no. 10 (1954): 612–30; Hans Pfaffenberger, "Hilfe für unsere Mischlingskinder—aber wie?" *Neues Beginnen* 8 (1955): 113–15; Rudolf Sieg, "Mischlingskinder in Westdeutschland: Eine anthropologische Studie an farbigen Kindern," *Beiträge zur Anthropologie* 4 (1955): 9–79; Gustav von Mann, "Zum Problem der farbigen Mischlingskinder in Deutschland," *Jugendwohl* 36, no. 1 (January 1955): 50–53; Hans Pfaffenberger, "Zur Situation der Mischlingskinder," *Unsere Jugend* 8, no. 2 (1956): 64–71; Herbert Hurka, "Die Mischlingskinder in Deutschland. Ein Situationsbericht auf Grund bisheriger Veröffentlichungen," *Jugendwohl* 6 (1956): 257–75; and Klaus Eyferth, "Die Situation und die Entwicklungsaussichten der Neger-Mischlingskinder in der Bundesrepublik," *Soziale Arbeit* 7, no. 11 (November 1958): 469–78; Klaus Eyferth, "Gedanken über die zukünftige Berufseingliederung der Mischlingskinder in Westdeutschland," *Neues Beginnen* 5 (May 1959): 65–68. Press reports appeared widely in newspapers and in magazines such as *Stern, Der Spiegel, Quick,* and *Revue.*

For a discussion of German women's fraternization with American soldiers, and one German community's response, see Maria Höhn, *GIs and Fräuleins: The German–American Encounter in 1950s West Germany* (Chapel Hill: University of North Carolina Press, 2002).

4. See Heide Fehrenbach, " 'Ami Liebchen' und 'Mischlingskinder'—Rasse, Geschlecht und Kultur in der deutsch-amerikanischen Begegnung," in *Nachkrieg in Deutschland*, ed. Klaus Naumann (Hamburg: Hamburger Edition, 2001), 178–205.

5. In the American zone of occupied Germany, marriage between U.S. soldiers and German women was permitted during 1947, but continued to be officially discouraged and subject to rigorous review and approval of one's officer and military chaplain. Evidence suggests that in large measure, such officers refused permission to interracial marriage applications. National Archives, College Park, Maryland. Office of the Military Government of Germany—U.S. (hereafter OMGUS), Circular 181.

6. The federal ministry of the interior petitioned state ministries of the interior in the former French and American zones of occupation for a head count of "Negro mixed-blood children" in November 1950. By mid-1951, a survey of all occupation children was initiated by the Deutscher Verein für öffentliche und private Fürsorge, which requested separate tabulation of white and black children. This survey was undertaken with the assistance of the state ministries of the interior as well as state and local youth offices, and commanded the interest of the federal ministry of the interior and the foreign office. In 1955, a federal nationwide survey of all occupation children was taken. See Bundesarchiv Koblenz (hereafter BAK), B153: Bundesministerium für Familien- und Jugendfragen, no. 342: Fürsorge für uneheliche Kinder von Besatzungsangehörigen, insb. für Mischlingskinder. Also see Bayerisches Hauptstaatsarchiv (BayHStA), MInn 81089 and Hauptstaatsarchiv Stuttgart (HstAStg) EA2/007, Nr. 1177.

7. For an expanded discussion of issues surrounding adoption, see Heide Fehrenbach, "Of German Mothers and '*Negermischlinge*': Race, Sex, and the Postwar Nation," in *The Miracle Years*, ed. Hanna Schissler (Princeton: Princeton University Press, 2001), 164–86.

8. A dominant feature of this postwar liberal discourse was the instrumentalization of race for the purpose of rehabilitating postfascist German identity and masculinity. On this point, see Heide Fehrenbach, "Rehabilitating Father*land*: Race and German Remasculinization," *Signs: Journal of Women in Culture and Society* 24, no. 1 (Fall 1998): 107–271; also Susan Jeffords, "The 'Remasculization' of Germany in the 1950s: Discussion," *Signs* 24, no. 1 (Autumn 1998): 163–69.

9. This shot occurs in *Toxi* at 0:37:28–0:38:00.

10. "Ich möcht' so gern nach Hause geh'n, ay ay ay. / Die Heimat möcht' ich wiedersehen, ay, ay, ay, ay / Ich find' allein nicht einen Schritt, ay, ay, ay / Wer hat mich lieb, und nimmt mich mit? ay, ay, ay."

11. My point here is not to minimize the suffering of marginalized and institutionalized children, but to make the point that the film, in formulating the "problem" it seeks to solve, shifts the focus from racism (a white-generated problem) to the children themselves. The sociological data on interracial children in postwar Germany show that just over 10 percent of the children were uncared for by their mothers or mothers' relatives. Nonetheless, commentators continually assumed that black German children were in the main raised in institutions and not by their families. This assumption, of course, affected both the way the "problem" of the children, and its solution, were formulated. For a longer discussion, see Fehrenbach, "Of German Mothers."

12. To be fair, this occurs before Theodor learns his lesson as a result of Toxi's unexpected disappearance. Nonetheless, even after his conversion, and just before Christmas Eve, we see a scene in the kitchen between the cook and the police investigator in which the latter discloses that he has learned the identity of the ailing grandmother who left Toxi

on the doorstep. When asked why he had not made a more general announcement of the fact, he responds that he wanted the child "to enjoy a peaceful Christmas first," thus indicating that her status is the home was necessarily temporary and nearing an end.

13. Again, the interracial children were "raced" as black rather than white. The pull of blood was never perceived to work in the direction of their white mothers.

14. My friend did not see the film as a child, nor, I suspect did most Afro-German children at the time.

15. For a discussion of how these issues were represented by social welfare workers, psychologists, academics, educators, and state officials, among others, see my discussions in "Of German Mothers" and " 'Ami Liebchen.' "

16. My discussion of this film will necessarily be schematic since it is based upon descriptions culled from film bills, publicity, press reports, and a more detailed novelized account of the film. Despite multiple attempts with German film archives and the German film company holding its rights, I have been unable to locate or gain access to either a film or video copy of *Der dunkle Stern*. Unlike many films from the 1950s, it has not been screened on German television, perhaps for obvious reasons, given the film's narrative. See Lia Avè, "Der dunkle Stern: Ein Roman," *Hermes Film-Roman Magazin* 17 (Munich: Hermes Film- und Bühnen-Verlag, n.d.).

17. This is a quotation from the publicity material of WEGE Film for *Der dunkle Stern*. Schriftgutarchiv of the Stiftung Deutsche Kinemathek, Berlin.

18. Avè, "Der dunkle Stern," 5.

19. For a longer discussion of the ideology of the postwar *Heimatfilm*, see Heide Fehrenbach, *Cinema in Democratizing Germany: Reconstructing National Identity after Hitler* (Chapel Hill: University of North Carolina Press, 1995), esp. 148–68. For a discussion of postwar films that respond more overtly to the war and its aftermath, see Robert G. Moeller, *War Stories: The Search for a Useable Past in the Federal Republic of Germany* (Berkeley: University of California Press, 2001), 123–70. The history of the modern concept of *Heimat* is explored in Celia Applegate, *A Nation of Provincials: The German Idea of Heimat* (Berkeley: University of California Press, 1990) and Alon Confino, *The Nation as Local Metaphor: Württemberg, Imperial Germany and National Memory, 1871–1918* (Chapel Hill: University of North Carolina Press, 1997).

20. "Ich will Bäuerin werden. Wie ich das heute in der Schule gesagt habe, haben alle gelacht. Dabei ist es doch das Schönste was es auf der ganzen Welt gibt. Es ist schön, durch die Getreide zu gehen, wenn die Aehren schon ganz hoch sind. Es ist schön, die Kühe auf die Alm zu treiben. Sie haben grosse und kleine Glocken um den Hals hängen und es bimmelt und läutet durcheinander, so wunderbar wie in der Kirche. Es ist schön, frühmorgens auf dem Feld zu sein, wenn die Sonne aufgeht, und den ganzen Tag mit den Knechten und Mägden zu arbeiten. Um am schönsten ist das Erntefest. Da freuen sich alle und tanzen und singen. Ich möchte einen fleissigen Bauern heiraten und einen Hof haben und viele Bauernkinder."

"Sie würden ihn schon kriegen!" meinte er darum . . .

"Sie wird ihn nicht kriegen." Fräulein Riegers Antwort war mutlos und endgültig. Oder glaubte Herr Doktor vielleicht, dass jemand von den Bauernbuben die Moni zum Altar führen würden? . . .

"Na also! Und gerade das Negermädchen . . ." Was tat es, dass das Kind eine besondere Liebe für das bäuerliche Leben mitbrachte, ja, geradezu ein ausgesprochenes Talent für Stall und Feld zeigte? Dieser Berufswunsch musste ein nebelhafter Traum bleiben, ohne geringste Aussicht auf Verwirklingung. "Tja,—und dann unser kleines Dörfchen hier! Solange es ein Kind ist, gehts ja noch—aber wenn sie mal siebzehn oder achtzehn ist, da werden sie sie hier wohl rausbeissen—wie einen fremden Hund!" Avè, "Der dunkle Stern," 8.

21. At the end of *Der dunkle Stern*, Moni joins the community of circus performers and ponders her fate: "Would she really become a trapeze artist in the world-renowned act of the Bellanis? Really a famous, if also dark, star in the circus heaven as was predicted? She wished it from the bottom of her heart because she must—no, she wanted to—find a new *Heimat* in this colorful world." Avè, "Der dunkle Stern," 55.

22. It is interesting in this connection that neither Celia Applegate nor Alon Confino discusses the relationship of Jews to "*Heimat*" in their studies. For examples of postwar *Heimat* histories that build their mythology on descriptions of racial violence (especially black-on-white rape and murder) see Rudolf Albart, *Die letzten und die ersten Tage: Bamberger Kriegstagesbuch 1944/46* (Bamberg, 1953) and Hans Rommel, *Vor zehn Jahren. 16.–17. April 1945. Wie es zur Zerstörung von Freudenstadt gekommen ist* (Freudenstadt, 1955); for a brief analysis of this mythology see Fehrenbach, "Rehabilitating Father*land*," 110–12. For a critical discussion that deals explicitly with the issue of race and *Heimat* after 1945 in terms of social experience, see Höhn, *GIs and Fräuleins*, 85–125.

23. Also of interest in this regard is that 1950s' *Heimatfilme* sometimes did thematize integration—both the need for newcomers to adapt to local ways and the need for locals to accept the new arrivals. But this applied exclusively to white ethnic German refugees from the former eastern reaches of the Third Reich. Perhaps the most popular of these *Heimatfilme* was *Grün ist die Heide* (1951).

24. Avè, "Der dunkle Stern," 50 and 55.

25. The instances of this are too numerous to list, but a couple of the more popular article titles are "Toxi speilt ihr eigenes Schicksal" or, in the case of *Der dunkle Stern*, "Toxi landet im Zirkus," "*Der dunkle Stern*—ein neuer Film mit Toxi!" In the credits for *Das Haus in Montevideo*, Elfie Fiegert is listed as Toxi Fiegert.

26. In 1967, for example, *Welt am Sonntag* published a feature article on black Germans titled, "Die 'Toxis' sind erwachsen—und haben Heiratssorgen" [The 'Toxis' are grown up—and have marriage worries], *Welt am Sonntag*, 26 March 1967. This article clipping was found in BAK, B189/6858: Bundesministerium für Jugend und Familie, "Untersuchung des Situation der Neger-Mischlingskinder in der Bundesrepublik."

6

WILL EVERYTHING BE FINE?

ANTI-RACIST PRACTICE IN RECENT GERMAN CINEMA

Randall Halle

Nabou (Kati Stüdemann), Afro-German, techno-punk, and lesbian, stands at the window of a subway kiosk where she works. The lace hat of her uniform perched awkwardly on top of her hair, she cuts a comic figure. In a counter-shot we find a customer asking for that European confection known in German as a *Negerkuß*, a "nigger kiss"—cookie on the bottom topped by a mound of marshmallow and all dipped in chocolate so that it comes to a point.[1] Nabou at first responds to the request with incomprehension, but the customer in counter-shot persists with her request. Nabou's boss intervenes, demanding that Nabou carry out her job politely. Nabou demands that either the customer order a *Schokokuß*, a "chocolate kiss," the new name that circulates in a more racially sensitive German vocabulary, or the customer receives nothing at all. In the face of the others' continuing incomprehension and her boss's attempt to smooth things over, Nabou explodes in anger and storms off. The customer and boss express only confusion, the boss now demanding from a distance that Nabou give the customer "a nice nigger kiss." Nabou departs, quipping at the white German women, "aw kiss yourselves." The scene has the possibility to be central to a tragic story, especially in a post-unification Germany where since 1992 violent attacks by the far right on "foreigners," that is, those who look, think, or act different than the popular imaginary of the white racist, have increased steadily to sixteen hundred.[2] However, this is a film by Angelina Maccarone, and that means humor, entertainment, and

161

enlightenment. The spectator can sit back and expect to laugh, not at but with the film's main characters as they confront the challenges presented by life in the new Federal Republic of Germany (FRG).

Angelina Maccarone's film *Alles wird gut* (Everything Will Be Fine) premiered at the New York Gay and Lesbian Film Festival in 1997, then had its German debut on television in the Fall of 1998 in the successful movie series "Wild Hearts" (*Wilde Herzen*).[3] *Everything Will Be Fine* takes as its subject the antics of two Afro-German women, Kim and Nabou.[4] To summarize the plot, Nabou is stalking her ex-girlfriend, the blue-haired punk Katja (Aglaia Szyszkowitz), who happens to live in Kim's building. Kim (Chantal de Freitas) is a successful advertising executive and workaholic whose personal life and apartment are equal messes. As chance would have it, she hires Nabou as cleaning help. Nabou cleans relatively well, but in the course of time, Nabou adds to the chaos of Kim's personal life; they develop mutual feelings for each other. Nabou begins to forget Katja and Kim begins somewhat to forget her pending marriage to her boss, Dieter Lauer (Uwe Rohde). Yet even after a night of passion with Nabou, Kim drifts toward an engagement with Dieter. Nabou, having learned not to leave relationships to chance, intervenes to prevent the wedding proposal. A "happy end" results when the guy doesn't get the girl in the end.

In the 1990s comedies in Germany were in. Since the collapse of the film market in the early 1960s, German productions had not captured more than 10 percent of the domestic market. The films that were produced, and especially those that were exported, were presented as the best of Germany and were consumed everywhere as signs of the epitome of high cultural film art. Suddenly in the mid 1990s the attendance numbers at German films doubled due to the work of a new generation of producers and filmmakers whose films bore little resemblance to the work of Wenders, Herzog, or Fassbinder. They distanced themselves from what they characterized as the difficult, melancholic, New German Cinema. Their style, gloss, and seamless edits sought to approach the culture industry of Hollywood on its own terms. Those critics who grew up on the high culture of German art film suddenly found their screens filled with contributions to popular culture and decried it as the end to German film art.

Everything Will Be Fine belongs to the Comedy Wave. It is a classic narrative film produced with fast camera work and high gloss worthy of a slick Hollywood film with a much higher budget. Especially in the beginning, the dual lines of the plot rely heavily on the sequencing of shots so that through tracks and pans the camera follows one lead character,

Nabou, as she races around in space, until she passes Kim. The camera's attention then turns to develop this second narrative line, only to pan and track onto the previous line when "chance" brings Nabou back into the frame. As their lives intertwine and they share more filmic space, the camera stabilizes. Further, the film draws on a specific use of filters and colors to convey certain emotional conditions and experiences, moving from cool blue to warm brown and on to hot red tones. The semiotics of this color key, while not universal, is rather uncomplicatedly trans-European. Its richness sets a foil to the possibility of a black/white schematism that might cling to the narrative. Further the narrative relies on visual gags along with humor of language and behavior of the type found in the best of Hollywood's screwball comedies. Hamburg and Afro-Germans offer the certain "indige-nousness," specificity, or local color that is praised as the basis of the good European film, while pacing and plot carry the story beyond. The narra-tive thus remains both general enough for international audiences, and yet culturally specific enough for Germany.

The comedy was produced for simultaneous film distribution and television release, a long-time policy of the public television station ZDF. In this manner, the public money sponsors especially young filmmaking talent, and television stations build up their own film library rather than add to the trade imbalance by purchasing programming from the media giants of the U.S. When one such film as *Everything Will Be Fine* finds its international premier in New York, and further successes on its U.S. run, this production strategy gains further credence. Furthermore the suc-cess of this "minor" production drew the attention of the U.S. majors and Maccarone received an offer to make films for the Samuel Goldwyn Com-pany, a subsidiary of MGM.

Reviewing the film history of the 1990s, we can easily agree that a shift in German film production to popular culture took place, but in the middle of these developments it almost appeared as if there were no other developments, no other genres present. The noise around the Comedy Wave drowned out all other discussions. However, it is now possible to review those developments in a more differentiated fashion. Film art of a certain kind might have been (temporarily) out, but artful and political films did not disappear. A comedy that brings audiences from Berlin to New York to laugh with Afro-German lesbians is not a traditional comedy. *Everything Will Be Fine* proved to be a smart, savvy film that pushed and transformed generic conventions to bring forward an artful, political, *and* entertaining final product. When we examine *Everything Will Be Fine,* we recognize that along with the comedy's shift to popular culture, it proved capable of accomplishing a shift to public culture with the antiracist and antihomophobic aspects of the plot. The union of comedy and multicultural concerns was unique in German film history. The following section will explore more closely the film's position in a longer history of "multicultural" filmmaking in the Federal Republic of Germany (FRG). Then I will go on to examine the film's immediate relationship to the Comedy Wave, after which I will take up the film's antiracist strategies. Finally, I will end by considering subsequent developments in the representations of Afro-Germans.

Everything Will Be Fine is a significant contribution to the development of Afro-German cultural identity. Moreover, it represents its own background out of which it emerges: a combination of filiative determination and conscious political affiliation. Pivotal in Kim and Nabou's relationship to each other, and the viewer's relationship to both, is the scene in which they trade stories about growing up. This scene performs the first aspect of Afro-German identity, the filiative dynamic. Going through Kim's photo album, they find a level of trust and comfort with each other to share obviously painful stories about their family, their background, and the traumas of growing up black in Germany. The stories are told, to the viewer's perspective, in an elliptical, even telegraphic fashion, and although the viewer may wish for more information, it is clear that Kim and Nabou understand each other very well. Instead of biography, the dialogue quickly shifts to fantasy as the two invent a fictional familial relationship. They enjoy making up a story of two mulatto sisters saved from jungle cannibals by Catholic missionaries and raised dancing and singing in Germany, until Kim realizes that her colleagues at work would indeed believe such a ridiculous scenario.

The film refuses to dwell on the biographies of Kim and Nabou, with good reason. Such explanations of background with their quasi assertions of "Germanness" or at least justifications of belonging to the German filiative community are not necessary for white Germans. For characters like Dieter, Katja, or even Nabou's exotic roommate, Guiseppa (Isabella Parkinson), there is no ethnic background profile necessary. In fact, Guiseppa's attempts to heighten her exoticism by affecting a fake Italian accent only provide a comedic element to the film. Nevertheless the bonding that takes place between Kim and Nabou over their family histories smartly displays the significance of breaking out of isolation and finding someone with a common background. Within the racist parameters of the society they inhabit, difference is not chosen but forced upon them, and the shift into the fantasy scenario, their quick rapport and

Figure 6.1. Film still from *Alles wird Gut* [Everything Will be Fine], directed by Angelina Maccarone, 1997). Left to right: Kim, Nabou, Kofi.
Photo courtesy of Nord Deutscher Rundfunk (NDR).

enjoyment, underscores how such bonding offers a necessary emotional vent in the face of imposed difference.

In a further scene Nabou joins her old friend Kofi and Kim in a Tai Chi session out in the open on Hamburg harbor. This scene might appear as a bit of filler, but it displays the second dynamic and actually gives the shape of political consciousness and identity to these experiences of filiative determination. As Kofi reveals to Nabou "embarrassing" moments from Kim's past, he assumes the role usually occupied by the mother of a new partner on the first visit home. However, it is a different kind of family album that Kofi pulls out, as he taunts Kim with memories of her Angela Davis haircut. Such allusions provide vignettes from the emergence of a radical Afro-German consciousness. The scene is again elliptical, leaving the viewers to their own devices to learn more about Afro-German history; nevertheless it provides a sense of the significance of this politicization. The development of a shared identity is figured visually as the three practice their Tai Chi, Kofi and Kim moving fluidly in unison, the younger Nabou following along haltingly, awkwardly, yet happily. If much of the film explores scenes of imposed difference, here the viewer catches a glimpse of the significance of how difference can also be a form of development for an individual subject and a matter of collective determination as well. The politicized Afro-Germans evidence an ability to move together against imposed difference toward self-definition, though, to be sure, in the face of exterior alterity it is a difficult and never-ending movement.

While Afro-Germans have been active in literary production, *Everything Will Be Fine* is the first film that really focuses on the community. Its filmic prehistory is either a relatively simple one or part of a fairly complicated genealogy of minority representations. The history of Afro-Germans as such in film is limited. In the postwar period, *Toxi* (Robert Stemmle, 1952), the story of a precocious abandoned Afro-German child, stands out as a significant but isolated contribution.[5] In this film there is a clear opposition between white German citizen and nonwhites as foreign others. Thus even though, as the narrative unfolds, acceptance of the character Toxi into the adoptive family comes to symbolize a healthy transformation of the family, literally a form of denazification into positive liberalism, the film finds its resolution only when Toxi's American father appears to take her "home." Toxi's mother is German, and all her life has been spent in Germany, but because her blackness presents itself as a foreign element the film suggests that her place is really somewhere else, "with her own kind."

Beyond *Toxi*, until the 1990s in general Afro-Germans disappear from visual culture. In the representations of black characters in German filmmaking we find primarily "foreigners," whether Americans or Africans. Brief scenes in Rainer Werner Fassbinder's *Die Ehe der Maria Braun* (The Marriage of Maria Braun, 1979) or Jutta Brückner's *Hungerjahre* (Hunger Years, 1980) contain good examples of such characters. Afro-German actor Günther Kaufmann, a member of Fassbinder's troupe and his sometimes lover, appeared in significant roles in numerous films, for instance as the drunken G.I. that Maria yells at, but never as an explicitly Afro-German character. Werner Herzog marks a sort of exception in New German Cinema on the basis of his then-frequent depictions of blackness; however for Herzog, blackness again became the signification of mythical foreignness in itself. In *Wo die grünen Ameisen Träumen* (Where the Green Ants Dream, 1984), on the surface a film that indicts the Australian treatment of its native population, Herzog offers an exoticizing vision of Australian aborigines such that they appear as an incomprehensible but authentic black other, filmed for the pleasurable consumption of Euramerican spectators. Other Herzog films offer at best cynical comments on the contact between the colonial bearers of great European culture and the simple childlike natives of, for instance, *Fitzcarraldo* (1982), or on the black threat in *Aguirre* (1972) and *Cobra Verde* (1987).[6] The conquistadors of *Aguirre* travel as white Europeans through the South American rainforest, refusing assimilation to the "foreign" world around them. This refusal is in part the beginning of their end. Percy Adlon's *Bagdad Café* (1988) intensified this dynamic by constructing the character of Jasmin (Marianne Sägebrecht) as a caricature of the Bavarian abroad. In comparison the caricature embodied by the African American character Brenda (Carol Pounder) fades into the background.[7]

Following Fassbinder's *Angst essen Seele auf* (Fear Eats the Soul, 1973) and through the 1980s, films that addressed minority existence in Germany tended to focus primarily on the conditions of guest workers and especially the Turkish minority. Helma Sanders-Brahms's *Shirins Hochzeit* (Shirin's Wedding, 1975), Jeanine Meerapfel's *Die Kümmeltürkin geht* (Melek Leaves, 1985), Jan Schütte *Drachenfutter* (Dragon Chow, 1987), or Hark Bohm's *Yasmin* (1988) are perhaps the most significant of these early films.[8] They are films undertaken by directors who live outside of the communities portrayed. These films tended to construct immigrant communities, in particular Turkish presence, as a failure of transcultural integration deriving especially from the gender oppression in those communities. Fassbinder's were exceptions in that they concentrated on the prejudices and aggression immigrants face at the hands of the dominant community. In the other works, images of conservative gender dynamics, women's oppression, and spousal abuse, although problems of a dominant German society, came to form the central filmic preoccupation with the minority (Muslim) populations. These films indicted Turkish society and held up German society as a space of liberal emancipation for oppressed women.[9] During this period, a few Turkish immigrant directors began to produce films, most widely known of which is Tevfik Baser with his films *40 qm Deutschland* (Forty Square Meters of Germany, 1985) and *Abschied vom falschen Paradies* (Farewell to False Paradise, 1988). Baser, like his German colleagues, concentrated on the oppression of Turkish immigrant women, although in the end of his films German society does not appear as such a positive site of emancipation.

In the 1990s in the face of the rise of neo-Nazi organizations and well-publicized attacks on blacks in Germany, filmic representations of racial dynamics increased and more German directors produced films in support of a growing discourse of multiculturalism and antiracism.[10] Attention specifically focusing on the role of blackness in German society received support and recognition when the German documentarist Pepe Danquart won an Oscar for his short film *Schwarzfahrer* (Black Rider, 1992). Set in

Berlin, the film attempted to confront racist stereotypes and the question of rising racism through a form of short fable. On a hot summer day with the sun brightly bleaching out colors, a black man (Paul Outlaw) gets on a crowded streetcar and sits quietly, as an old woman (Senta Moira) next to him begins a racist diatribe. The passengers stare on in silence, some even nodding in agreement as her vitriol continues. In its surprise ending, the film imbues the "black rider" with an ability to act; he grabs the ticket of the woman and swallows it just as the conductor arrives. A sudden shift takes place, a play on the term *Schwarzfahrer* as someone who rides public transportation without paying, and the woman finds herself trying to explain why she is "riding black." Her stammering does not affect the conductor, an agent of bureaucratic equality, and he removes her from the streetcar.[11] The film invites the viewer to applaud the cleverness of the black man, yet behind the good intentions of the film there is a failure to overcome a limiting otherness. The character is identified in the film indeed simply as *der Schwarze*, "the black man," the only racial/ethnic designation, whereas the other characters are identified by what they do or their age. The black man remains primarily outside of language, and throughout the film there are shots that highlight his color as point of visual alterity. It is possible that he is Afro-German but that is not of interest to the film, rather he appears without background as the symbolization of a multicultural society in which the white and nonwhite Germans must learn to find their way. Ultimately this blackness as a point of alterity consumes a more complicated reading of him even as the film attempts to develop an antiracist viewing position. While the problem of the film is the behavior of the old white woman, the black other does not or cannot speak for himself so the film must speak for him.

In 1994 director Doris Dörrie premiered her film *Keiner liebt mich* (Nobody Loves Me), in which there is a similar reliance on blackness as the embodiment of multiculturalism.[12] Dörrie relies on the perspective of her main character, Fanny Fink (Maria Schrader), as she engages with the diverse residents of her apartment building. The film presents this community through magical realist conventions, leaving the hallway to appear like a fairy tale or wonderland. In this setting, Fanny meets the embodiment of exoticism, Orfeo de Altamar, a dying, gay, Afro-German drag queen, East German space alien, and former cook-turned-fortuneteller. Orfeo is played by Pierre Sanoussi-Bliss, in real life an East German Afro-German former cook turned actor. At the time, the role of Orfeo was the most significant Afro-German film character to cross the screen since Toxi. Like Toxi, who belonged in America with her father, Orfeo appears as an alien, literally belonging on the planet Arcturus. Unlike Toxi, however, Orfeo's central problem is not derived from being Afro-German. Indeed the diegesis of the film provides knowledge of the various complicated aspects of the character only slowly and not as a coherent identity. He is an exotic black man such that when building manager slumlord and yuppie Lothar Sticker (Michael von Au) identifies his "true identity" as Walter Rattinger, cook from East Berlin, his domestication into just an Afro-German seems a disappointment to the viewer.

However Orfeo is a complicated character, and Dörrie plays with the viewer's perspective to develop a few antiracist scenes. For instance, a short and humorous scene has Orfeo in the pedestrian zone at a table offering his services as fortuneteller. Business is slow. He flips his sign to indicate that he is there to collect money to "return" to Africa. As he occupies this role as other, performing an abjection of blackness, an elderly woman immediately gives him money, indicating her pleasure at sending the likes of him back to Africa. The humor in the scene relies on the viewer's knowledge at this point that Orfeo is an Afro-German Ossi, allowing the spectator to laugh at the aggression of the old woman and admire Orfeo's ability to manipulate the imposition of otherness, that is the racism of other Germans, to his advantage. Like the black man of *Schwarzfahrer*, however, Orfeo must be a trickster, a clever character who delights the viewer and thereby wins sympathy.

Alongside German representations of racial and ethnic others, already in the 1980s, in the wake of the earlier successes of feminist and gay films, a new set of filmmakers began to emerge from out of the German minority communities. Tevfik Baser was mentioned earlier. In the 1990s Turkish "Kanak" films appeared on the scene.[13] In the 1980s, a few films stood out as projects undertaken by black directors, primarily Africans attending film school in Germany. A few directors received the support of money and broadcast time from West German television (WDR) for some projects oriented toward portraying the lives of people of color in Germany. Films in this group include: *Ich, deine Mutter* (I, you mother, Safi Faye, 1980), *Europa mein Traum* (Europe, my dream, Masseye Niang, 1982), *KuKuRantumi: The Road to Accra* (King Ampaw, 1983), *Africa am Rhein* (Pape B Seck, 1985), and *Haitian Corner* (Raoul Peck, 1988).[14] Nevertheless, these were not the representations of Afro-Germans, but strictly speaking of Africans or Afro-Caribbeans in Germany. Such representations were building, however, especially in literature with the works of May Opitz and Katerina Oguntoye.

Everything Will Be Fine thus appears in the culmination of this development, a film emerging out of the Afro-German community. To be sure the director, Angelina Maccarone, is not Afro-German; however she is a lesbian and the daughter of an Italian guest worker, familiar with the problems of (ethnic) minorities in Germany. The film script was a collaborative project between Maccarone and Fatima El-Tayeb. Together they developed a film that is smartly aware of the antagonism of dominant German culture toward the Afro-German minority and that seeks to provide insight into the lives of Afro-Germans and the confrontation with quotidian racism. The film further benefited from the presence of talented and professionally trained Afro-German actors whose career possibilities were expanding in part because of media interest in multicultural representation.

Chantal de Freitas, who plays the character Kim, represents one of the most significant Afro-German actresses currently active in film and television. Freitas studied at theater school in Frankfurt am Main and at the famous Circle in the Square Theater in New York City. She first came to public attention in Germany with her role as Silke in *Stadtgespräch* (Talk of the Town, Rainer Kaufmann, 1995), although she had already appeared in a number of films by then. Here she played in a supporting role alongside the then brightly ascending star of lead Katja Riemann. De Freitas made television history in 1998 by accepting the role of Commissar Carol Reeding in the new run of *Polizeiruf 110.*[15] De Freitas was thus an obvious and significant choice for the leading role of Kim in *Everything Will Be Fine*. Pierre Sanoussi-Bliss, who plays in the supporting role of Kofi, has likewise had a significant career that began in the former GDR. He has appeared on the stage, in film, and television.[16] Sanoussi-Bliss, however, has been outspoken in his astonishment at the role of race in the FRG "that first became a problem after the *Wende*."[17] Especially in the media industry he had to confront sudden barriers to his career that he had never experienced before: "It's always, a black lead actor could not be imposed upon [*zumuten*] the German public."[18] After playing the male lead Orfeo in *Keiner liebt mich* he received an offer, like de Freitas, to appear as Commissar on a different long-running West German police show, *Der Alte*. In the narratives of the show, the private lives of the characters play little part, such that while Sanoussi-Bliss's presence was significant for the representation of minorities in the German media, it was not significant for the representation of minority "problems."

Everything Will Be Fine is both a comedy and lesbian film, two interconnected aspects that complicate its genealogy further and add to its significance for German film history. In Germany in the mid 1990s a wave of comedy films appeared that marked a fundamental transformation of the film landscape toward popular and entertainment film. While this general shift toward entertainment film remains, in the history of the Comedy Wave, *Everything Will Be Fine* marks if not its actual end, then a significant change in the genre.[19] Drawing from Bordwell's work on classic Hollywood narrative, David N. Coury suggested that "what these new films have in common structurally is their reliance on traditional elements of the classic cinema: causality, linear narrative, closure, and the most necessary element of all, a happy end."[20] Certainly after decades of the open or melancholic end serving as a trademark of European art films, the abundance of happy endings was remarkable. Certainly *Everything Will Be Fine* had one. However beyond Coury's observations of structural traits we can recognize that in terms of plot, there is also a common theme that keeps the audience laughing: heterosexuality. In all these regards *Everything Will Be Fine* certainly is part of its genre.

The beloved institution of heterosexuality has gone through many transformations and borne many jibes and attacks in the century of cinema. In Hollywood, the crisis of heterosexuality has always been a significant aspect of the comedy genre. For instance, crises abound in the screwball comedy where the plot often runs according to schemes like: girl meets boy, girl falls in love with boy, girl has twenty four hours to convince boy that he is marrying the wrong girl. Much of the narrative energy of the comedy genre thus derives from attempts to attach libidinal desire to a "proper" object, meaning that the majority of the film is spent with desire out of control and oriented toward "improper" objects. Perhaps the best example of such improper proper alignments of desire comes at the end of the screwball classic *Some Like it Hot* (Billy Wilder, 1959), when in response to Daphne's revelation that she is really "a man" Osgood Fielding III utters the famous line "Well, nobody's perfect" and they speed off presumably to live happily ever after.

In the German Comedy Wave of the 1990s, a crisis of heterosexuality also drives the plots. In terms of plot development, the films evidence two general generic patterns, refined by the gender of the main protagonist. If the film focuses on a male protagonist, we find a character hampered by his own chauvinism.[21] If the main character is female, she is a dynamic but anxious individual struggling both to find a partner and establish a career for herself. Her job prospects are shaky, and the world is filled with insensitive machos.[22] A further figure often appears as either second lead or as main supporting character—the figure of the gay man. In such a plot configuration, the heterosexual male passes through a "temporarily gay" narrative,[23] learns to be more "sensitive," and thereby becomes an acceptable partner. The heterosexual female learns through her interaction

Figure 6.2. Film still from *Alles wird Gut* [Everything Will be Fine], directed by Angelina Maccarone, 1997). Kim with Dieter and Mrs. Lauer. Photo courtesy of Nord Deutscher Rundfunk (NDR).

with the gay character to be independent and confident and at that point a heterosexual relationship becomes possible.

In *Everything Will Be Fine* the main character, Kim, occupies the position of the typical female protagonist. Her boss and possible fiancé represents the ineffectual German male, although this time not because he is a macho but because he is not dynamic enough. In a play on his name, he is literally referred to as the "lauer Dieter," lukewarm Dieter. Nabou and her roommate Guiseppa appear in roles similar to that typically occupied by the gay male. However, in the final resolution of this film, rather than restoring Kim and Dieter to a happy heterosexuality, Nabou's presence undoes heterosexual norms altogether. For its narrative motivation, the film relies on a form of triangulation with Kim as the beloved object establishing a line of rivalry between Dieter and Nabou. A great deal of the humor in the second half of the film, however, relies on a comedy of errors derived from the presumption of heterosexuality and the resulting lesbian invisibility. Only Nabou is aware that she is Dieter's rival. Dieter fails consistently to recognize who Nabou really is. His own assumptions and stereotypes lead him to understand her as Kim's younger, crazed sister and he tries to treat Nabou as an ally in his attempts to draw Kim to him.

As a result of this shift in the pattern of triangulation, Kim's desires and agency come to play a more significant role in the narrative development than would otherwise be afforded the female beloved of a triangle. In the end Kim chooses literally to jump the heterosexual ship, swimming away from the boat, on which Dieter had intended to propose to her, toward Nabou. In a traveling far shot, the camera displays how Kim and Nabou swim to a buoy, their own island in the unstable waters. Dieter and co-workers are left behind on the boat, perplexed and, from the perspective of narrative development, justly diminished.

The lesbian resolution to the heterosexual crisis offered by *Everything Will Be Fine* marked a distinct transformation of the Comedy Wave. Of course the lesbian basis to the narrative does not surprise, given Maccarone's filmography.[24] *Everything Will Be Fine* made its way to New York as part of the developments of international New Queer Film. In the late 1980s, gay- and lesbian-themed film won general critical notice, such that Hollywood even launched its own Gay Wave with films like *To Wong Foo, Thanks for Everything, Julie Newmar* (Beeban Kidron, 1995) or *In and Out* (Frank Oz, 1997). While *Everything Will Be Fine* is part of these developments, it also paid savvy attention to the generic developments of the German film context, combining national and international dynamics. Moreover if the film's subversion of the heteronormative conventions of the Comedy Wave foregrounds the sexual dynamic in the film, its antiracist aspects should not fade into the background. Rather, both mark a further transformation of the genre.

Films like *My Beautiful Launderette* (Stephen Frears, 1985), *Young Soul Rebels* (Issac Julien, 1991), *Les Roseaux sauvages* (Wild Reeds, André Téchiné, 1994), or *Lola und Bilidikid* (E. Kutlug Ataman, 1999) have explored the dynamics of gay life within European minority communities, *Launderette* even as a comedy. However, through this exploration of a dou- bly determined minority status, *Everything Will Be Fine* helped propel the German Comedy Wave from popular to public culture. This shift is sig- nificant in that the Comedy Wave was much criticized in its turn to enter- tainment as an apolitical betrayal of the legacy of the German New Wave. Here *Everything Will Be Fine* might be understood as accomplishing a hybrid of comedy and *Problemfilm*, the "social problem film." This rein- fusion of political concerns into the Comedy Wave expands the potential reach of the film beyond the audiences of the arthouse theaters.

The social problem film is a genre that had disappeared from the screens, but in Germany during the 1950s and 1960s it had brought for- ward for popular consumption exposés of cultural decline.[25] It sought in this regard to expand the public sphere by offering contributions to public debates. They often focused on youth culture, and attendant problems of sexuality, alcohol and drug use, joblessness, etc. Even though these films now appear as a form of camp, they were never intentional comedies. *Everything Will Be Fine* appears in its historic juncture as a response to two films in particular: *Anders als Du und Ich* (Different from You and Me, Veit Harlan, 1957), which warned its postwar audiences about the dangers homosexuality presented to its contemporary youth,[26] and *Toxi*, which, although often classified as a children's film, presents a vehicle for portraying the social problem of Afro-German children. These films, however, serve as foils rather than precursors to *Everything Will Be Fine* because they approached the subculture or minority milieu as a threat to dominant German society. *Everything Will Be Fine* inverts this perspective, relying on humor to approach the problems the minority experiences in interactions with the dominant society. With its foregrounding of the problems of Afro-Germans, the "enlightenment" goals of the problem film fill *Everything Will Be Fine* and imbue the comedy with seriousness and purpose. Various "humorous" scenes of foreclosure actually add to the political potential of the film as comedy. For instance, when Kofi realizes that Kim is falling in love with Nabou and sincerely congratulates her on her new romance, Kim immediately responds: "For what then? Black lesbian in Germany?"[27] As if her life were not already complicated enough.

Richard Dyer noted in regard to "images of" studies (e.g., images of blacks in German film) so central to antiracist work[28] since the 1970s that they ran the risk of replicating a power imbalance against which they actually sought to work.

> Looking, with such passion and single-mindedness, at non-dominant groups has had the effect of reproducing the sense of the oddness, differentness, exceptionality of these groups, the feeling that they are departures from the norm. Meanwhile the norm has carried on as if it is the natural, inevitable, ordinary way of being human.[29]

It is significant to note, however, that *Everything Will Be Fine* offers a new negotiation of "differentness," or alterity. While the film focuses on a non-dominant group, it does not make "Afro-Germaness" the problem. Rather the problem is the situation in which Afro-Germans find themselves, the situation of a hostile Germany. It is the "norm," the white German, that is the problem in the film, yet in its indictment of current social conditions, the film refrains from relying on a racial essentialism, which would instantiate a reverse racism. The black/white divisions portrayed in the film are cultural not biological; the conditions of alterity are not essential, they are contingent.

With Nabou's calling out "Kiss yourselves!" the culturalist and non-essentialist aspects of the film's antiracism becomes clear. As Nabou turns her back on the kiosk the viewer is positioned to follow Nabou and not remain behind. Throughout, the film uses humor as a vehicle to sensitize and raise the consciousness of a mass audience, members of which might have indeed remained behind at the kiosk; however, the viewer is pulled into a position of insider in these jokes. The joke is on the overt racists like the driver who yells "We're not in Africa," and also on the well-intentioned liberals caught in racialist presumptions, like the customers at the kiosk, or Kim's co-workers who cringe in fear at Nabou because of their willingness to believe her to be dangerous, even a cannibal. Here the humor relies on the viewer seeing through the characters' prejudice, stereotyping, and ignorance. The viewer who laughs along does not remain behind with the boss and customer at the kiosk, but follows Nabou and is thereby incorporated into an antiracist community that is not distinguished by racial difference.

In this regard *Everything Will Be Fine* relies on spectatorial strategies developed in the history of Queer filmmaking. Earlier gay and lesbian films, developed within and for "the Movement," invoked both an identification *with* and a type of typification that allowed for an identification *as*. The audience for Rosa von Praunheim's *Nicht der Homosexuelle ist pervers* (Not the Homosexual is Perverse, 1970) or Frank Ripploh's *Taxi zum Klo* (Taxi to the Toilet, 1981) were invited both to identify with the main homosexual protagonist and also to go beyond simple classic dramatic conventions—to self-identify as gay. New Queer Cinema sought a cross-over potential in order to win a market that went beyond the gay and lesbian audience. The cross-over was made possible through the assertion of an identification *with* that did not also demand an identification *as* gay or lesbian. In regard to sexuality, that is certainly the case in *Everything Will Be Fine*. However, there is a modification in regard to issues of race: the audience is certainly not required to identify as Afro-German but is definitely invited to identify as a new German, one who can inhabit a Germany defined by heterogeneous cultural parameters. In effect, the film makes it possible for the audience to experience its laughter as part of an antiracist movement.

For audiences outside of Germany, especially U.S. audiences, the lives portrayed in *Everything Will Be Fine* can too quickly lose their cultural specificity and become enfolded in other racial contexts, for instance the conditions of African Americans as minority. It must therefore be kept in mind that in terms of contemporary racial dynamics Afro-Germans confront fairly unique conditions. In the U.S., France, England, or any country that accepts the possibility of immigration, there is no question that citizens derive from different ethnicities. Germany, however, defines citizenship primarily through blood, making it next to impossible to immigrate to Germany. There is therefore a presumption of a homogeneous German culture that combines easily with a racialized presumption of dominant society that Germans are white.[30] Afro-Germans, however, present a challenge to these kinds of presumptions in the dominant society in which they live. Afro-Germans confuse the white racialist imaginary that projects a homogeneous physical and cultural belonging. Yet in this context a form of alterity clings to Afro-Germans that denies a legitimate belonging to hyphenated existences and imbues them with foreignness. In this respect Afro-Germans experience many of the same prejudices experienced by Turkish-Germans or members of immigrant communities. However, unlike Turks and Turkish-Germans who belong to distinct communities defined by language, dress, religion, cuisine, and so on, Afro-Germans live dispersed among the dominant community and thus their alterity is not defined by specific practices. For members of this minority an odd condition develops in which Afro-Germans born and raised in Germany to German parents are nevertheless required in their daily lives to prove their "Germanness."

Everything Will Be Fine thematizes this dynamic. In scenes from the film where Nabou is complimented on her German, asked about her ability to endure the cold, and so on, or in the scenes where Kim confronts the liberal awkward racism of her "well-intentioned" colleagues, the viewer experiences quotidian denials of their belonging. Yet beyond the narrative of the film, we see this dynamic in the reporting around the cast. From media discussions we know that of the actors in *Everything Will Be Fine*, Pierre Sanoussi-Bliss's father was from Guinea, and Chantal de Freitas's father was from Panama. Such demarcations of belonging are not solely experiences of Afro-Germans; given the "exoticism" of her last name, we can even learn that Macarrone's father was the first Italian guest worker in Pulheim. However, when such background information fails in the reporting on the other members of the cast, as it does, its absence indicates the presumption of homogeneity. In support of an unsatisfying multicultural discourse, the media are compelled to address in some fashion the presumption of who a German is.[31] The hyphenated existence as Afro-Germans (or Italo-Germans, or Turkish-Germans, and so on) must be biologically traced out, but precisely this biological tracing of a well-intentioned multiculturalism perpetuates racialist essentialism.

For its part, *Everything Will Be Fine* displays the vision of Germany that the conservatives and far right decry, one in which images of a monolith of unified German culture give way. Nevertheless, while the film displays an expanded vision of cultural belonging, it proves suspicious of *Multikulti* essentialism. It displays the problems of cultural displacement and foreclosure that set the limits to multiculturalism, and it pushes beyond multiculturalism to raise problems of intercultural and transcultural dynamics as well. Supporting characters in the form of Guiseppa, Nabou's roommate, and Kofi, Kim's best friend, help construct such complications in the film.

Guiseppa's Italian ethnicity helps undermine a simple black/white schematism. Through Guiseppa's presence "whiteness" loses a presumption of homogeneity and the category of German as such proves open to all forms of intercultural hybridization. Yet unlike Kim and Nabou vis-à-vis their existence as Afro-Germans, Guiseppa does not experience her being Italo-German as anything more than a form of background, which in the film poses no barrier to her belonging. Guiseppa is free to adorn her life with esoteric wisdom, contact the other side via the spirit of Greta Garbo, introduce the Swahili phrase *hakuna matata*, and in general present herself as a ready target for Nabou's accusation that Guiseppa is a cultural imperialist. Guiseppa responds by claiming an exoticism based on her ethnicity but it presents itself only through her ability to mimic the most clichéd of Italian accents, certainly not the basis for a believable performance of identity. Ultimately the dynamic represented here by Guiseppa's "assimilation" presents a foil to the racialist foreclosure of belonging experienced by Kim and Nabou for whom then the performance of Afro-German identity is equally response and imposition.

Kofi on the other hand was once a student of German from Ghana, whose dissertation now lies moldering on a shelf somewhere. He is a sort of reverse ethnologist, who has studied German culture and can be trusted to know more about it than those who lay claim to belonging by birth. Yet he knows he could never be a Germanist in Germany. The academy, apparently unwilling to accept the success of its own education, requires that German culture be taught in the classroom only by those who can perform a belonging to it. For Kofi this foreclosure is clearly a point of frustration. He presents the possibility of willing acculturation. Kofi is not simply an African in Germany, rather he is an Afro-German by desire. That he announces to Kim that he wants to return to Ghana after all these years is not a sign of his shortcomings in negotiating Germanness or the impossibility of transcultural assimilation, but rather precisely a result of the barriers to assimilation caused by institutional racial definitions of belonging.

Recalling Dyer's warning, we can recognize that the film performs a work of enlightenment and tolerance, and yet it refrains from exoticizing the Afro-German characters. While clever and resourceful, they are not tricksters but rather simply talented and successful. Their representation does not respond to the racial dynamic in Germany with naïve faith in multiculturalism but allows Afro-Germans to speak outside of stereotypes and clichés. However, the film runs into a different problem when ultimately negotiating the place of Afro-Germans in the dominant society. We can return to the final scene discussed earlier and realize that if Kim is jumping the heterosexual ship, she is also jumping the full German boat. She leaves behind the boring security and tolerance of Dieter for a future of only questions; the baffled partygoers look on, uttering comments like "*andere Länder, andere Sitten*" [other countries, other customs], inadequate attempts to assess the developments—and therefore comic. Yet as Kim jumps ship, we should recall the fates of Toxi and Orfeo, who find their "real" homes elsewhere outside of Germany. In *Everything*'s ending, there is a suggestion that like belongs with like, although the film does struggle against such readings. To be sure, the women have bonded and fallen in love through scenes of shared experiences and mutual understanding, and it is not their shared ethnicity that binds them together as much as their shared experiences in a hostile Germany. However, they must swim away, although in their case it is not to a place of stability toward which they swim, rather they arrive at the buoy and create their own island, the existence of which is precarious and circumscribed, as enacted by the final encircling shot.

Since *Everything Will Be Fine*, Afro-German presence in the media has increased, along with general minority visibility, but no films have appeared that have offered the same type of representations or engaged in the same form of antiracist work. What has appeared has been both positive and negative. Sanoussi-Bliss not only found the role on television discussed above, he also appeared in two feature films. Doris Dörrie drew on his talents again in her film *Bin ich schön* (Am I Pretty, 1998). In this film, Sanoussi-Bliss appeared alongside a panoply of stars from the history of German film. His role was a rather odd background character, exotic, black, naked, Spanish, and apparently over-sexed, in short a character unfortunately based in many of the clichéd images of blackness. With *Zurück auf Los* (Back to Go!, 2001), Sanoussi-Bliss found himself in front of and behind the camera; he wrote the filmscript, starred in it, and had his film directorial debut. This film again draws strongly from his own biography, but here he plays a complicated character who "happens to be Afro-German" along with gay, HIV-positive, former East German, in love, out of work, and a number of other qualities. Indeed the motivation of the film's narrative seems to draw primarily from representing how such an accretion of qualities confronts the society in which he lives. This is obviously a strategy of representation that differs greatly from *Everything Will Be Fine*.

Given the limited number of representations of Afro-Germans, it is not possible to identify trends or consistent strategies of representation as such. Furthermore, for critics it is not necessary to insist on a positive image aesthetic in future productions. At this point what really matters most is a simple increase in the presence of Afro-Germans and Afro-German issues in all the media to the point where they can come to occupy a normalized and naturalized position within German society in all its real existing diversity—including the diversity within the Afro-German community itself.

Notes

1. It is also known as a *Mohrenkopf,* a "Moor's head."

2. Attacks on "foreigners" take place on the average of over one hundred per month, although there is debate as to the accuracy of these numbers. The statistics kept by the *Bundesamt für Verfassungsschutz* represent the number of reported attacks, hence it can be easily assumed that given the nature of the attacks there are a significant number that remain unreported. See http://www.verfassungsschutz.de/. The *Dokumentations- und Informationszentrum für Rassismusforschung e. V.* organized in 1994 as an independent organization to collect information about racism in Germany. For further information see their informative website at http://www.dir-info.de/index.shtml.

3. The program *Wilde Herzen* was produced through the decade of the 1990s and described its profile as strongly connected to the successes of its contemporary German film. In addition to *Everything*, it co-produced and served as the television venue for such films as Detlev Buck's *Männerpension* (Jailbirds, WDR), Rolf Silber's *Echte Kerle* (Real Men, BR), Hans-Christian Schmid's *Nach fünf im Urwald* (After Five in the Jungle, BR/SWR) and Wolfgang Becker's *Das Leben ist eine Baustelle* (Life is All You Get, WDR). Further description of the series can be found under http://www.das-erste.de/wildeherzen/staffel9.asp.

4. See also the film book, Fatima El-Tayeb and Angelina Maccarone, *Alles wird gut* (Berlin: Orlanda Frauenverlag, 1999).

5. I will keep my remarks on this film brief. See Heide Fehrenbach's discussion (chapter 5) in this volume for a full and detailed analysis.

6. For a discussion of the work of Herzog in relation to race and neocolonialism see John E. Davidson, "As Others Put Plays upon the Stage: Aguirre, Neocolonialism, and the

New German Cinema," *New German Critique* 60 (1993): 101–32; and Lutz P. Koepnick, "Colonial Forestry: Sylvan Politics in Werner Herzog's *Aguirre* and *Fitzcarraldo*," *New German Critique* 60 (1993): 133–59.

7. See Barbara Mennel and Amy Ongiri, "In a Desert Somewhere Between Disney and Las Vegas: The Fantasy of Interracial Harmony and American Multiculturalism in Percy Adlon's *Bagdad Café*," *Camera Obscura* 44 (2000): 151–77.

8. For discussions of this dynamic from the period, see Helma Lutz, "Orientalische Wirklichkeit: Das Bild der Türkin in der Literatur konfrontiert mith Selbstbildern," *Informationsdienst zur Ausländerarbeit* 4 (1989): 32–39; Helma Lutz, "Die 'orientalische' Frau in westlichen Diskursen," *Peripherie* 37 (1989): 51–66; and in general the discussions in *"Getürkte Bilder": Zur Inszenierung von Fremden in Film*, ed. Ernst Karpf (Marburg: Schüren, 1995).

9. Indeed in these films "Turkish" society appears as a homogeneous misogynistic entity, effacing real differences that structure the Turkish diaspora in Germany, for example the ethnic difference between Turks and Kurds, or real differentiations on the basis of class, secularization, education, and so on. In these films the headscarf became the *sine qua non* of pre/anti-modernity and German filmmakers did their best to "save" Turkish women from Turkish men.

10. For a discussion of racist images from this period see R. Riepe and G. Riepe, *Du Schwarz, ich weiß: Bilder und Texte gegen alltäglichen Rassismus* (Wuppertal: Hammer, 1992).

11. For a further discussion of the film and especially the role of the conductor see Doron Kiesel, "Das Schweigen der Fahrgäste: Zu *Schwarzfahrer* von Pepe Danquart," in Karpf, *"Getürkte Bilder.*"

12. For an extended discussion of the film see Margaret McCarthy, "Teutonic Water: Effervescent Otherness in Doris Dörrie's *Nobody Loves Me*," *Camera Obscura* 44 (2000): 177–202.

13. Kanak music, literature, and film represents a new minority awareness especially among Turkish-Germans. The works of directors Fatih Akin, Yüksel Yavuz, and Kutlug Ataman are perhaps the best known. It is interesting to note that in the history of representation of Turks in Germany, beyond the types of the oppressive man and oppressed woman, the criminal is the most notable other type. Kanak films did not break with this type and tended to focus on the gangsta Turk, a dangerous member of the underworld who belongs to predominant German anxieties and stereotypes about the Turkish population.

14. For a brief discussion of these films and the general conditions of film production for black filmmakers see Maureen Blackwood and June Givanni, "Black Film-Making in Europe," *Screen* 29, no. 4 (1988): 114–20.

15. This series, a police drama, had been the most successful television series of the former GDR and it developed further after German unification to compete successfully with the long-running West German series, *Tatort*. The new *Polizeiruf* retained a long history of creative and even critically progressive crime narratives, especially in comparison to the more conservative and straightforward stories of *Tatort*. *Polizeiruf* focuses more sharply on the lives of the police investigators alongside the episode's crime investigation. Hence in a television landscape lacking in diversity, this background made *Polizeiruf* an obvious place to find an Afro-German woman in a position of authority and success. As of the episodes in 2000, Dennenesch Zoudé, a younger actress with an already impressive acting background, has taken over the role of Commissar Reeding.

16. See Frank Junghänel "Statt der Engel," *Berliner Zeitung*, 9 February 2000; Claudia Becker, "Wo ein Engel für schöne Träume sorgt," *Berliner Morgenpost*, 30 October 1999: n.p.; Susanne Lost, "Der Neue beim 'Alten,'" *Berliner Morgenpos*, 30 May 1997; Matthias Oloew, "Vom gelernten Koch zum Profi-Schauspieler," *Tagesspiegel*, 10 September 1996: n.p.

17. Oloew, "Vom gelernten Koch zum Profi-Schauspieler."

18. Ibid.

19. In 1994 the Comedy Wave took off with the surprise success of *Der bewegte Mann* (Maybe, Maybe Not, Sönke Wortmann). Dörrie's *Nobody Loves Me* premiered in the same year and was not as successful but is now in retrospect being understood as part of the Comedy Wave as well. For a detailed discussion of the Comedy Wave, especially with focus on the role of heterosexuality, see Randall Halle, " 'Happy Ends' to Crises of Heterosexual Desire: Toward a Social Psychology of Recent German Comedies," *Camera Obscura* 44 (2000): 1–41; see further David N. Coury, "From Aesthetics to Commercialism: Narration and the New German Comedy," *Seminar* 33 (1997): 356–73.

20. Coury, "From Aesthetics to Commercialism," 356.

21. He is on the streets having been abruptly dismissed from a relationship as a result of his insensitivity and/or philandering. While he wants it, this character is incapable of being in a relationship, and this forms his central motivating conflict. *Der bewegte Mann, Echte Kerle* (Real Men, Rolf Silber, 1996), *Werner, daß muß kesseln* (Werner, Eat my Dust, Udo Beissel and Gerhard Hahn, 1996), *Männerpension* (Jailbirds, Detlev Buck, 1996), *Allein unter Frauen* (Alone Among Women, Sönke Wortmann, 1991), *Nur über meine Leiche* (Only Over My Dead Body, Rainer Matsutani, 1995) all provide variations on this generic theme.

22. *Abgeschminkt* (Makin' Up, Katja von Garnier, 1993), *Das Superweib* (The Superwife, Sönke Wortmann, 1996), *Ein Mann für jede Tonart* (A Man for Every Melody, Peter Timm, 1993), *Stadtgespräch* (Talk of the Town, Rainer Kaufmann, 1995), *Irren ist männlich* (Father's Day, Sherry Hormann, 1996), *Die Putzfraueninsel* (The Isle of Cleaning-women, Peter Timm, 1996), all revolve around these same problems.

23. The idea of a temporary gay narrative is derived from Chris Straayer's work on the temporary transvestite. See Chris Straayer, *Deviant Eyes, Deviant Bodies: Sexual Re-Orientation in Film and Video* (New York: Columbia University Press, 1996).

24. In 1992 she won a film script competition in Hamburg with a coming-out comedy. This script, *Kommt Mausi Raus*, turned into Maccarone's co-directorial debut in 1995. Its success served as the basis of her master's thesis two years later, "Eine Mainstream-Leben Komödie und ihre kultur- und filmhistorischen Voraussetzungen." It also accounted for the support she received for *Everything* and in turn for *Ein Engel schlägt zurück* (1998).

25. This genre especially enjoyed popularity from the 1930s through the 1960s, and in the U.S. context is perhaps best known now through the ever-popular screenings of *Reefer Madness* (1936).

26. This film was directed by Veit Harlan, one of the most significant directors of propaganda films during the Nazi era. His anti-Semitic *Jud Süß* was mandatory for SS officers and his *Kolberg* was used to encourage the civilian population to carry on the fight even after the military collapse. Harlan was the center of highly controversial denazification hearings, and was allowed to return to filmmaking in the 1950s. *Anders* was his attempt to contribute to the new film and political culture of the young Federal Republic.

27. She states "Zu was denn? Schwarze Lesbe in Deutschland."

28. Of course "images of" studies can be undertaken for other reasons, e.g. images in the media of women, gays, blacks, Turks, Germans, and so on motivated by anti-misogyny, anti-homophobia, and so on.

29. Richard Dyer, "White," *Screen* 24 (1988): 44.

30. There is not enough space to discuss German immigration policies, especially given that a number of attempts have been undertaken to reform them since unification. However, throughout the 1990s, in the midst of discussions of the "Foreigner Problem," the German government was actively recruiting "Germans" among Russia's ethnic minorities to "return" to Germany. Until 2000 a third generation child of German immigrants from overseas could with ease receive German citizenship while a third generation Turkish child who had spent all his or her life in Germany experienced only the greatest of difficulties. A new law is now in effect that should make the process somewhat easier. Reform efforts continue. For more information see http://www.bundesauslaenderbeauftragte.de/ themen/staats.stm, http://www.einbuergerung.de/, and http://www.antirassismus.com/.

31. A further example of this dynamic can be recognized in Sanoussi-Bliss's film roles where a great deal of his own biography often clings to his characters. Born in Berlin in 1962, his acting career began in the GDR. After first training as a cook he attended the Ernst Busch acting school where he was the first black acting student in the GDR. He received a steady position on the *Staatsschauspiel* in Dresden, from 1987 until unification. In 1990 he began successfully to find his way in the new Federal Republic first as an independent actor and then as director for stage and now screen. He lives his private life as an out gay man. Orfeo in *Keiner liebt mich* and Sam in *Zurück auf Los* both are gay former East Germans. In the course of the film we learn that Orfeo had been a cook. In the case of *Zurück* Sam struggles in the entertainment industry and in the East Berlin gay scene. It might not be unheard of in the culture industry that a well-known actor's life becomes material for a film; however it is uncommon that films develop their plot lines on the basis of the available actor's life.

7

WRITING DIASPORIC IDENTITY

AFRO-GERMAN LITERATURE SINCE 1985

Leroy Hopkins

Beginning in the late 1980s a new voice began to emerge on the German literary scene. Germans of African and/or African American descent began to speak out against the everyday racism and discrimination that was depriving them of their cultural identity as Germans. More than just articulating their victimization, these Black Germans sought to expose the origins of their victimization and in the process challenge and redefine German cultural identity to include the perspectives of race and gender.

To achieve this goal it was necessary to create a group identity through organizational activities that would encourage Germans of color to reflect on what it had meant to grow up Black in German society. As a consequence, many of the texts produced were autobiographical in nature. Surprisingly, to date few of the published texts have been authored by men. Women have been in the forefront both in the organizational as well as the publishing activities. Without slighting male authors such as Michael Hyperion Küppers or Peter Dernbach, at this point in time, Afro-German literature is primarily women's literature. In the following, we shall first consider the context and the implications of Afro-German organizational work before proceeding to a general consideration of literary texts with special emphasis on autobiography.

Surveying the German literary scene of the 1970s and 1980s, Barbara Kosta notes what she terms an "unprecedented surge of autobiographical expressions" by women.[1] What was unprecedented about the autobiographies was their appearance at a time when the concepts of authorship, the self, and self-representation were not just challenged but considered antiquated by philosophers and cultural critics. Kosta argues, however, that the autobiographies from the two decades before reunification represent a reconceptualization of a genre firmly rooted in the Western literary canon.

Unlike the traditional, male-dominated autobiography, the texts by women demonstrate what Kosta characterizes as a "shift from an interest in displays of individualism as objective testimonies of historical processes to an interest in subjective interpretations of life."[2] Contrary to the declarations of the death of the author and literature itself, German women writers reconstituted the author as a structural organizing principle of the literary text but without the hegemonic claim to authority found in traditional personal narratives. According to Kosta this "destablization of monolithic notions of self and author, authoritative orginator and proprietor of the text, has allowed for the inclusion of hetereogeneous voices."[3]

Inclusivity is a significant concern because, as Kosta notes, elimination of the auctorial voice subverts the attempts of traditionally marginalized groups such as women to gain access to the literary mainstream and posits the traditional, patriarchal narrative structure as the only possible subjectivity.[4] Thus the reconceptualized narrator must be valorized because:

> By maintaining a signature, important extratextual references such as race, class, gender, ethnicity, and the cultural and historical background of the author are preserved as significant markers. The author, consequently, is read as one possible site of meaning, as a point of departure and not as a focus of absolute meaning or conclusion.[5]

Kosta thus asserts the inherently democratic and integrative character of German women's autobiographical literature and locates the origin of this new subjectivity in the "politicization of the personal" in Germany, which she identifies as a result of the women's movement and the 1968 student revolt.[6] Although she places women's autobiographies of the 1970s and 1980s in the context of the women's movement of that era and the "rediscovery" of the tradition of female self-representation, Kosta fails to include in her study another literary phenomenon from the same period: the emergence of an Afro-German literature. This oversight, while perhaps unintentional, points to one difficulty which Afro-German writers—most of whom are women—confront in their attempt to enter the literary mainstream.

The publication in 1986 of *Farbe bekennen*[7] was largely ignored by the German literary establishment. Even today, although the major texts published by Afro-Germans appear in a leading feminist publishing house (Berlin's Orlanda Frauenverlag), critics either ignore the literary productions of Black Germans or relegate them to the sociological realm. For years after 1986 texts dealing with Germans of African or African American descent could be found on those bookshelves devoted to the problems of the *Ausländer* (foreigners) in the Federal Republic. It was not until 1992 that a major publishing house (Fischer Verlag) issued *Farbe bekennen*; characteristically it was put into the series *Die Frau in der Gesellschaft* (woman in society), an obvious attempt to stress the documentary over the literary quality of the anthology.

The reason for this relegation to the sociological realm is perhaps grounded in the Afro-Germans' motives for writing. Individually and as a group they have begun a far-reaching cultural project intended to establish a new identity for themselves by challenging basic and cherished assumptions about German cultural identity. The oral histories and historical essays published in *Farbe bekennen* are components in a project intended to legitimize the racialized self, free it from isolation, and expose the racism and sexism that have existed throughout German history and especially since 1884 when Germany began establishing a colonial empire in Africa and the Pacific.

Rather than reading Afro-German texts as a reminder that recent German history still had unresolved issues, the German reading public perceived them as statements of victimization rooted in the unfortunate decisions of a few. It was easy to categorize the stories as sociological studies, since Afro-Germans were, for the most part, the offspring of African-American G.I.s and Africans who had come to the Federal Republic after 1945. In essence, the German literary establishment and reading public did not believe that Afro-German texts had literary quality or were relevant to mainstream literary concerns. There was, after all, no racism in Germany. All of that unpleasantness had disappeared with denazification.

To counter this exclusion an Afro-German cultural program emanating from the grassroots organizations, the I.S.D. (*Initiative Schwarze Deutsche*/ Initiative of Black Germans) and ADEFRA (*AfroDeutsche Frauen*/ Afro-German Women) soon took form between 1986 and 1990. The various magazines, *Onkel Toms Faust, Afrekete, afro look*, and *Strangers*, the national summits (*Bundestreffen*), a Black History Month celebration in Berlin, and the more recent Black Culture calendars and the *Afronetz* are all components in a strategy designed to achieve what during the heyday of the American civil rights movement was known as "consciousness-raising." Research, analysis, and publication of the essential facts about the contacts between Germans and the indigenous populations of the African continent were important for two reasons.

First, Germans of African or African American descent not only lived in isolation from each other but were as a group quite heterogeneous. Lacking a thorough knowledge about their personal background and cultural heritages they were easy prey for the stereotypes and prejudices about people of color anchored in the German language. Second, if the group was to coalesce and have an impact on German society, it must present itself not only as a contemporary but also as a historical phenomenon. Given the magnitude of its dual task of individual and group organization for social change, it was only logical that the emerging Afro-German community would seek a model for its cultural campaign.

That model was implicit in the information presented by Audre Lorde. Black Americans have come through and are still in the midst of a seemingly never-ending struggle to define and assert themselves as individuals. Although to my knowledge no explicit reference to him is made in the various Afro-German programmatic statements, W. E. B. DuBois's concept of the "double consciousness" described quite accurately the plight of the Black German. As DuBois notes in *Souls of Black Folks*:

> After the Egyptian and Indian, the Greek and Roman, the Teuton and Mongolian, the Negro is a sort of seventh son, born with a veil, and gifted with second-sight in this American world—a world which yields him no true self-consciousness, but only lets him see himself through the revelation of the other world. It is a peculiar sensation, this double consciousness, this sense of always looking at one's self through the eyes of others, of measuring one's soul by the type of a world that looks on in amused contempt and pity. One ever feels his twoness—an American, a Negro; two souls, two thoughts; two unreconciled strivings; two warring ideals in one dark body, whose dogged strength alone keeps it from being torn asunder.[8]

Without suggesting slavish imitation, it is noteworthy that in attempting to find their own voice Afro-Germans employed a discursive strategy also used by the emerging Black communities in the Atlantic world in the eighteenth and nineteenth centuries: autobiography.

By telling their own story, Afro-Germans have attempted to liberate themselves from the strictures and barriers erected against them by a society whose ultimate control over their destiny was visible in the very process of naming. The controversy over what to call Americans of African

descent, which extended from William Whipper's[9] rejection of the term
"colored American," to W. E. B. DuBois's insistence that the "n" in "Negro"
be capitalized, to the more recent changes from "Negro" to "Black" to "Afro-
American" and finally to "African American" all prefigure the Afro-German
rejection of terms such as "*Besatzungskind*," "*Mischling*," "*Mulatto*," or
"*Neger.*" To some observers this reaction seems unnecessarily hypersensitive
but in a true biblical sense reality is what we name it and Afro-Germans—
as well as African Americans—reject the notion that others can categorize
and thus ultimately control them.

The autobiographical statements or oral histories in *Farbe bekennen*
are more than just an assertion of individualism. Much like the slave
narratives of the nineteenth century they are designed above all to establish the veracity of the teller and to put a human face on a development
long ignored by the German public, that is, the transformation of a
supposedly monocultural country into not only a multicultural but also a
multiracial and multi-ethnic society. Beyond positing their racialized identity
as Germans, the voices in *Farbe bekennen* also document the pervasiveness of
sexual and racial oppression in German society beginning at the linguistic
level.

Two ISD brochures from the late 1980s summarize rather succinctly
the programmatic goals and objectives of Black Germans and offer insight
into their concept of cultural identity. Emphasizing that their history had
its roots in the late nineteenth century, Afro-Germans situate themselves
in a phase of German history which some contemporaries try to repress.
The oppressive and exploitative German colonial system and the genocidal
racial policies of the Nazis are the background that shapes that historical
period. A common denominator that unites nineteenth- and twentieth-
century Germany is a racism that many Germans prefer to believe no
longer exists.

For them the everyday racism and discrimination encountered by
people of color in Germany are the unfortunate by-products of a xenophobia caused by the unprecedented influx of foreigners into the Federal
Republic. If there were no foreigners, then there would be no problems.
Thus the official response to the increase in violence against people of
color in the years preceding and immediately following reunification was
to discuss ways in which to regulate and ultimately reduce the influx of
foreigners. That response blamed the victim for his victimization and
ignored the fact that many of the targets of the violent outbursts were people of color—some of them Germans. As a consequence, German cultural
identity became an underlying topic of public discourse. Who exactly was

German? If blood rather than law was to be the standard by which Germaness was to be judged, what should be done with the immigrants whose children had become acculturated after almost two generations in the Federal Republic? Furthermore, what was to be done for those Germans of African or African American descent?

The response orchestrated by the ISD to the emerging debate on German cultural identity was a series of demands. Besides official recognition of their status as victims of Nazi persecution with a legitimate claim to compensation, they also demanded official action against the rising tide of xenophobia and fascism that manifested itself in the attacks on Afro-Germans as well as the asylum-seekers, Sinti, Roma, and other persons of color in the Federal Republic. The call for a cessation of support for racist regimes such as the apartheid government in South Africa was coupled with the demand to terminate German economic exploitation of the so-called third world. These last two demands, which originate in a sense of solidarity with people of color around the globe, reveal an important feature of Afro-German cultural identity. Afro-Germans are internationalists who seek to redefine German identity not in terms of a specific national setting or cultural tradition but as a feature of a development that has occurred on a global scale: the African diaspora.

A diasporic consciousness is indicated in a second brochure published by the ISD in 1989, in which reference is made to the importance of cooperative efforts with "Gruppen aus der weltweiten Schwarzen Bewegung" (groups from the worldwide Black movement).[10] In Fischer Verlag's 1992 reprint of *Farbe bekennen*, Katharina Oguntoye and May Opitz are much more specific when they laud their book for having contributed to a growing awareness of the "*Schwarze Diaspora*" among Black Germans. It is this international consciousness that enriches but also complicates the Afro-German identity construct. Rather than asserting their rootedness in traditional German cultural values such as order, *Heimat*, linear time, and so on, Afro-Germans use the categories of race and gender in an effort to reinterpret German history and thus legitimize their own sense of double-consciousness.

Internationalization is only one stratagem employed by Afro-Germans to establish their cultural identity. A substantive and promising tool for their project of cultural affirmation has been the literary text. Two genres predominate up to now: the lyric and the epic. In both, the desire and even the need for self-representation is an overriding concern. The texts in *Farbe bekennen* draw on both genres to lend an additional impact to the lives presented, but the book's chief aim is to put Black German lives in an historical context. For that reason, the purely literary texts in the anthology yield to testimonials about the confrontation with sexism and racism leading to the emergence of a new awareness and acceptance of a personal commitment to social activism.

The lyrical texts in the ISD's magazine reflect this evolving consciousness. A deliberate international note was struck in the provocative title of the first magazine, *Onkel Toms Faust* (Uncle Tom's Fist). Apparently the title proved too controversial even for some Afro-Germans[11] and it was quickly changed to the more neutral *afro look*. Despite the tactical failure manifest in the change in title the reference to Harriet Beecher Stowe's abolitionist classic is indicative of another aspect of Afro-German cultural work: the promotion of literary works of the African diaspora.

From the outset the magazines publicized and promoted translations of African and African American literature. The late Vera Heyer, an unsung heroine of the early phase of the movement, was one of the individuals involved in the compiling and publishing of lists of Black literary works available in German translation. Those lists were circulated among interested Afro-Germans and also published in the magazines. Besides literature, other artistic forms also found support in the magazines. The very talented Afro-Belgian a capella women's group Zap Mama received favorable reviews as did the inimitable Nina Simone.

The progression of magazines has apparently been halted—funding has always been a difficult problem. Most recently, the internet has helped bridge the communication gap. *Afronetz*, which emanated for some time from the University of Kassel, provided an important forum for the exchange of news items, discussions, and also private inquiries. The latest development is the appearance of an electronic newsletter, certainly a less expensive way of maintaining contact with the readership.

Over the past decade the Afro-German readership has been exposed to a small number of significant literary publications beginning with the volume *Macht der Nacht, eine schwarze deutsche anthologie* (Power of the Night, a Black German anthology).[12] The decision to publish their own material probably was the result of the authors' inability to interest any of the mainstream publishing houses in their work. The authors reflect an essential element in the then-emerging cultural program: coalition building.

Besides Germans of Asian descent, Afro-Germans have actively cultivated alliances and coalitions with other marginalized groups such as Jews, Arabs, and Turks. Publications such as *Geteilter Feminismus, Wege zu*

Bündnissen, or *Entfernte Verbindungen*[13] document the bridge-building that is central to the cultural work of the Black German women. *Macht der Nacht* adds a new note by incorporating texts by men and women of varying backgrounds and experiences. Michael Hyperion Küppers, for example, is a multi-media artist who studied at Duke University with Henry Louis Gates. Sheila Mysorekar is an Indian German who lived in Brazil.

An international context is easily found in the various texts in the anthology. The juxtaposition of German and English language texts combined with clear evocations of the African American experience in texts such as "It's Nation Time" or "Listening to Malcolm X" not only establish a tangible international context but also serve as a counterpoint to texts such as those by Magali Schmid:

> It's Afro Time
> Händesschütteln hie, Küßchen da
> Das Bewußtsein auf den Schultern
>
> Aber ja nicht zuviel zeigen,
> Zeig ja nicht Deine Verletzbarkeit
>
> Deinen wunden Punkt
> Das Bewußtsein drückt auf den Schultern
> Ich weiß Du möchtest schreien, daß Fenster aufreißen
> Und schreien,—
> Aber zeig ja nicht Deine Verletztbarkeit[14]

The tension in this poem between forced external tranquility and suppressed inner rage leads into an emotional cul-de-sac of internalization and stoic denial in the face of discrimination and racism. Schmid recreates the frustration of this text in another entitled:

> Einsamkeit
> Gemeinsam aber doch alleine
>
> Einsam gehst Du durch die Straßen dieser kalten Stadt!
> Du sehnst Dich nach—Anerkennung
> Wird jemand sie Dir geben können?
> Werden "Sie" Dir dies geben können?
> Nein, Deine Seele schreit sie Schreit nach dem Etwas
>
> Sie schreit nach Anerkennung
> Die "Sie" Dir nie geben werden[15]

The uncertainty and isolation permeating these lines have their correspondent expression in another shorter text by the same author:

Weiß, Schwarz—Oder Sind Es Nur Farben

Ich gehe durch die Straßen—
Aufrecht aber doch gebückt
Stolz, aber doch unsicher,
Gleichgültig aber doch betroffen[16]

The antitheses expressed in these lines capture the ambivalence of the racialized self. The duality of the double consciousness manifests itself in the contradictions in posture and emotional states of a self alternating between independent pride and abject dependency.

The emotional pathology described in Schmid's text is countered by the defiant tones of Sheila Mysorekar's:

It's Nation Time!
Chicago Angola Tamil Eelam
Feine Fäden aus Gold und Blut
Aber jetzt
   Jetzt ist Zeit
Zu lang haben wir gewartet
Wir sind überall
   Schau dich um
In der Métro in Paris in Marseille in Lille
Dunkle Lippen gedrehte Ringe
Ein schräger Blick
Dasselbe Understanding im supermarket in
Leicester Liverpool Notting Hall
Kinky hair with glittering gel
Slow smile and hands slapping
There we are we are here
   What's the time
Rumba in Dresden
Im Ruhrpott werde scharfe Soßen gemischt
Schwarze Stimmen in Berlin und Köln
   . . . . Und geballte Fäuste
wie spät ist es
   spät ist es
   what's the time
   now

> beat the drum
>   dance
>   dance the nation dance
> it's NATION TIME !
> Viele sind wir
> Und jetzt
> Jetzt ist Zeit
> Jetzt ist die Zeit
> Gekommen[17]

This poem deserves greater recognition than it has received. The well-crafted cadence and rhetorical flourishes in the text place it in the forefront of the multicultural literature emerging in Germany. Unlike Magali Schmid's isolated and frustrated self, here a defiant "we" announces its birth. National boundaries and cultural distinctions fade before the sheer force of a new global awareness that unites historical enemies (England, France, and Germany) and challenges traditional cultures with its proponents' kinky hair, rhythmic dances, and spicy foods. The call to nationhood is both a legitimization of the racialized self and an affirmation of the struggle that precedes true selfhood and independence.

A more recent example of coalition-building between Afro-Germans and other marginalized groups is the anthology *Talking Home.*[18] Although published in Amsterdam the anthology's subtitle underscores an important step in the process of self-definition: "*Heimat aus unserer eigenen Feder. Frauen of Color in Deutschland*" (Home out of our own pens: Women of Color in Germany). Different from the other collaborative writing enterprises involving Afro-German women, this anthology is intended to deal with the issue of gender directly. In the preface the editors reiterate their intention to publish an anthology of texts by "Frauen/Queers of color in Deutschland."[19]

Even in exploring the boundaries of acceptable sexuality the editors and contributors stake out new terrain for themselves. "Queer" has for them the same broad implications as "Black" does for the Afro-Germans:

> "Queer" to us signifies the attempt to resist the strictures of prescribed role models—whether in a hetero or a homosexual life style. Ultimately, each can decide what is queer because we wanted to offer enough latitude. Many dislike the term "Lesbian" others do not see themselves subsumed in "dyke," etc., some are "bi" and still others do not want to define themselves. The choice of language was optional for each contributor as well. We

welcomed different languages and linguistic styles because they are the expression of our reality. Many of us use several languages.[20]

The anthology fulfills all that the editors promise. Sixteen authors explore in texts written in English, German, Spanish, and Turkish the vagaries of everyday life in a society that rejects them because of their skin color and their sexual orientation. There are also texts that deal with personal relationships and the emotional life of an outsider. Above all, however, the anthology treats the theme of "home" and the vicissitudes of self-definition in a society that does not accept otherness.

Even a cursory survey of Afro-German lyric would be incomplete without a consideration of the achievement of May Ayim (1960–1996). Although not the only Afro-German poet, May Opitz (Ayim after 1990) has been the only one to reach a mass audience with her poems. Two volumes of her poetry—one posthumous—were published by Orlanda Frauenverlag and have been well received. For our purposes it is expedient to concentrate on the volume published during Ayim's lifetime.

Blues in schwarz weiss (Blues in black and white, 1995) contains texts written between 1978 and 1994.[21] One poem in the collection, "nachtgesang" (Night song, 1992), was republished as the title poem in a 1997 compilation of texts from Ayim's estate. Both volumes are organized into cycles. In *blues in schwarz weiss* the cycles bear the titles of "am anfang war das wort," "zeitenwechsel," "die zeit danach," "aus dem rahmen," "blues in schwarz weiss," "berührung," "himmlisch," "nachtrag," and "nachwort." Each cycle contains a text bearing the cycle's title.[22]

Besides personal statements dealing with relationships and the art of writing there are a number of poems that speak directly to Afro-German identity issues. The first such poem is "*afro-deutsch I*" (1985) in which the reader is exposed to a series of stereotypical reactions of white Germans to Black Germans, for instance the assumption that mulattoes can overcome their alleged inherent inferiority because of access to German education and culture, or, because of their skin color Black Germans should have a special relationship to and bear a greater responsibility for improving conditions in Africa.

These racist statements ignore European agency in the cycles of war, poverty, and social instability that have debilitated Africa for centuries. Likewise, the presumption of European superiority is built on the enforced inferiority of other peoples. The implication that access to the advantages available in German society is open to everyone ignores the reality of everyday life in Germany where people of color find themselves exposed to all types of discrimination. Because of this discrimination the Afro-German is robbed of his identity and dehumanized.

Dehumanization is alluded to in the text by the reference to Afro-Germans not as persons but as a *"interessante Mischung"* (an interesting mixture). It is against their depersonalization through terms such as "mulatto" that Afro-Germans rebel because it robs them of agency and relegates them to the purely biological realm. This not-so-subtle rejection had its correspondence in May Ayim's own life when her mother had her institutionalized. The pain from the experience permeates several of the poems in the collection, especially *"dunkelheit"* (darkness, 1991) and *"nichtig"* (insignificant, 1992).

Complicating the situation of the Afro-Germans is an attitude depicted in *"afro-deutsch II"* (1985). This text demonstrates a tendency among white Germans to diminish the situation of Afro-Germans through invalid comparisons to other groups. For example, in the text an Afro-German woman is told that she should be glad that she is not a Turk. The implication is that her victimization is somehow less important because there are others who are supposedly more victimized. The insidious aspect of this comparison is that the situation of Turks and Afro-Germans is caused by *"Ausländerhetze,"* suggesting that like the Turks Afro-Germans are really foreigners.[23]

A feminist note is also sounded in this text. An obviously feminine voice states that she has the same problems as an Afro-German and one cannot always blame skin color for one's problems.[24] The significance of the Afro-German woman's situation is further trivialized by the comparison to women in general and to a friend specifically who is obese. The ultimate result of trying to equate the oppression of one group with that of another is stated insightfully by Ayim in the following passage:

> Ich finde überhaupt,
> daß die schwarzen sich noch so 'ne natürliche
> Lebenseinstellung bewahrt haben.
> Während hier: ist doch alles ziemlich kaputt.
> Ich glaube, ich wäre froh, wenn ich du wäre.
> Auf die deutsche Geschichte kann man
> ja wirklich nicht stolz sein,
> und so schwarz bist du ja auch gar nicht.[25]

The anxieties and problems of Afro-Germans are seemingly neutralized by their transformation into contemporary noble savages whose natural state contrasts favorably with the decadence of Germany. The speaker's wish to change places is minimalized by the assertion that the Afro-German is not really that Black. Race as a category in German life is devalued by such comparisons.

A telling response to the all-pervasive racism is found in the text "die zeit danach" (the time after, 1987). Dedicated to the memory of Dr. Martin Luther King, who is addressed as "brother," the text builds on his famous "I have a dream" speech to fashion a powerful statement on race just one year after the appearance of *Farbe bekennen*. Contrasting her dream with Dr. King's, Ayim interjects a note of militancy that calls into question the efficacy of rhetoric as a means for social change. The compelling rhetoric of Dr. King's speech has been:

> [. . .] konserviert
> konserviert und verkauft, Bruder
> postkarten und poster
> dreizeiler in einem geschichtsbuch
> >>I Have A Dream<<
> ein abgeschlossener Roman
>
> sie haben
> vergangenheit daraus gemacht
> weiß wie tränensalz
> und da wo ich lebe
> würden sie es >bewältigt< nennen, Bruder.[26]

The reference to "bewältigt" evokes Germany's relationship to its recent history and suggests that the racism of the Nazi era is linked to contemporary racism because of the reaction it elicits: denial and displacement. As with Dr. King's dream, conservation of the rhetoric permits one not to deal with the substance of the dream.

To counteract public indifference Ayim declares:

> ich trage meinen traum
> hinter
> erhobener faust
> in pfefferfarben
> und fange ganz klein an
> fange endlich an
> mit meiner schwester
> und meiner freundin an der hand mit
> meinen brüdern und

> wenn es sein soll
> auch allein
> —damit es endlich anders werden
> muß![27]

This obvious militancy is just one aspect of the Afro-German community dynamic. The title poem of the collection reflects the internationalization that lies at the core of Afro-German identity. In the year of German reunification Ayim reflected on the differences that divide the world and concluded:

> es ist ein blues in schwarz-weiß
> 1/3 der welt
> zertanzt
> die anderen
> 2/3
> sie feiern in weiß
> wir trauern in schwarz
> es ist ein blues in schwarz-weiß
> es ist ein blues[28]

Elsewhere in her text Ayim identifies some of the members of the two-thirds of the world who are given the blues:

> das wieder vereinigte deutschland
> feiert sich wieder 1990
> ohne immigrantInnen flüchtlinge jüdische
>   und schwarze menschen
> es feiert im intimen kreis
> es feiert in weiß
> doch es ist ein blues in schwarz-weiß
> es ist ein blues[29]

The exact nature of this exclusion and its mechanisms Ayim interprets as:

> 1/3 der welt vereinigt sich
> gegen die anderen 2/3
> im rhythmus von rassismus sexismus and antisemitismus
> wollen sie uns isolieren unsere geschichte ausradieren
> oder bis zur unkenntlichkeit
> mystifizieren
> es ist ein blues in schwarz-weiß
> es ist ein blues[30]

From these excerpts it is clear why May Ayim is celebrated as the poetic voice of the Afro-Germans. Besides being one of the early organizers of the movement she contributed the historical essays that provided a context for the oral histories in *Farbe bekennen*, but it was as a creative writer that she was able to give voice to the key issues of the Afro-German movement. Her lyrics are original and demonstrate a comfort with the modern literary tradition that encompasses the engagement of Brecht or Enzensberger. She also draws, especially in this poem, on the African American tradition as embodied by Langston Hughes, another poet who used the Black idiom of lament, the blues, to speak out on the contemporary condition.

Beyond the realm of the lyric, the appearance of prose forms has gone hand in hand with Afro-Germans' attempts to define themselves both synchronically and diachronically. Exploration of their history has also brought a degree of complexity and richness to their cultural identity, which is quite familiar to individuals living in multicultural societies such as the U.S. The 2000 federal census with its attempt to define what is an American by allowing respondents to select from a list of various ethnic heritages has its correspondence in the efforts to define who is an Afro-German. Research into Germany's colonial history makes this question even more cogent.

Who is an Afro-German? Do the offspring of German colonizers in Namibia, Togo, Cameroon, or Tanzania have the same status as the children of the African students and workers who came to Germany after 1884 and in greater numbers after 1945? What about the children born after 1945 whose fathers were African American soldiers? It is not my intent to suggest a specific ranking or hierarchy; instead, I merely want to point out of the complexity of Black German identity as exemplified in the story of the young Black German woman whose father was a native of Liberia but the descendant of repatriated African-Americans.

As Afro-Germans have repeated themselves, the only commonalties in their experience have been race and gender. The men have been reluctant to discuss gender issues, which has caused some tension in the movement. In general, we can conclude that the process of Afro-Germans' socialization has been affected by these factors, though the great variety makes it misleading to generalize about their backgrounds. The complexity of their situation is represented in three autobiographical texts have appeared since 1986: May Opitz/Ayim's "Aufbruch" (Departure), Ika Hügel-Marshall's *Daheim unterwegs. Ein deutsches Leben* (translated as *Invisible Woman: Growing Up Black in Germany*, 1998), and Hans J. Massaquoi's *Destined to Witness* (1999).

May Ayim's text appeared, of course, in *Farbe bekennen* and differs stylistically from the other personal narratives.

Several of the texts in *Farbe bekennen* interweave lyrical and narrative passages to achieve a specific effect. May Ayim's text is an attempt to transform prose into poetry, as is apparent in the opening sentence: "An dem Tag, als ich geboren wurde, kamen viele Geschichten meines Lebens zur Welt" (The day I was born, many stories of my life came into the world).[31] While recognizing the legitimacy of the various narratives, of the various truths about her, the narrator states she is telling *her* story as she experienced it without any apologies for the preponderance of negative experiences.

Unlike the traditional structure of the other texts that employ first-person narration, Ayim's text intersperses third-person narration into the deconstruction of a childhood that consisted of institutionalization, adoption, psychosomatic illness, fear, and unpleasant reminders of her otherness. The impact of the hostility and everyday racism on her consciousness is artistically recreated in the use of the third person "kind" to suggest a powerless and victimized subject:

> Kindheit ist, wenn kind sich viele Gedanken macht, und die
> Wörter, die kind spricht, nicht verstanden werden. Kindheit
> ist, wenn kind ins Bett macht und die Eltern das Resultat mit
> Schlägen kommentieren. Kindisch ist, wenn kind alles falsch
> macht, ungezogen ist, nichts kapiert, zu lahm ist und immer
> wieder die gleichen Fehler macht.
>
> Kindheit ist, wenn kind immer wieder ins Bett macht und
> keiner versteht, daß kind das nicht tut, um seine Eltern
> zu bestrafen. Kindheit ist, mit der Angst vor Schlägen zu
> leben und damit nicht fertig zu werden. Kindheit ist, jede
> Bronchitis zu bekommen und immer wieder zur Kur
> geschickt zu werden[32]

The repetition of the phrase "Kindheit ist" and the relative simplicity of the sentence structure contrast markedly with the content—the pathology of growing up different in a society that does not tolerate difference.

Ayim confides in the reader that her childhood drove her not only to rebel but also to entertain thoughts about suicide or at least the desire not to exist. Lacking in the narrative is a description of how she came to balance this negativity with fantasies of escape, especially to Africa where everyone would resemble her, and her German parents and siblings, when they came to visit, would be the outsiders. Then she could make them understand what her life was like in Germany.[33] Interestingly enough, this dream of being Black, as Ayim terms it, was destroyed by meeting her father who was darker than she. To her naïve question as to whether all people in Africa were so dark, her father replied affirmatively. This obviously false revelation destroyed her dream because she was still different.

To come to herself, as it were, she had to leave her milieu and reflect on what she had experienced. Exactly what led to her breakthrough is not explicitly stated but suggested in the statement: *"Der Umstand, nicht untertauchen zu können, hat mich zur aktiven Auseinandersetzung gezwungen, die ich nicht mehr als Belastung, sondern as besondere Herausforderung zur Ehrlichkeit empfinde."*[34] May Ayim's personal narrative presents a triumphant subject that has overcome adversity to evolve towards emancipation or, as she formulates it: "Ich habe mich auf den Weg begeben" (I began my journey).[35]

Ika Hügel-Marshall's text has one advantage over May Ayim's: it is a book-length publication and allows the author to reflect more extensively on her life. Superficially, Hügel-Marshall had experiences similar to those of Ayim. Both were institutionalized and were "problem" children. One significant difference was the nationality of their fathers. Ayim's father was from Ghana but Hügel-Marshall's father was an American G.I. Both men were prevented by law and circumstance from living with their daughters. Fraternization was strictly forbidden by the U.S. occupation forces and after returning to the U.S. the likelihood of a Black soldier bringing home a foreign bride was not always an option.

Like Ayim, Hügel-Marshall describes how she overcame isolation and adversity to achieve a positive self-image and assume a role in the struggle against sexism and racism. The link to Ayim is more than just a similarity in their life experiences. The title of Hügel-Marshall's text, *Daheim unterwegs* (At home in transit), derives from Ayim's poem *"entfernte Verbindungen"* (distant connections), which was also the title of the anthology for which Hügel-Marshall was both a contributor and coeditor along with Ayim and four other women. Publisher of that anthology and most of the Afro-German texts, including Ayim's and Hügel-Marshall's autobiographies, is Berlin's Orlanda Frauenverlag, where Hügel-Marshall has worked since 1990. It is no exaggeration to state that women and women's issues form an important part of Hügel-Marshall's identity. Her national identity is as complex as that of other Black Germans with many of whom she shares the following sentiment:

> Germany is my home even though up to today I have not learned to love the country. For me there is no other country, no other home, no language

which could bring my father closer. But hearing the word "father" which is
spoken so often and in so many places, every time I feel the same deep pain.
I want to know who I am. [36]

The figure of the father looms large in Afro-German literary texts. The
father is not only the source of the racialized identity, he is also the missing
ingredient in the Afro-German identity, the familial love and acceptance
that were frequently absent in childhood. For Hügel-Marshall the search
for her father was synonymous with the search for her own identity, an
identity that was evolving and being refined by new experiences.

Gender is the other important factor in Hügel-Marshall's narrative.
Her account of her mother and grandmother reflects extraordinarily mature
and compassionate insights into the motives of the two most important figures of her childhood. Her grandmother acted instinctively to protect her
from the barbs and taunts of a racist environment and thus earned her
undying love and respect. The mother is a much more complex character.
Not as heroic as the grandmother, she is helpless to prevent the institutionalization of her daughter. Despite her mother's weakness, the narrator indicates her understanding that her own victimization is also her mother's or,
as she concludes: "In my heart I feel the love and unarticulated fear of my
mother; in close contact with discrimination she, who is white, has to, in her
own way, integrate the hate and racism of whites in her life and survival." [37]

The relationship to her white half-sister is equally complex. As adolescents, a pivotal event in their relationship occurred in a disco. Accompanying
her sister, the narrator is shocked by her sister's denial of their sisterhood
when one of the sister's acquaintances inquires as to the identity of the
narrator. Nevertheless, the narrator cannot bring herself to hate her sister.
Instead, she seeks the sister's help to write a letter to the absent father in
the U.S. The letter is returned as undeliverable, but the narrator's life takes
a positive turn when she finds work in a group home and begins her studies at Frankfurt's Fachhochschule.

Her experiences in the group home and her success in breaking the
cycle of victimization and dehumanization present in that environment
are an important step towards coming to grips with and overcoming her
own victimization. Even a failed marriage to a white German proves to be
another important step in her self-actualization. She summarizes her experience and her insight:

> Whites don't have to deal with racism. Whites don't have to question their
> values. Quite the contrary, for them questioning means questioning their

privileges—and who is willing to do that? Who can afford to do that? It is therefore not so much the recognition that all whites are racist but more how whites deal with this fact.[38]

With these axiomatic insights the narrator examines her own reactions to the racism she had experienced, and decides to externalize her anger, and, in effect, work to change her environment. With her new attitude towards her racist milieu the narrator assumed a critical position vis-à-vis the women's movement. She organized a "WG" (communal household) with some white friends and got involved in the turbulent political life of Frankfurt in the 1970s and 1980s. Her entry into feminist circles helped her to perceive inherent differences tied to race. Those differences become apparent in the description of how the "WG" was furnished. The other women brought their furniture as well as much of the kitchen equipment. By contrast, the narrator gathered her furnishings from the "Sperrmüll" (trash left roadside for collection) on Frankfurt's streets and refurbished it.

That simple act underscored the class differences between white and black feminists. The middle-class, white women brought a portion of their privileged lives into the new setting. Also in the midst of the political activities—participation in the weekly demonstrations, organization of a Frauenhaus, a feminist library, a Frauenkneipe, a motorcade protesting the ban on abortion, etc.—the narrator remarks that the feminists were fighting individually and as a group for equality and against oppression but not against racism.[39]

The reason for this omission is apparently a difference in class interests. To the narrator it is clear that the white feminists were not interested in the history of Black women. This disinterest for her is synonymous with racism. When she challenged her friends on the issue their response only affirmed her insight. They claimed to be different from other women. They were, after all, feminists and had no antipathies for Black people. They recommended "Laß doch mal deine Hautfarbe aus dem Spiel, wenn du uns etwas sagen willst" (Don't always bring up your skin color if you want to say something to us).[40] They were thus unwilling to examine their own prejudices and automatically assumed that because they were struggling against the patriarchy that they were not racists. Racism and sexism are linked but not identical.

The narrator's response is telling. She stated she felt robbed of her face and denied the right to feel the way she did. Her friends further criticized her for being too subjective, too sensitive. According to the white feminists the narrator used her race to control and manipulate.[41] Rebuffed, the narrator withdrew and became introspective. Self-hatred as well as frustration grew in her but enrollment into a Tai kwan-do course introduced her to a woman (Sunny) who was more solicitous of her feelings and even drew her attention to the Afro-Germans.

Initially reluctant to meet others with life experiences similar to hers the narrator eventually established contact and was surprised at the warm welcome she received. The result is a transformation that even her white friends noticed. By joining the Afro-German movement the narrator not only overcame her social isolation but also her self-hatred and the negative stereotypes imposed on her by her environment. This transformation was also facilitated by her study of Black literature and history, which in turn reawakened her interest in finding her father.

A move to Berlin opened new perspectives for Hügel-Marshall. There she not only joined Orlanda Frauenverlag but her relationship to Dagmar Schultz, the publisher of Orlanda, brought her into contact with American feminists and especially Audre Lorde. Although the narrative does not dwell at length on specifics, it is abundantly clear that Lorde had a profound impact on her. After 1990 whenever Lorde visited Berlin she lived with Hügel-Marshall and Dagmar Schultz. The narrative mentions extensive discussions between Hügel-Marshall and Audre Lorde on racism and feminism. Hügel-Marshall's decision to write her personal narrative resulted from the years in Berlin and her interaction with Lorde and other Black feminists.

Afro-German literature is not yet two decades old, and it has a small but growing corpus of texts, many of them personal narratives. One of the most recent, titled "*Erste Begegnung mit dem Vater*" (First encounters with father) appeared on *Afronetz* in 2000. Most of the texts have been written by women and, using the criteria set forth by Barbara Kosta, the narrator is not merely content to recreate her victimization. Instead, she relates how a new level of consciousness evolved and empowered her to cope with and overcome her vicitimization. In a very real sense the Afro-German autobiographies are a reconceptualized *Bildungsroman* in which the narrator, instead of being reintegrated into the world and achieving harmony, gains insight into the processes that oppress her and takes action to effect change. The empowerment for this self-realization is gained through the integration of the individuals into the group (an as-yet-unrealized goal in the real world). The racialized self overcomes its isolation to join the collective, the diasporic community of people of color.

This transformation is not always unproblematical, as demonstrated by May Ayim's initial dismay when confronted with the Blackness of her father. Idealization of the diasporic community is a cul-de-sac that can only impede full integration. Hügel-Marshall's account is for the moment the best example of a personal narrative in which the evolution of a diasporic consciousness is presented succinctly and effectively. It is an organic process that evolves from experience. Just as in the classical *Bildungsroman*, the author's development through experience and introspection is both logical and compelling. Her evolution into a woman of color who can critically analyze her situation and take appropriate actions makes her narrative at least as attractive as Frederick Douglass's account of his rise from slavery.[42] Unfortunately, the German reading public seems to have taken little notice of Douglass's interesting work.

Let me close with a few brief remarks about the only Afro-German personal narrative composed by a man. Hans J. Massaquoi's *Destined to Witness* (or its more revealing German title *Neger, Neger, Schornsteinfeger*) is a literary phenomenon that can only be compared to Harriet Beecher Stowe's *Uncle Tom's Cabin* in terms of its reception by the German reading public.[43] It also offers a telling contrast with Frederick Douglass's autobiography. A comparison of the reception of these two nineteenth-century texts with Massaquoi's on both sides of the Atlantic creates an interesting perspective on the reception of Afro-German literature, and especially Ika Hügel-Marshall's autobiography.

Within a year after Stowe's semi-fictional account of Josiah Henson's life appeared in 1852, five publishing houses in Leipzig and Vienna issued their own versions of the novel. J.J. Weber Verlag's translation ran through three editions in 1853 alone. Almost contemporaneous with *Uncle Tom's Cabin* was Douglass's autobiography, published in German translation in 1860 by Hamburg's Hoffmann und Campe Verlag. While Stowe's novel reached an unusually large audience in the German-speaking world, Douglass's autobiography went through only one edition and was apparently ignored by most critics except for one review that appeared in the relatively obscure "*Illustriertes Familienbuch zur Unterhaltung und Belehrung häuslicher Kreise*" in Triest.[44] A second edition was not published in Germany until 1965 when, characterisitically, an edition appeared in the GDR.

The discrepancy in the German reading public's reaction to Uncle Tom and to Frederick Douglass may be a matter of chronology. By the time Douglass's story appeared it is possible that interest in that topic had been exhausted. More likely, the difference is rooted in the nature of both narratives. The image of the African that predominates in Stowe's text is the subservient victim, the improvident object who requires the help of others to deal with life's problems. Douglass, on the other hand, presents the account of his self-emancipation and self-determination. Douglass not only freed himself from bondage but also became a most compelling leader in the struggle that ultimately ended that bondage.

Nineteenth-century German readers' predilection for Uncle Tom suggests that it was the docile African that corresponded best with their own preconceived notions of Africa and the African character. Hegel had after all proclaimed Africa as a continent without history, that is, without culture. The certainty of the African's inferiority to the European was a useful starting point for the aspirations for colonial empire, which some Germans considered important to their national destiny in the nineteenth century. Perceived intrinsic inferiority of the African was, of course, a keystone of the scientific and pseudo-scientific discourse on race that extended from the early writings of Germany's Johann Friedrich Blumenbach to the racist diatribes of France's Gobineau or England's transplanted Germanophile Houston Stewart Chamberlain.

Like Stowe's classic, Massaquoi's autobiography has taken the German reading public by storm. Since its appearance in the early Fall of 1999 up to late 2000, *Neger, Neger, Schornsteinfeger* has remained in the top five of the German bestseller list as reported by *Der Spiegel*. It was serialized in the author's hometown of Hamburg by the daily newspaper and, reportedly, a feature film is planned. A difficult question is why the difference in the reception of these two Afro-German authors, Ika Hügel-Marshall and Massaquoi?

One answer may be historical perspective. Ika Hügel-Marshall, although a most exceptional woman, is nevertheless typical of the majority of Afro-Germans born after 1945: she lived in isolation, suffered from the overt racism of her working-class environment, and languished during childhood in institutions into which her mother had been forced to place her because a father was not present. During her formative years her environment and not she herself made important decisions such as career opportunities. Hügel-Marshall's life story is her struggle to define herself both as a person and a woman. Massaquoi, on the other hand, can boast of connections to important players and events in recent German history. His grandfather was a Vai chieftain from Liberia who first served as a language informant for Hamburg's Kolonialinstitut and then as consul to Weimar Germany. Massaquoi's father's family belonged to the circle of powerful families that controlled Liberia during most of its history. As such he has a touch of royalty about him that lends his alterity an aura of exoticism.

Just as the German elite of the eighteenth century willingly stood as godparents for the offspring of their court Moors, so too is the German reader apparently drawn to the account of the Afro-German boy who survived, as they did, World War II at the side of his working-class white German mother. The hint of romantic fantasy comingles with a certain satisfaction at Massaquoi's admission that he, too, was initially mesmerized by Hitler. Unlike the *Besatzungskinder* (occupation children) Massaquoi returned first to the country of his father, then to the United States, where he continues to live as an American citizen of Afro-German descent.

Although he does not explicitly state it in his account, it seems clear that Massaquoi's perspective is radically different from that of the majority of Afro-Germans. Born a German, he nevertheless did not write his autobiography in German. It was translated by his German publisher. He apparently did not choose the German title, which places the whole narrative in a slightly different light. The English title emphasizes the author's experiences during a very tumultuous time in world history. The German title, on the other hand, uses a children's rhyme to focus attention on how the author differed from the society in which he was born.

Massaquoi does not explicitly describe the sense of belonging to a diasporic community, in part because he has no need to. For many Afro-Germans the idea of a diaspora appears to be surrogate for the missing father, the sense of community that was denied them in their youth. Although Massaquoi grew up without his father, he knew where he was, and when circumstances permitted, he joined him. That decision was, however, just another phase in his maturation process. Realizing that living in Liberia was a cul-de-sac for him, Massaquoi decided to join relatives in America, which was just another step in his efforts to improve his life situation. Ironically, the diasporic community where he finally gets a start in life is peopled by his white relatives. The later success and status, which he achieved in America, justified that move.

This last fact is important because to the German reader Massaquoi is really an American and not an annoying reminder of the deeply ingrained racism in their society. Ika Hügel-Marshall represents by contrast the German past, present, and future, which has yet to be "overcome." She represents in fact a dual challenge for German society: not just a woman but also a woman of color. In the nineteenth century Frederick Douglass and the women of Seneca Falls ultimately parted company because of their disagreement over the prioritization of women's rights and the rights of Africans. Afro-Germans seem to be equally split on this issue, as some discussions in the last few issues of *afro look* seem to indicate. Unfortunately, until an Afro-German male writes his autobiography it will remain a matter of speculation as to the difference that gender as well as race plays in the emerging Afro-German literature. One thing is certain: the discussion of gender will also have to include sexuality, a topic that is a difficult one for Afro-German as well as African-American men.

Notes

1. Barbara Kosta, *Recasting Autobiography: Women's Counterficitions in Contemporary German Literature and Film* (Ithaca: Cornell University Press, 1994), 1.

2. Ibid., 3.

3. Ibid.

4. Ibid., 4.

5. Ibid., 5.

6. Ibid., 6.

7. May Opitz and Dagmar Schultz (eds.), *Farbe bekennen* (Berlin: Orlanda Frauenverlag, 1986), translated by Anne V. Adams under the title *Showing Our Colors: Afro-German Women Speak Out* (Amherst: University of Massachusetts Press, 1992).

8. W. E. B. DuBois, *Souls of Black Folk*, ed. Donald B.Gibson (New York: Penguin, 1989), 5.

9. William Whipper (1804?–1876), noted African-American abolitionist, philanthropist, and intellectual.

10. Both ISD brochures provided the author by Eleonore Wiedenroth of the Frankfurt/Main ISD.

11. The title creates an oxymoron, i.e., Uncle Tom, the ultimate symbol of acquiescence, and the fist, the symbol of resistance to oppression. It is perhaps an intentional reference to the upraised fists popularized by the Black nationalist movement of the 1960s and the protest exhibited in 1968 at the Olympic games by African-American athletes who responded to the playing of the American national anthem with a gloved fist salute.

12. Initiative Schwarze Deutsche (ISD), *Macht der Nacht, eine schwarze deutsche anthologie* (Munich, 1991–2).

13. Ute Annecke et al. (eds.), "Geteilter Feminismus. Rassismus. Antisemitismus. Fremdenhaß," in the series *beiträge zur feministischen theorie und praxis* 13 (1990): 27 (2nd edition Cologne: 1991); May Ayim and Nivedita Prasad (eds.), *Dokumentation Wege zu Bündnissen. Dokumentation der Tagung von/für ethnische und afro-deutsche Minderheiten*, Bremen, 8.–10. Juni 1990; *zweiter bundesweiter Kongreß von und für Immigrantinnen, Schwarze deutsche, jüdische und im Exil lebende Frauen*, Berlin 3.–6. Oktober 1991 (Berlin: ASTA Druckerei der FU Berlin, 1992); Ika Hügel et al. (eds.), *Entfernte Verbindungen* (Berlin: Orlanda Frauenverlag, 1993).

14. "It's Afro Time/ Handshaking here, kiss there/ Consciousness on our shoulders/ But don't show too much,/ Don't show your vulnerability, your wound.

"Consciousness presses on our shoulders/ I know you would like to scream, rip open the window/ and scream—/ But don't show your vulnerability." Hügel et al., *Entfernte Verbindungen*, 11.

These and following translations are mine and are an attempt to reflect the spirit of the text. No attempt has been made to correct obvious orthographical errors in the original texts, such as the obvious "daß" for "das" Fenster.

15. "Loneliness/ Together but still alone/ Lonely you wander through the streets/ of this cold city!/ You long for—recognition/ Will anyone be able to give it to you?/ Will 'they' be able to give you this?/ No, your soul screams, it screams for something/ It screams for recognition/ Which 'they' will never give you." Ibid., 9.

16. "White, Black—or are they only colors/ I go through the streets/ Upright but yet bowed/ Proud but yet insecure/ Unconcerned but yet affected." Ibid., 8.

17. "It's Nation Time!/ Chicago Angola Tamil Eelam/ Fine threads of gold and blood/ But now/ Now is time/ Too long we have waited/ We are everywhere/ Look around/ In the Metro in Paris in Marseille in Lille/ Dark lips twisted rings/ A wry look/ The same understanding in the supermarket in/ Leicester Liverpool Notting Hall/ Kinky hair with glittering gel/ Slow smile and hands slapping/ There we are we are here/ What's the time/ Rumba in Dresden/ In the Ruhrpott spicy sauces are being mixed/ Black voices in Berlin and Cologne/ . . . . . And clenched fists/ how late is it/ it is late/ what's the time/ now/ beat the drum/ dance/ dance the nation dance/ it's NATION TIME!/ Many are we/ And now/ Now is time/ Now the time has/ Come." Ibid., 18.

18. Olumide Popoola, Beldan Sezen (eds.), *Talking Home* (Amsterdam: blue moon press, 1999).

19. Ibid., 1.

20. "Queer bedeutet für uns der Versuch, sich nicht den Zwängen der vorgeschrieben Rollenmodelle zu beugen. Sei es nun im heterosexuellen oder im homosexuellen Leben. Wer letztendlich was als queer verstand blieb jeder selbst überlassen, denn wir wollten einen breiten Raum bieten. Manche mögen den Begriff 'Lesbe' nicht, andere sehen sich nicht in 'dyke' etc., manche sind 'bi' und wieder andere wollen sich schlichtweg nicht definieren.
"Auch die Wahl der Sprache war jeder freigestellt. Im Gegenteil, unterschiedliche Sprachen und Sprachstile waren uns willkommen, denn sie sind Ausdruck unserer Lebensrealität. Viele von uns bewegen sich in mehreren Sprachen." Ibid.

21. May Ayim, *blues in schwarz weiss* (Berlin: Orlanda Frauenverlag, 1995).

22. The titles of the cycles are: "in the beginning was the word," "time change," "the time afterwards," "out of context," "blues in black and white," "touching," "heavenly," "postscript," and "epilogue."

23. Ayim, *blues in schwarz weiss*, 25.

24. Ibid.

25. "I think/ that the Blacks have retained a natural/ perspective on life. On the other hand everything/ here is quite broken/ I think I would be happy if I were you./ One really cannot be proud of the/ German history, and besides you are/ not that Black." Ibid.

26. "[. . .] conserved/ conserved and sold, brother/ post cards and posters/ terzetts in a history book/ >I have a dream</ a completed novel/ they have made past out of it/ white like salty tears/ and there where I live/ they would call it 'overcome', brother)." Ibid., 54.

27. "I carry my dream/ behind/ a raised fist/ in pepper colors/ and begin quite small/ finally begin/ with my sister/ and my friend by the hand, with/ my brothers and if/ necessary/ also alone—so that things must finally change." Ibid.

28. "it is a blues in black-white/ 1/3 of the world dances the other 2/3 to pieces/ they celebrate in white/ we mourn in black/ it is a blues in black-white/ it is a blues." Ibid., 82.

29. "the reunited Germany/ celebrates itself 1990 again/ without immigrants refugees jewish/ and Black people/ it celebrates in an intimate circle/ it celebrates in white/ but it is a blues in black-white/ it is a blues." Ibid.

30. "1/3 of the world unites itself/ against the other 2/3/ in the rhythm of racism/ sexism and anti-semitism/ they want to isolate us erase our history/ or mystify it to the point of indecipherability/ it is a blues in black-white/ it is a blues." Ibid.

31. In Opitz and Schultz (eds.), *Farbe bekennen*, 202.

32. "Childhood is when child thinks a lot and the words/ that child speaks are not understood. Childhood is/ when child wets to bed and the parents comment on the/ result with blows. Childish is when child does everything/ wrong, is discourteous, understands nothing, is too slow and makes the mistakes again and again./ Childhood is child wets to bed again and again and no one/ understands that child doesn't do that to punish his parents./ Childhood is living in fear of blows and not coping with it./ Childhood is catching every form of bronchitis and being/ sent to the spa again and again." Ibid., 203.

33. Ibid., 205ff.

34. "The circumstance of not being able to submerge oneself forced me into the active struggle, which I no longer feel is a burden but a challenge to be honest." Ibid., 207.

35. Ibid.

36. "Deutschland ist meine Heimat, auch wenn ich das Land bis zum heutigen Tag nicht liebengelernt habe. Für mich gibt es aber kein anderes, keine andere Heimat, keine Sprache, die mich meinem Vater näher bringen könnte. Doch bei dem Wort Vater, das so oft und an vielen Orten ausgesprochen wird, verspürte ich jedesmal den gleichen tiefsitzenden Schmerz. Ich will wissen, wer ich bin." Ika Hügel-Marshall *Daheim unterwegs. Ein deutsches Leben* (Berlin: Orlanda Frauenverlag, 1998), 11.

37. "Im Herzen fühle ich die Liebe und unausgesprochene Angst meiner Mutter, in engem Kontakt mit Diskriminierung, sie, die weiß ist, muß auf ihre Weise den Haß und Rassismus von Weißen in ihr Leben und Überleben integrieren." Ibid., 43.

38. "Weiße müssen sich nicht mit Rassismus auseinandersetzen. Weiße müssen nicht ihre Werte in Frage stellen. Ganz im Gegenteil, denn für sie bedeutet In-Frage-Stellen, ihre Privilegien in Frage zu stellen—und wer ist freiwillig dazu bereit? Wer will sich das leisten? Es ist also weniger die Erkenntnis, daß alle Weißen rassistisch sind, als vielmehr, wie Weiße mit dieser Erkenntnis umgehen." Ibid., 78.

39. Ibid., 82.

40. Ibid., 83.

41. Ibid., 84.

42. *Narrative of the Life of Frederick Douglass, an American Slave*, 1845.

43. Hans J. Massaquoi, *Destined to Witness: Growing up Black in Nazi Germany* (New York: William Morrow and Co., 1999).

44. For more details on Douglass's reception in Germany see my article " 'Fred' vs 'Uncle Tom': Frederick Douglass and the Image of the African American in 19th Century Germany," in *etudes germano-africaines* 9 (1991): 67–78.

8

THE SOULS OF BLACK *VOLK*

CONTRADICTION? OXYMORON?

Anne Adams

"The term Afro-German is still new in West Germany. It came to life when a few women of African-German descent met in 1984 with the Afro-American writer Audre Lorde and decided to define themselves instead of constantly being defined by others."[1] These opening statements by May Ayim (née Opitz) at the 1994 PANAFEST arts festival in Ghana would introduce to a welcoming Pan-African audience the "new kids on the block" of the African diaspora: Afro-Germans. The coincidence—maybe—of place, time, and identity, of Ayim's talk is useful for contextualizing Afro-German consciousness within a framework of the African diaspora. Indeed, this would be the last invited talk on the subject of Afro-German identity that activist/writer Ayim would give; the inspiring spokeswoman for Afro-German consciousness would take her own life the following year, at the age of thirty-six. The place, Ghana, is the adopted homeland and final resting place of W. E. B. DuBois, the "Father of Pan-Africanism"; the time, 1994, is one hundred years after DuBois's student sojourn in Ayim's native country and final resting place, Germany. The fact that the stimulating, international city of Berlin was the place where both DuBois and Ayim sojourned and came into political maturity may not be a coincidence. For DuBois the attraction was the distinguished faculty of the Friedrich Wilhelm University of Berlin (now the Humboldt University); for Ayim, it was the cosmopolitan character of the city, which tolerated racial, ethnic, and cultural diversity more than other places in her country. But what is an intriguing coincidence is the fact of DuBois's residence in 1892–94 in the Oranienburg Strasse in the district of Kreuzberg, a few doors away on the same street as the current offices of the *Initiative Schwarze Deutsche* (Initiative of Black Germans), or ISD, of which Ayim was a co-founder in 1984. Like Ayim a century later, DuBois was a precursor of African diaspora individuals whose intellectual and human-rights careers would bring them to Germany, in general, and Berlin, in particular.[2] Since any legitimate consideration of the relationship of people of the African world to the European world must ultimately refer to the work of W. E .B. DuBois, these coincidences—maybe—between Ayim and DuBois enhance our discussion of Afro-Germans.

> The problem of the twentieth century is the problem of the color line [the relation of the darker to the lighter races of men]. . . . The modern world must needs remember that in this age . . . the millions of Black men in Africa, America, and the Islands of the Sea, not to speak of the brown and yellow myriads elsewhere, are bound to have great influence upon the world in the future, by reason of sheer numbers and physical contact. . . . If, by reason of carelessness, prejudice, greed and injustice, the Black world is to be exploited and ravished and degraded, the results must be deplorable, if not fatal, not simply to them, but to the high ideals of justice, freedom, and culture which a thousand years of Christian civilization have held before Europe.[3]

When DuBois published this prescient admonition in his seminal work *The Souls of Black Folk* in 1903, his two-year sojourn as a student in Germany was already a decade behind him. But DuBois's identification of the color-line as the *twentieth* century's most virulent social ill resonates today in Germany as loudly as it did in the U.S. at the dawn of the last century. In fact, Germany seems to be an instance where the "problem of the color line" takes on new meaning, here, at the dawn of the twenty-first.

DuBois would remember his Berlin years (1892–94) as one of the most pleasant and stimulating periods of his young life. He reveled in the European education, culture, and company to which he was exposed. His emulation of the Kaiser's image is by now well known. Excelling as a scholar, he worked on his dissertation under the tutelage of some of the University of Berlin's most respected professors, barely missing attaining his doctorate there because of technicalities regarding residence requirements.[4] Intellectually, he felt a strong affinity with contemporary German philosophy, including that of G. F. W. Hegel. Nevertheless, DuBois's philosophical sympathies were not devoid of sobering contemplations of race and culture issues. DuBois's biographer David Levering Lewis remarks on the ambivalence: "There were numerous instances in which European culture and racial identity grappled with each other—instances in which he became acutely aware at some level of a conflict between culture and destiny. . . . 'how far can love for my oppressed race accord with love for the oppressing country?' "[5]

But DuBois was, after all, a foreigner, an *Ausländer*, who clearly enjoyed the positively perceived special attention he received as an exotic novelty. Ayim, phenotypically quite similar to DuBois, and also a scholar, was, a hundred years later, in fact a German who would struggle daily against being perceived and treated as an exotic foreigner sojourning for a finite period, but in fact belonging to the "oppressed race" and native to the "oppressing country."

Lewis suggests that DuBois's Germany "had been *a culture in search of a nation.*"[6] In that light we might suggest that the Germany of today—bearing out DuBois's color-line prophecy—is *a nation challenged to re/search its culture.* Within a century following DuBois's sojourn in Germany, the book *Farbe bekennen* was published, proving that Germans included numbers of the "darker races" of which DuBois had written in *The Souls of Black Folk.* Unlike other Western European nations, whose histories of conquest, slavery, colonialism, and postcolonialism have resulted in the (often grudging) acknowledgment of their "multiracial" populations, Germany has held on to different notions about race and nationality. For all of the permutations resulting from their national history, Germans generally continue to consider Germany racially and culturally as a relatively homogeneous society, signified by the racial, cultural, and political signifier *das deutsche Volk*, though allowing that many "foreigners," several generations in residence, also share German physical space as fellow citizens: Germans, but not German, as Ayim was once told. Consequently, the phenomenon of the "Black German" is inconceivable for anyone who subscribes to the notion of *das deutsche Volk* (like the resurgent neo-Nazis) because "Black" cannot be conceived of as an attribute of "German." And "Afro-German"—also a racial as well as socio-political signifier—would sound patently oxymoronic. Thus the phenomenon of the "Afro-German" as German Black folk (or Black *Volk?*), suggests a parallel identity for DuBois's notion of "two souls": "One ever feels his two-ness,—an American [substitute 'German'], a Negro." If we may assume, for the moment, that that two-ness, German and Black/African, a) is relevant for the Afro-German experience, and b) that that two-ness is the basis for identifying as part of an African diaspora—an idea presaged by DuBois's theory—then it is instructive to consider the ways in which the African diaspora manifests itself among Afro-Germans.

At this juncture a note on terminology, as used in this paper, and as used by Germans who identify in some way with a Black community, in speaking and writing of themselves, is appropriate. Ayim, as noted at the beginning of this chapter, attributes Afro-Germans' act of naming themselves to the specific influence of Audre Lorde. The ISD, formally registered as *Initiative Schwarze Deutsche und Schwarze in Deutschland* (Initiative of Black Germans and Blacks in Germany), uses the German adjective-noun phrase "*Schwarze Deutsche*," which translates to "Black Germans." In conversation among themselves, Blacks who live in Germany but are of no white parentage frequently use "Afro(s)" to refer specifically to those born of white German and Black (i.e., African or African-descended) parentage, as Ayim referred to herself and others. Many of Ayim's fellow Afro-Germans, however, also use the term "Black Germans" to refer to themselves, as evidenced by the ISD's name. In everyday spoken use, the three terms "*Afro-Deutsche*," "*Schwarze Deutsche*," and "*Schwarze*" are active, depending upon the specific situation. Ultimately, the nomenclature signifies a racial/social identity, that is, a Black identity in Germany and a Black diaspora identity in the world, an identity constructed from the fabric of their experience and self-affirming connections. Hence, the terminology used in the paper will reflect all those as well. The discussion that follows will demonstrate that, while Afro-Germans' references to themselves as a *Black German community* are explicit, their references to themselves as part of a *Black diaspora* are implicit. A discussion of "Black diaspora" concludes this chapter.

Construction and Function of Afro-German Community

The life-altering meetings alluded to in Ayim's 1994 Ghana talk among groups of women of African-German descent, the Afro-American writer Lorde, and her feminist-activist-writer partner Gloria Joseph took place on more than one occasion, in more than one German city. Lorde, who by then was frequenting Germany primarily for medical treatment, would make a point of seeking out and bringing together Black German women, listening to the women speak of their feelings of isolation, of "otherness," and non-belonging within their otherwise white families, communities, schools, etc. At one such meeting in 1987 in Frankfurt where I served as interpreter, Lorde replied to the Afro-German women by saying, You don't have to live your lives as marginalized, outcast Germans. There is a whole other half of you, your Black self, that can be embraced by the Black diaspora. So, rather than viewing yourselves merely as outcast, half-caste Germans, you can view yourselves as Afro-Germans. In effect, Lorde was "inviting" these Black Germans spiritually to assume their birthright membership and identity in the Black diaspora as a complement to their birthright German nationality.

But even as those women were being invited to participate in a larger Black diaspora, which included Afro-Caribbean-Americans Lorde and Joseph (and African American me)—even as the Afro-Germans were being embraced, in the mid-1980s, by a larger Black family—they were still only beginning to discover their connections to each other as Black Germans. This would become an encounter of acknowledgment of their common situation followed by tentative, apprehensive, movement toward "community." Up until this time they had lived as individuals, subscribing, like *all* Germans, to negative definitions of Black Germans, and, as an ironic consequence, avoiding interaction with others like themselves. Having no life-support systems from childhood, no native institutions as a base for "community," Afro-Germans had to consciously *construct their own*, starting at the age of self-conscious young adults. The wordsmith Lorde, in creating a name for those Black Germans, was assisting them in reinventing themselves. Such a *sui generis* creation of an identity and the community that would spring from it is unique in the Black diaspora, where otherwise the communities, now centuries old, originated from migrated *groups*—whether forced or voluntary—who carried with them some basic cultural material for identity and community, which would be adapted in the new environment. Adopting in the mid-1980s the term "Afro-German," modeled obviously on "Afro-American,"[7] which has not only racial but also ethnic, that is, cultural and social, political, and historical connotations, those Black Germans were simultaneously connecting themselves with the rest of the "Afro-" world, the African diaspora.

To review briefly some of the articulations by Afro-Germans themselves regarding their consciousness of their racial situation, Ayim wrote in 1994,[8] "Germany still does not perceive itself as a country of immigration, still Black and German are considered as an exotic combination. Anyone who doesn't look typically German—which means essentially the Aryan ideal—apparently doesn't belong."[9] Becoming conscious of their common situation, and coming together around their common issues, the Afro-Germans would come to adopt, into their German discourse, the diaspora-adapted English concept of "community" as well as the terms "*Schwestern und Brüder*" (sisters and brothers) to address each other, in some written contexts: "and even if the Black community in this country is small, it is there, active, and constantly growing."[10] And so, as Ayim started off her

Ghana address, *naming themselves* in the mid-1980s as a way of identifying and defining themselves, took on a spiritual as well as socio-political signification. By 1995 Ayim would write an entry for the encyclopedia *Ethnische Minderheiten in der Bundesrepublik Deutschland* (Ethnic Minorities in the Federal Republic of Germany): " 'Afro-German' " is a self-definition formulated in the early '80s by German women of African and Afro-American descent, as an approach to questions of their identity, and has since come into wide usage."[11] This formulation reiterates the statement published in the ISD's introductory brochure:

> Our definition is not restricted to skin color, but includes all minorities affected by racism. With terms such as "Black Germans" and "Afro-Germans" as expression of our "multi-cultural" background we are defining ourselves instead of being defined. To meet each other, to have exchange and to share was and is for many a new experience. What we have most in common is isolation, the feeling of being enclosed in primarily white social relations, without support of a Black community. Of course, we are also very diverse, through our socialization, our characters, our ages, our interests, through our experiences in family and occupation, as hetero- and homosexual women and men and in our relations to the non-European part of our heritage.[12]

But, of course, finding each other and naming themselves, while psychologically therapeutic, is only the first step. The Black Germans' approach to constructing community is articulated by Ayim and another cofounder of the ISD, John Amoateng-Kantara, in the following terms:

> *May*: We call ourselves "Initiative of Blacks in Berlin" and are Black Germans, aware of their isolation and who want to get out of it. As a child, growing up in a white foster family, I was the only Black person. At school and later at university in Bavaria I was also alone. Here in Berlin I began to meet other Blacks. . . . The idea of organizing ourselves gradually crystalized. We put notices in newspapers and used word-of-mouth publicity for our project. About thirty people came, between the ages of 14 and 28. Our group consists of Afro-Germans, in the majority, Afro-Britons, and even Afro-Russians.
>
> *John*: To me the impetus for many to join our group is an emotional one, namely to meet other Black Germans. Up to now most of us were living in isolation. We lacked a disciplined working and committed group to get us together.[13]
>
> *May*: Of course it's important for us to know more about African history, progressive Black movements and about the struggle in South Africa. Sure, we can point to the fact that there were great Black civilizations, that Blacks have achieved much and have contributed to progress, but that won't

change anything in the status quo. We don't yet have the power to make our wishes felt.[14]

The impetus to *construct institutions* as a realization of the impetus to come together as a "community," as we have seen in the above quotations from Ayim and Kantara, first took form, quite naturally, in the major cities of Berlin and Frankfurt, beginning in the mid-1980s. Gradually coming to life in other locations, notably Cologne, Munich, and Hamburg, and in varying forms, the result is an identifiable network of *institutions*—organizations, organs, projects, businesses, annual events—that both contribute to and draw their life from the increasingly visible *community* of Black Germans. While most are, obviously, locally focused, some of the regular, annual events, bring together Afro-Germans from all sectors of the country. Further, activism in the form of demonstrations and other public responses to escalating racial violence have mobilized Afro-Germans and coalition partners from around the nation. Two examples are, first, the successful pressure on companies manufacturing a popular form of chocolate candies to replace the name "*Negerkuss*" (Nigger Kiss) with "*Schokokuss*" (Chocolate Kiss), and second, the demonstrations and boycotts in the city of Aschaffenburg in the summer of 2001 following the police killing of a twenty-five-year-old Senegalese resident in her estranged husband's apartment.

In offering an overview of the representative institutions of the Black German community, it is critical to note the diversity within the self-acknowledged Black community itself. The obvious core group are the biracial Germans, of whom one parent is white German, most often the mother, and the other parent, most often the father, is continental African, African American, or African Caribbean, etc. While some of the biracial individuals have both parents in their lives, a far greater number have at best only the German parent. Numerous are those, like Ayim, who grew up with neither of their biological parents and were adopted or reared in foster homes by white German families. But in addition to biracial individuals, large numbers of Africans, sometimes refugees, sometimes students or workers, have immigrated into Germany, especially in the last couple of decades, in the era of awakening Black German consciousness. Particularly those Africans who came as children, including some refugees raised in German foster homes—therefore, virtually acculturated as Germans—also identify as Afro-Germans and make up a constituent part of that community. And so, when we look at an inventory of organizations and other institutions of the Black German community, we see a host of configurations. An overview of the eight most vigorous of these testifies to that complexity in the Afro-German "community."

The ISD was originally founded as the Initiative Schwarze Deutsche and later expanded to the Initiative Schwarze Deutsche und Schwarze in Deutschland. A registered umbrella group in existence since 1986, it operates in several major German cities, particularly collaborating in public political activism anywhere in the country and sponsoring intra-group social support. ADEFRA (the acronym for Afro-Deutsche Frauen [Afro-German women]) is a registered Afro-German women's group, founded simultaneously with the ISD, and also operating in several major cities; it provides a support-group sisterhood for Afro-German women, initiating woman-focused projects. In 1989 Black History Month was established in Berlin on the American model and provides public programs, including children's events, in the spheres of history, culture, arts and letters, political issues, and on Black Germans and African/diaspora more broadly.

*afro look: eine zeitschrift von schwarzen deutsche*n (Afro Look: A Magazine of Black Germans), later becoming *afro look: eine zeitschrift von schwarzen menschen in deutschland* (Afro Look: A Magazine of Blacks in Germany), was originally the quarterly publication of ISD and subsequently became independent. *afro look* contains articles and creative writing by and about the Black German community and relevant African/diaspora subjects, written mostly in German, but with individual contributions occasionally also in English and French. While the change of ownership reflects merely the vicissitudes of the young and fragile organization, the change in subtitle, occurring in 1994, clarified the implicit diasporic identification that had defined the ISD and its organ from their inception, as stated on the masthead page under the heading "*Wir über uns*" (Who we are): "We are Black Germans/Afro-Germans, who were born in the FRG [Federal Republic of Germany] or have spent a significant part of our lives here." A 1995 editorial reporting on the ISD's tenth national meeting mentions the change in label:

> In 1985 Black Germans from around the country met for the first time in Wiesbaden. One result of this first national meeting of Black people in Germany was the founding of the ISD—Initiative of Black Germans. . . . The concept of ISD was later expanded, after much discussion of our basic principles, as indicated in the magazine title.[15]

The African Courier is an English-language monthly newspaper containing articles of national political and social interest for Africans in Germany. The "Showing Our Colors" youth exchange program provides

Figure 8.1. ISD Bundestreffen 2003 (National annual meeting of initiative of Blacks in Germany).
Photo courtesy of Ibiajulu O. Amuro.

Figure 8.2. Sankofa-Bundestreffen 2001. (Sankofa is an annual meeting of Black families in Germany.) Photo courtesy of Yonis Ayeh.

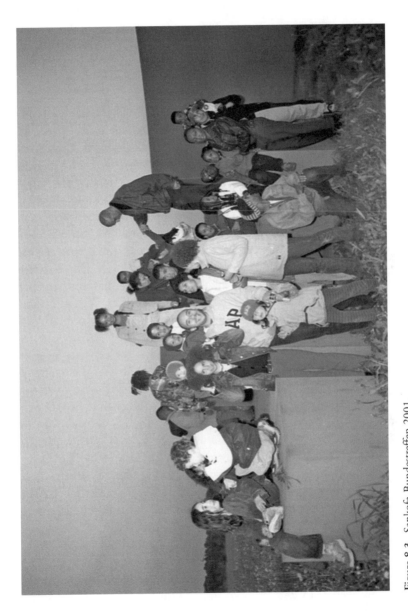

Figure 8.3. Sankofa-Bundestreffen 2001. Photo courtesy of Yonis Ayeh.

an opportunity for Black German youth to visit and interact with Black communities in the U.S. and vice versa, as a way of extending the borders of Black diaspora identity. The annual Bundestreffen (National Retreat) is an intra-group retreat for Afro-Germans to share with, strengthen, learn from, and support each other in their daily lives. The Sankofa Kinder-Bundestreffen (Sankofa Children's National Retreat), an intra-group retreat for parents and children, emphasizes identity-formation and other child-rearing issues for Blacks in Germany.

Beyond these institutional "products" for social, political, cultural, emotional collectivity, what are the forms of intellectual, creative, artistic, scholarly products that contribute to the further development of an Afro-German "community"? What forms of analysis, theorizing, criticism, aesthetic vision, and representation are there to further crystallize and voice the consciousness of community? In the vacuum of "traditions" beyond their German sources, in the virtual absence of a *community* history and culture, where shall inspiration and antecedents be sought for most Afro-Germans? For many, it is through a reconstructed connection with Africa, sometimes, though not always, informed by a journey there. For others, it is a borrowing or adaptation from other sources of the diaspora, notably the U.S. but also Britain as well as the Netherlands, or from a self-affirming consumption of cultural products from and about other parts of the Black world. Oprah Winfrey, whose talk-show is aired without German dubbing (one of the only U.S. TV shows not dubbed) and at the unlikely hour of one a.m., is an example of achievement for many Afro-German women. London's annual version of Caribbean Carnival attracts Afro-Germans for an occasional therapeutic immersion in Black life and energy. At home in Germany the celebration of Kwanzaa has been adopted from its African American origins. Afro-German programs and publications frequently use African figures, for instance, Ghanaian Adinkra proverbial figures, or terms such as "sankofa," for symbolic expression. Black Germans with school-level English skills are constantly looking for German translations of African/diaspora literary works. Afro-Germans who read English more fluently consume and cite writings by diaspora social and political activists, from Sojourner Truth and Frederick Douglass to Mumia Abu-Jamal. As the first literary expressions of their own diaspora identity, poetry—as exemplified in Ayim's two volumes,[16] and published in other volumes[17] as well as in *afro look*—introduces the timbre of Afro-German voices. Expanding these beginnings are autobiographical works, notably Ika Hügel-Marshall's *Daheim Unterwegs*, with the problematic English title of *Invisible Woman*,[18] and Hans-Jürgen Massaquoi's *Destined to*

Witness,[19] with the problematic German title of *Neger, Neger, Schornsteinfeger* (Nigger, Nigger, Chimneysweep), both of which are discussed by Leroy Hopkins in Chapter 7 of this volume.

For theoretical and scholarly writing, however, in the absence of mainstream recognition as legitimate subject matter, academic and other intellectual work about Afro-Germans in their own country has been largely self-initiated and self-executed on the margins of established centers of intellectual inquiry. Since Ayim's 1986 thesis at the University of Regensburg and its publication in *Farbe bekennen*, a few other academic studies, mostly masters theses, such as Katharina Oguntoye's in 1995,[20] and graduate seminar papers, along with one or two doctoral dissertations, such as Fatima El-Tayeb's in 2000,[21] have been produced. It is encouraging to know that the publisher where it all began, Orlanda Frauenverlag, now plans to publish a series of such academic studies expressly for the purpose of putting them into the wider academic arena to support formal research in the area. In addition other collections of theoretical, critical, and social-scientific essays, especially in collaboration with other German minority scholars, have recently appeared.[22]

Self-initiated productions by Afro-Germans in the film medium, reaching a wider public than the written word, have in a few instances found production backing in established institutions. Providing substance not only to Afro-German consciousness, such works articulate an Afro-German perspective for the mainstream audience. Of the narrative film production from the creative mind and perspective of Afro-Germans, Fatima El-Tayeb's and Angelina Maccarone's *Alles Wird Gut* (Everything Will Be Fine, 1997), the comically incisive first example, is discussed by Randall Halle in Chapter 6 of this volume. The title is a German rendering of the Swahili *"Hakuna Mutata,"* an articulation of against-the-odds confidence in the outcome of a seemingly hopeless situation, which is at some point in the film pronounced in its original form. Considering the Swahili phrase in its spontaneous English rendering, "No problem" (as, for instance, in the caricature of Jamaican attitude) invests the German title with an "Afro" discursive character not otherwise discernible in the German title (nor the title's English version).

But the genre of documentary film by Afro-Germans plays a different role in shared Black community-consciousness as well as informing the wider German public. With the authority to make choices and decisions about subjects, perspective, topics, supplemental sources, and other aspects of presentation of Afro-German documentary material, the documentary filmmakers are adding a critical dimension to Afro-German cultural production. Filmmaker John Kantara has directed two documentaries on Afro-Germans for the German public television station Zweites Deutsches Fernsehen (ZDF). His *Blues in Schwarz-Weiss* (Blues in Black and White), which borrows its title from an Ayim poem, documents the lives of two women and two men, growing up in East and in West Germany, of different generations, from survivors of the Third Reich to younger adults. Represented posthumously but as a leitmotif of the whole film is the life of Ayim, while the other three subjects are presented in their own contemporary contexts: septuagenarian Theodor Wonja Michael speaks about his youth in the Nazi era; Aminata Cissé Schleicher is shown in postwar and reunification-era Leipzig; and contemporary businessman Tyron Ricketts represents Black media aspirants with the commitment to shield them from exploitation. Kantara's *Und wir waren Deutsche* (And We Were Germans) features Hans-Jürgen Massaquoi, an Afro-German survivor of the Third Reich who eventually emigrated to the U.S., became a successful editor for *Ebony* magazine, and in retirement has written his autobiography *Destined to Witness*, mentioned above. Connecting the survival stories of both an Afro-German and a Jewish-German victim of Nazism, the film moves from Massaquoi's own reflections, after a comfortable life in the U.S., toward his reunion after fifty years in his hometown of Hamburg with his childhood Jewish friend Ralph Giordano. John Kantara has recently shot footage for a third Afro-German documentary, an interview with concentration camp survivor Gert Schramm.

Another Afro-German film, which takes to another level the violence of German life upon the soul of a Black German, is Bronwen Okpala's work *Dreckfresser* (Dirt Eater). Receiving high critical praise, this debut work, produced as the director's final project for certification from the Berlin Film Academy, was screened in art theaters as well as on television. *Dreckfresser* documents a dramatically classic case of the objectifying media-mutilation of an Afro-German "pretty face." Filmmaker Okpala brings distinctly Afro-German sensibilities to the tragic case of a handsome, virile, young Black policeman in Dresden, plucked and groomed as a model for a new advertising campaign—if not gimmick—of "The Saxon Man." The adulation distorts his self-identity, causing actions that ultimately bring all of the forces of the media and law enforcement powers down on his head, until he figuratively is feeding on dirt. Most recently, in response to escalating violent attacks on Black Germans, some resulting in death, Tyron Rickett's short film *Afro-Deutsch*, which was screened in art theaters, dramatizes the ever-present danger in the lives of Afro-Germans. That danger, which so frequently takes the form of gang attacks on a lone Black man, materialized in June 2000, when a longtime Angolan resident and family man, Alberto Adriano, was fatally beaten in Dessau by a gang of skinheads while walking home one evening. In an effort to raise consciousness and funds to fight racist violence, a group of prominent Afro-German hip-hop artists and singers, including Xavier Naidoo and Adé Odukoya, organized the project "Brothers Keepers" to produce the CD single and video "Adriano (Letzte Warnung)" (Adriano [Last Warning]), which is also discussed in the introduction to this volume.

The foregoing inventory of film projects presents merely a catalogue of media initiatives by Afro-Germans that have come to fruition in the past five years and are making their way into the public arena. They are given attention in this paper, however, because of the special gratification the creators derive from airing them for, and receiving feedback from, the Afro-German community. Some of the projects, for example, Okpala's *Dreckfresser*, Rickett's *Afro-Deutscsh*, and Kantara's in-progress documentary on Buchenwald survivor Gert Schramm, were shared first at Afro-German gatherings before their public screenings. The Brothers Keepers video "Adriano (Letzte Warnung)," for which Afro-Germans in Berlin had been recruited as extras for the crowd scene, was first screened before an Afro-German audience. This experience had the exhilarating effect of a family video but for a political and philanthropic purpose. Such moments of mutual affirmation effect a sense of shared ownership and representation for the collective Afro-German community.

Ayim, with an M.A. degree in sociology and training in speech pathology, possessed the insight and language—poetic as well as scientific— to analyze the social and psychological aspects of the Afro-German experience. In addition to her poetry, she published and left behind essays and other articles, which were posthumously published in a volume with the title *Grenzenlos and Unverschämt* (Brazen and Borderless) in 1997. In an essay, "White Stress and Black Nerves," Ayim noted that the "Black community" is by no means homogeneous and that the politically motivated desire for unity is often frustrated because of the community's diversity (in such factors as education level, economic status, professional status, political consciousness level, and the nature of the individual's family background, and, infrequently, the specifics of status as Black Germans, for instance, bi-racial native German or African-born immigrant, etc.).[23] Since the time of Ayim's writing, in the 1980s and 1990s, the Afro-German community continues to increase in size and diversity, with Afro-German families—couples or single parents—notably raising their children with Afro-German consciousness. All of the formal programs, such as Black History Month and annual retreats, include programming for children for the purpose of exposing them to educational materials featuring Black children, providing positive self-images and acquaintance with Black peoples elsewhere in the diaspora—exposure which is entirely absent from their school materials—and helping them to cope with the marginalization, stereotyping (especially gendered racial stereotyping) or other forms of discrimination they experience in school and elsewhere in their environment. To that specific end ISD has established a Kids' Annual Retreat for Afro-German children and their parents, to provide an actual community experience and, hence, identity—something the parents did not enjoy—for the upcoming generation of Afro-Germans.

All of the material products discussed to this point—the publications, films, programs, organizations, etc.—serve as one type of manifestation of community. But "community" and "identity" are less often manifested by such visible, tangible products and more often manifested as a *sense* of shared heritage and experience, an empathy, generating a *sister- and brotherhood*. Because community among Afro-Germans has been, for the most part, formed from *individuals* gravitating toward each other, rather than from families or cultural enclaves or other micro-institutions, the simple need for *being with one's own kind* is a major function of the Afro-German community. Hence, emotional and social needs are addressed by such things as frequent, organized, informal social gatherings such as dance parties or picnics, which happen in the various cities largely by "grapevine" publicity, usually drawing attendance from other cities within the region. Indeed the very fact of a "grapevine" is evidence of a community, in this case, one that is even interregional. These opportunities provide "family" for many isolated Afro-Germans. Thus it is in such largely social aspects that the community manifests itself with any frequency.

In addition to the opportunities for social encounter, electronic chat rooms and listserves keep up lively discussion on topics covering local and national topics of interest to Black Germans, often calling for concerted action, such as public demonstrations in response to escalating racial violence. Besides Germany-specific subjects, the cyber-community can be equally engaged in discussions about diaspora-related subjects elsewhere, ranging from the American Music Awards to Jesse Jackson's activities, to civil war in Congo or Sierra Leone. More importantly, though, for diaspora interests, "the electronic communication facilitates better access to and closer collaboration with other Black groups within and outside of Germany."[24] Of course, the original impetus, though not the official sponsor, of all the manifestations of community is the initiative of the ISD.

The young (fifteen-year-old) organization has a fragile history, reflecting the dynamics of constant self-reevaluation. Nevertheless, all of the other community products—the informal and the formal, the social, the cultural, and the political—can be viewed as byproducts of community activity of the ISD. It is significant that the young founders settled on the concept "initiative," which "in contrast to club or organization, expressed the innovative, active character of the new group."[25]

In spite of the emotional and psychological significance of the various forms of Afro-German community identity, they cannot neutralize the day-to-day reality lived by Afro-Germans. In real life an Afro-German, whose mother and mother-tongue are German, is usually perceived as a "foreigner" or an "immigrant." Consequently, such an individual is socially lumped together with those groups and, hence, is likely to be treated patronizingly, with curiosity, or with hostility, or some other form of discrimination at school, in the workplace, in the search for housing, etc. Earnest government efforts to quell the increasing volume of right-wing attacks—such as those portrayed in the film *Afro-Deutsch*—seldom acknowledge them as racially motivated, taking cover, instead, behind the euphemism "xenophobia," due to the extreme sensitivity about the phenomenon of "race" since the Jewish Holocaust. Thus, sharing a plight in part with resident foreigners and immigrants, Afro-Germans do frequently embrace and engage with individuals and collective projects of those groups as well. An example of such between-the-cracks status is the irony that Afro-Germans' Black History Month receives funding in part from a state office responsible for the welfare of foreigners living in Germany.

But for some white Germans who are enlightened enough to acknowledge the diversity of German society, and who understand that Black Germans are indeed Germans, the suggestion that this population group warrants special attention, even legislation such as anti-discrimination laws, is met with the attitude that, since they are all Germans, why single out that group for specific consideration? Recoiling from the prospect of once again (or still) constructing "race" as a category in German life after the history of the Jewish Holocaust, an acknowledgment of German society as multiracial is a hard pill for white Germans to swallow. Easier to swallow, it appears, is the concept of "*multikulturell*" (multicultural), embraced by the more liberal-minded. But as it is used in writing and in speech most often in its slang, therefore diminished, form, the concept of a "*multikulti*" German society is laden with the grudge of political correctness and the lack of a sincere embrace by mainstream society. As articulated by journalist and ISD executive council member Jeannine Kantara, "Nevertheless,

Black and German is still a contradiction. . . . [although] [n]ot for Black Germans themselves. The problem lies rather with a society that isn't willing to give up its white self-image. The multicultural society is in fact multi-ethnic. 'Culture' just sounds less threatening."[26]

With such social, cultural, and intellectual activity and productivity by Afro-Germans now clearly burgeoning, and with their very presence and appellation gaining some visibility in print and electronic media, the question arises why there is not yet acknowledgment of their existence as a legitimate German minority community? There is as yet no academic or other authoritative recognition of this population as an identifiable component of the German population. Interest, however, on the part of a department such as European Ethnography at Berlin's Humboldt University suggests that consideration within the academy as the next critical site of intellectual activity is, to say the least, timely.

Afro-Germans and African Diaspora

What did it mean, back in the mid-1980s, for any of those Afro-German women, who may not ever have been embraced by their own Black parent or any other Black person, to be embraced by the African diaspora? Lorde, child of Afro-Caribbean parents, born and raised in the U.S., shared neither their mother tongue nor their fatherland nor their German culture. How to include Afro-Germans in the "Black Folk" of which DuBois wrote a century ago? How do Afro-Germans fit into the African diaspora?

Shared African origins do not in themselves constitute African diaspora. Rather, the presumption that Black people worldwide share a community is based primarily in geopolitical orientation, rather than portable cultural retentions. Thus, launching a debate on definitions of "African diaspora," the editors of a special issue of the *African Studies Review* remind us that "diasporic identities are socially and historically constituted, reconstituted, and reproduced; and that any sense of a collective identity among Black peoples in the New World, Europe, and Africa is contingent and constantly shifting."[27] This theoretical articulation of the slipperiness of African diaspora is indeed useful in searching out African-diaspora consciousness among Afro-Germans.

The meaning of the phenomenon "African diaspora" is, today, not only debated—even disputed—but is the subject of energetic scholarly activity, replete, even, with discussion of the term's "indisputabl[e] . . . politics of usage."[28] The Winter 2000 issue of the African Studies

Association's journal *ASA Review* is devoted to a discussion of Africa's diaspora. (In fact, one contributor bitingly remarks on the global studies
bandwagon onto which diaspora studies gets shoved, a bandwagon for
those scholars escaping from the crumbling "academic Berlin Wall"[29] that
was area studies.) But, sarcasm aside, the authors of the focal article,
"Unfinished Migrations: Reflections on the African Diaspora and the
Making of the Modern World,"[30] Tiffany Patterson and Robin Kelly,
problematize DuBois's 1947 notion of the natural development of an
African diaspora for which Africa was the homeland: "The idea of one
Africa to unite the thoughts and ideals of all native peoples of the dark
continent belongs to the twentieth century. . . . Various groups of Africans,
quite separate in origin, became so united in experience and so exposed to
the impact of new cultures that they began to think of Africa as one idea
and one land."[31] The theoretical debate on diaspora, intelligently waged
by Patterson and Kelly and the several scholars responding to their paper,
incorporates the broadest range of considerations, including the cultural,
political, geographic, and historical concepts of national or diasporan
identity and the creation of community.

The academic debate offers valuable material for theorizing the
unique formation of Black diaspora community and identity among Afro-
Germans. Considering "the construction and reproduction of diasporic
identities—the creation of a diasporan consciousness," Patterson and Kelly
suggest that transnational connections linking diasporas may or may not
invoke any perceived or imagined homeland but may, rather, be based in
"lateral connections," which refer to similar trajectories and adaptation to
the present location.[32] For those Afro-Germans of German mothers and
African fathers who grew up with both parents, the family typically spent
part of its life in the father's country before the children returned to
Germany with one or both parents. Those Afro-Germans obviously have a
substantive connection with the father's country. However, in the case of the
large percentage of Afro-Germans who have grown up with no acquaintance
with their fathers—African or Afro-Caribbean, or African American—it
stands to reason that the only country that Afro-Germans have any relationship to is Germany. Thus, for them Africa has no meaningful personal
reference. However, some of these individuals who know that their fathers
came from a particular country in Africa desire to find their father or at least
to know something about that country. Some have traveled to the country
of their father's birth in search of their father, a few with success. If and when
the paternal connection is made, the Afro-German feels some connection to
that country, but only a symbolic connection, as the Afro-German individual

has no substantive, identity-grounding experience with the father or his country of origin. Some Afro-Germans who know that their father came from the U.S. or the Caribbean also make efforts to locate their fathers. For all of these as well as for the many who do not find their fathers, their identity as Afro-Germans would seem to stand on such "lateral connections" or similar trajectories and adaptation to their presence in Germany.

For the significant number of Afro-Germans born in Africa and growing up in Germany, either as refugees or immigrants because of other "push factors," their trajectories have allowed for little, if any, retention of significant community and cultural forms. Hence, as children adapting to German life, their connection to their African origins retains unfortunately little positive memory to undergird a remote African identity. Nevertheless, numerous individuals in this category identify as Afro-German and are enthusiastic and appreciated members of the Afro-German community.

Thus, the reference to a real or imagined Africa is not critical for an Afro-German diaspora identity. Cheryl Johnson-Odim, a respondent in the Patterson/Kelly debate, raises complexities inherent in conceptualizing diaspora community in very different ways:

> Community boundaries, it seems to me, imply a sense of active connectedness on shared things [resulting in an identity that] can be as loose as . . . a sense of comfort around "x" because of unspoken, shared meanings— a recognition of oneself in another. Identity is important for people's understanding of who they are—at least "compared to what?" or perhaps "compared to whom?"[33]

This "recognition of oneself in another," the understanding of oneself in comparison to "others," would describe the early experience, before the 1980s, that would have brought Afro-Germans, strangers, wary of each other, into contact. Marginalized because "different" in comparison to the majority population, they could recognize themselves in each other, as they vented to Lorde. Or, as Kantara writes in an *afro look* article, reflecting on the ISD's first ten years, "We'd see each other in the subway or bus, a fleeting eye contact, but usually without making any approach. Why not, remains speculative; it couldn't have been disinterest, or else there would be no ISD."[34] Even now, the tentative anticipation of an Afro-German attending her or his first annual retreat, at the urging of a friend, is characterized by a perhaps unacknowledged recognition of "a sense of comfort around [their blackness] because of unspoken, shared meanings." The same feeling of marginalization, if not also the self-recognition, can form the bond between Afro-Germans and other diaspora Blacks who as adults, perhaps as students or artists, migrate to or sojourn in Germany. It is a connection that is consciously pursued by the interaction of these individuals who find the sense of shared meanings of being Black in Germany. It is the "active connectedness," of which Johnson-Odim speaks, giving substance to the sense of community. Such connections are critically supported in the informal venues and given greater substance through the formal activities.

In the final analysis, Patterson and Kelly, citing Stuart Hall, conclude:

> The linkages, therefore, that tie the diaspora together must be articulated and are not inevitable. These linkages are always historically constituted. Furthermore, diaspora is both a process and a condition. As a process it is constantly being remade through movement, migration, and travel, as well as imagined through thought, cultural production, and political struggle. Yet, as a condition, it is directly tied to the process by which it is being made and remade. In other words, the African diaspora itself exists within the context of global race and gender hierarchies which are formulated and reconstituted across national boundaries.[35]

The dynamic diaspora-process of the Afro-German community, as remade through movement, migration, and travel, is a description of the Afro-German trajectory itself. African or Caribbean male students or workers in Germany (owing to historical circumstances such as colonialism and its aftermath), encountering German women with whom they produce children, and in some cases marrying, in many cases prevented legally from marrying, and in other cases severing or abandoning the relationship—this migration and movement is the very origin of much of the Afro-German population. Subsequently, while the majority of Afro-German linkages with wider diaspora take place within Germany, through movement and travels of diaspora people into Germany, there are also contacts through travels of Afro-Germans to other parts of the diaspora. Examples include participation in London's Black and Radical Book Fair and its Carnival celebrations; participation in minority and race-related conferences, as reported frequently in *afro look*; visits by Afro-German groups and individuals to Black communities in the U.S., as with the Showing Our Colors youth exchange program and ADEFRA members' talks to Black college students; and the relationship established between the historically Black Howard University and the "elder" of the Afro-German community, Theodor Wonja Michael, who spent a week in residence at the university in the fall of 2000.

As for Patterson's and Kelly's notion of the imagining of the diaspora linkage process through thought, cultural production, and political struggle, any issue of *afro look*, any program brochure for Black History Month can serve to illustrate those aspects of the process. Further, those two products of the Afro-German community exemplify the full diaspora scope that the community assumes. Concerning the initiation of Black History Month, Ayim cited the role model of the African American institution established in 1926 as Negro History Week by historian Carter G. Woodson.[36] Similarly, *afro look's* masthead states as part of its mission a contribution toward a Black diaspora community: "Open[ing] up or intensify[ing] the access to our Black cultures and our Black history . . . making a contribution to a Black community . . . in Germany and beyond its borders." Thus articles in the magazine include book reviews or interviews with African/diaspora cultural figures (e.g., Maryse Condé, bell hook, and Spike Lee) visiting Germany, usually on promotional tour. Other subjects explored in *afro look* are the Million-Man March in Washington, African women at the United Nations Conference on Women in Beijing, the new South Africa, and the status of Afro-Germans, individually and collectively.

Bearing out Patterson's and Kelly's characterization of political struggle as a constituent aspect of the process and condition of diaspora, the clearest evidence of the maturity to which the Afro-German community has developed is its political activism, primarily in response to acts of violence against Blacks (largely immigrant Africans), including police brutality, as mentioned earlier in this chapter. The escalation of such incidents to the highest levels since German reunification in 1990 has galvanized the Black community around the country to express its protest in organized demonstrations, as well as to call on the government to pass—and enforce—tougher laws to protect Blacks and other minorities from further incidents of brutality. To be sure, this political voice had been a basic tenet since the inception of the ISD, and there have been demonstrations and other forms of activism previously. However, the current level, with the example of the Brothers Keepers Project, indicates a stage of Black community that Ayim and other ISD founders envisioned.

Afro-Caribbean-American poet-activist Lorde, in inviting her German "sisters" to identify psychologically with that Black world, was inviting them to participate in the process and condition of African diaspora. Afro-German poet-activist Ayim, in addressing the PANAFEST Colloquium, inserted Germans into the Pan-African mix in the process and condition of the African diaspora. ISD and ADEFRA, by their missions, exemplify the process and condition of African diaspora. African diaspora as *condition* resolves any "contradiction" or "oxymoron" in "Afro-German"; African diaspora as *process* resolves the DuBoisian "twoness" in the souls of Afro-German Black Folk/*Volk*.

Notes

1. May Opitz Ayim, address at the second Pan-African Historical Theatre Festival (PANAFEST), Cape Coast, Ghana, 1994, culled from essays published posthumously in the collection *Grenzenlos und unverschämt* (Berlin: Orlanda, 1997). This appeared in English as *Borderless and Brazen*, Anne V. Adams, trans. (Trenton, N. J.: Africa World Press, 2002).

2. Paulette Reed-Anderson, *Berlin und die afrikanische Diaspora: Rewriting the Footnotes* (Berlin: Die Ausländerbeauftragte des [Berliner] Senats, 2000) chronicles sojourns by, for instance, composer Will Marion Cook, human rights activist Mary Church Terrell, and pan-Africanist activist George Padmore.

3. "To the Nations of the World," quoted in David Levering Lewis, *W. E. B. DuBois: Biography of a Race, 1858–1919* (New York: Henry Holt, 1993), 251.

4. Lewis, "Lehrjahre," Ch. 6 in *W. E .B. DuBois*, 117–49.

5. Ibid., 136.

6. Ibid. Emphasis added.

7. The term "African American" subsequently replaced "Afro-American" as a way of ascribing full value to the African heritage. It was a move of cultural politics in the U.S. and does not reflect comparatively on other groups in the Black diaspora that continue to use the "Afro-" prefix (e.g., Afro-Cuban, Afro-Brazilian, etc.).

8. This and subsequent quotations from Ayim, *Grenzenlos* bear the citation date of the collection (1997), although reference might also be made to the original date of the statement. All translations mine.

9. Ayim, *Grenzenlos*, 137.

10. Ibid.

11. Ibid., 139.

12. Ibid., 155–56.

13. Ibid., 45.

14. Ibid., 47.

15. Elizabeth Abraham, "10 Jahre Initiative Schwarze Deutsche & Schwarze Menschen in Deutschland," *afro look* 18 (1995): 31.

16. May Ayim, *Blues in Schwarz-Weiss* (Berlin: Orlanda Frauenverlag, 1995) and *Nachtgesang* (Berlin: Orlanda Frauenverlag, 1997).

17. E.g., Olumide Popoola and Beldan Sezen (eds.), *Talking Home: Heimat aus unserer eigenen Feder—Frauen of color in Deutschland* (Amsterdam: Blue Moon Press, 1999); selections in *Junge Lyrik II: 50 Dichterinnen und Dichter, Jahrgänge 1959–1969* (Melsbach: Martin Werhand Verlag, 2000).

18. Ika Hügel-Marshall, *Daheim unterwegs. Ein deutsches Leben* (Berlin: Orlanda Frauenverlag, 1998), translated as *Invisible Woman: Growing Up Black in Germany* by Elizabeth Gaffney (New York: Continuum, 2001). I, as well as the German publishers, consider the English title problematic because of its obvious reference to the African-American

novel *Invisible Man* by Ralph Ellison. Because of the stature of Ellison's novel as a classic American fiction text *Invisible Woman*, which is not a novel but a personal testimony, could be judged on the basis of expectations generated by an unavoidable comparison with the Ellison text.

19. Hans-Jürgen Massaquoi, *Destined to Witness: Growing Up Black in Nazi Germany* (New York: William Morrow, 1999); *Neger, Neger, Schornsteinfeger. Meine Kindheit in Deutschland*, Ulrike Wasel and Klaus Timmermann, trans. (Bern: Fretz & Wasmuth, 1999). Many Afro-Germans whom I heard discuss the book recall being taunted by white German children with the chant "Neger, Neger, Schornsteinfeger," because of the soot-covered image of the chimney sweep, and, hence, find it difficult to see those words, even though (or especially) appropriated by an Afro-German.

20. Katharina Oguntoye, *Eine Afro-Deutsche Geschichte. Zur Lebenssituation von Afrikanern und Afro-Deutschen in Deutschland von 1884 bis 1950* (Berlin: Hoho Verlag, 1997).

21. Fatima El-Tayeb's dissertation for the department of history at the University of Hamburg later was published as *Schwarze Deutsche: Der Diskurs um "Rasse" und nationale Identität 1890–1933* (Frankfurt: Campus 2001).

22. Examples are Ika Hügel et al. (eds.), *Entfernte Verbindungen: Rassismus, Antisemitismus, Klassenenunterdrückung* (Berlin: Orlanda Frauenverlag, 1993); and Cathy Gelbin, Kader Konuk, and Peggy Piesche (eds.), *Aufbrüche: Kulturelle Produktionen von Migrantinnen, Schwarzen und jüdischen Frauen in Deutschland* (Königsberg/ Th: Ulrike Helmer, 1999).

23. Ayim, *Grenzenlos*, 130.

24. Jeannine Kantara, "Wohin geht die ISD," *afro look* 20 (1996): 9.

25. Ibid., 7.

26. Jeannine Kantara, "Schwarz. Und deutsch. Kein Widerspruch? Für viele meiner weißen Mitbürger schon," *Die Zeit* 37 (7 September 2000).

27. Tiffany Ruby Patterson and Robin D. G. Kelley, "Unfinished Migrations: Reflections on the African Diaspora and the Making of the Modern World," *African Studies Association Review* 43, no. 1 (April 2000): 19.

28. Brent Hayes Edwards, " 'Unfinished Migrations': Commentary and Response," *African Studies Association Review* 43, no. 1 (April 2000): 48.

29. Michael O. West, " 'Unfinished Migrations': Commentary and Response," *African Studies Association Review* 43, no. 1 (April 2000): 61.

30. Patterson and Kelley, "Unfinished Migrations," 11–45.

31. W. E. B. DuBois, *The World and Africa* (1946; reprint, New York: International Publishers, 1965).

32. Patterson and Kelly, "Unfinished Migrations," 15.

33. Cheryl Johnson-Odim, " 'Unfinished Migrations': Commentary and Response," *African Studies Association Review* 43, no. 1 (April 2000), 52–53.

34. Kantara, "Wohin," 7.

35. Patterson and Kelly, "Unfinished Migrations," 20.

36. Ayim, *Grenzenlos*, 156.

SELECTED BIBLIOGRAPHY

Arndt, Susan, ed. *AfrikaBilder: Studien zu Rassismus in Deutschland*. Münster: Unrast, 2001.

Avè, Lia. "Der dunkle Stern: Ein Roman." *Hermes Film-Roman Magazin* 17. Munich: Hermes Film- und Bühnen-Verlag, n.d.

Ayim [Opitz], May. "Die afro-deutsche Minderheit." In *Ethnische Minderheiten in der Bundesrepublik Deutschland*, edited by Cornelia Schmalz-Jacobsen and George Hansen, 39–52. Munich: Beck, 1995.

Ayim, May. *blues in schwarz weiss*. Berlin: Orlanda Frauenverlag, 1995. Translated by Anne Adams under the title *Blues in Black and White: A Collection of Essays, Poetry, and Conversations* (Trenton, N. J.: Africa World Press, 2003).

———. Nachtgesang. Berlin: Orlanda Frauenverlag, 1997.

———. "The Year 1990. Homeland and Unity from an Afro-German Perspective." In *Fringe Voices: An Anthology of Minority Writing in the Federal Republic of Germany*, edited by Antje Harnisch, Anne Marie Stokes, and Friedemann Weidauer, 105–19. New York: Berg, 1998.

——— and Nivedita Prasad, eds. *Dokumentation Wege zu Bündnissen. Dokumentation der Tagung von/für ethnische und afro-deutsche Minderheiten*. Berlin: ASTA Druckerei der Freien Universität Berlin, 1992.

Bauer, Wilhelm A. *Angelo Soliman, der hochfürstliche Mohr: ein exotisches Kapital* [sic] *Alt-Wien*. 1922. Reprint, edited and with an introduction by Monika Firla-Forkl. Berlin: Edition Ost, 1993.

Bechhaus-Gerst, Marianne and Reinhard Klein-Arendt, eds. *Die (koloniale) Begegnung. AfrikanerInnen in Deutschland 1880–1945. Deutsche in Afrika 1880–1918*. New York: Peter Lang, 2003.

Berman, Russell. "DuBois and Wagner: Race, Nation, and Culture between Germany and the United States." *German Quarterly* 70, no. 2 (1997): 123–35.

———. *Enlightenment or Empire: Colonial Discourse in German Culture*. Lincoln: University of Nebraska Press, 1998.

Biddiss, Michael. *Father of Racist Ideology: The Social and Political Thought of Count Gobineau*. London: Weidenfeld & Nicolson, 1970.

Blackshire-Belay, Carol Aisha, ed. *The African-German Experience: Critical Essays*. Westport, Connecticut: Praeger, 1996.

———, Leroy Hopkins, and David McBride, eds. *Crosscurrents: African Americans, Africa, and Germany in the Modern World*. Columbia, S.C.: Camden House, 1998.

Bley, Helmut. *South-West Africa under German Rule, 1894–1914*. Translated by Hugh Ridley. Evanston, Ill.: Northwestern University Press, 1971.

Bock, Gisela. *Zwangsterilisation im Nationalsozialismus*. Opladen: Westdeutscher Verlag, 1986.

Campt, Tina M. "Afro-German Cultural Identity and the Politics of Positionality: Contests and Contexts in the Formation of German Ethnic Identity." *New German Critique* 58 (1993): 109–26.

————. *Other Germans: Black Germans and the Politics of Race, Gender, and Memory in the Third Reich*. University of Michigan Press: Ann Arbor, 2004.

————, Pascal Grosse, and Yara-Colette Lemke Muniz de Faria. "Blacks, Germans, and the Politics of the Imperial Imagination, 1920–60." In *The Imperialist Imagination: German Colonialism and its Legacy*, edited by Sara Friedrichsmeyer, Sara Lennox, and Susanne Zantop, 205–29. Ann Arbor: University of Michigan Press, 1998.

———— and Pascal Grosse. "'Mischlingskinder' in Nachkriegsdeutschland: Zum Verhältnis von Psychologie, Anthropologie und Gesellschaftkritik nach 1945." *Psychologie und Geschichte* 6, no. 1/2 (1994): 48–78.

———— and Michelle Wright, eds. "Reading the Black German Experience." Special section of *Callaloo* 26, no. 2 (2003).

Cleaver, Tessa and Marion Wallace. *Namibia: Women in War*. London: Zed Books, 1990.

Cohen, Cynthia. "'The Natives Must First Become Good Workmen': Formal Educational Provision in German South West Africa and East Africa Compared." *Journal of Southern African Studies* 19, no. 1 (1993): 115–34.

Davidson, John E. "As Others Put Plays Upon the Stage: Aguirre, Neocolonialism, and the New German Cinema." *New German Critique* 60 (1993): 101–32.

DuBois, W. E. B. *The Autobiography of W. E. B. DuBois*. New York: International Publishers, 1968.

Ebeling, Hermann. "Berichte: Zum Problem der deutschen Mischlingskinder." *Bild und Erziehung* 7, no. 10 (1954): 612–30.

Ehmann, Annegret. "From Colonial Racism to Nazi Population Policy: The Role of the So-Called Mischlinge." In *The Holocaust and History: The Known, the Unknown, the Disputed, and the Reexamined*, edited by Michael Berenbaum and Abraham J. Peck, 188–12. Bloomington and Indianapolis: Indiana University Press, 1998.

El-Tayeb, Fatima. "'Blood Is a Very Special Juice': Racialized Bodies and Citizenship in Twentieth-Century Germany." *International Review of Social History* 44 (1999), Supplement 7, 149–69.

————. *Schwarze Deutsche: Der Diskurs um "Rasse" und nationale Identität 1890–1933*. Frankfurt: Campus 2001.

———— and Angelina Maccarone. *Alles wird gut*. Berlin: Orlanda Frauenverlag, 1999.

Emde, Helga. "An 'Occupation Baby' in Postwar Germany." In *Fringe Voices: An Anthology of Minority Writing in the Federal Republic of Germany*, edited by Antje Harnisch, Anne Marie Stokes, and Friedemann Weidauer, 80–88. New York: Berg, 1998.

Essner, Cornelia. "Zwischen Vernunft und Gefühl. Die Reichstagsdebatten von 1912 um koloniale 'Rassenmischehe' und 'Sexualität.'" *Zeitschrift für Geschichtswissenschaft* 45, no. 6 (1997): 503–19.

Eyferth, Klaus. "Gedanken über die zukünftige Berufseingliederung der Mischlingskinder in Westdeutschland." *Neues Beginnen* 5 (1959): 65–68.

———. "Die Situation und die Entwicklunaussichten der Neger-Mischlingskinder in der Bundesrepublik." *Soziale Arbeit* 7, no. 11 (1958): 469–78.

———, Ursula Brandt, and Wolfgang Hawel. *Farbige Kinder in Deutschland: Die Situation der Mischlingskinder und die Aufgabe ihrer Eingliederung.* Munich: Juventa, 1960.

Fansa, Mamoun, ed. *Schwarzweissheiten: Vom Umgang mit fremden Menschen.* Oldenburg: Isensee Verlag, 2001.

Fehrenbach, Heide. *After the Racial State: Black G.I.s and "Colored" Occupation Children in Postwar Germany.* Princeton: Princeton University Press, forthcoming 2005.

———. "'Ami-Liebchen' und 'Mischlingskinder'—Rasse, Geschlecht und Kultur in der deutsch-amerikanischen Begegnung." In *Nachkrieg in Deutschland*, edited by Klaus Naumann, 178–205. Hamburg: Hamburger Edition, 2001.

———. "Of German Mothers and 'Negermischlingskinder': Race, Sex, and the Postwar Nation." In *The Miracle Years: A Cultural History of West Germany, 1949–1968*, edited by Hanna Schissler, 164–86. Princeton: Princeton University Press, 2001.

———. "Rehabilitating Father*land*: Race and German Remasculinization." *Signs* 24, no. 1 (1998): 107–27.

Firla-Forkl, Monika. "Darstellungen von Afrikanern im Württemberg des 17. und 18. Jahrhunderts." *Tribus* (Stuttgart: Linden-Museum) 46 (December 1997): 57–79.

Fischer, Eugen. *Die Rehobother Bastards und das Bastardisierungsproblem beim Menschen.* Jena: Gustav Fischer, 1913.

Forgey, Elisa. "'Die große Negertrommel der kolonialen Werbung': Die deutsche Afrika-Schau 1935–43." *Werkstatt Geschichte* 9 (1994): 24–33.

Frankenstein, Luise. *Soldatenkinder: Die unehelichen Kinder ausländischer Soldaten mit besonderer Berücksichtigung der Mischlinge.* Munich: W. Steinebach, 1954.

Gelbin, Cathy, Kader Konuk, and Peggy Piesche, eds. *Aufbrüche: Kulturelle Produktionen von Migrantinnen, Schwarzen und jüdischen Frauen in Deutschland.* Königsberg/ Th: Ulrike Helmer, 1999.

Gilman, Sander. "Black Bodies, White Bodies: Toward and Iconography of Female Sexuality in Late Nineteenth-Century Art." In *Race Writing and Difference*, edited by Henry Louis Gates, Jr., 223–261. Chicago: University of Chicago Press, 1986.

———. *Difference and Pathology.* Ithaca: Cornell University Press, 1985.

———. *On Blackness Without Blacks.* G.K. Hall Publishers: Boston, 1982.

Gobineau, Arthur comte de. *Essai sur l'inégalité des races humaines.* 2d ed. Paris: Firmin-Didot, 1884.

Goldberg, David T. *Racist Culture: Philosophy and the Politics of Meaning.* Cambridge, Mass.: Blackwell, 1993.

Grimm, Reinhold and Jost Hermand, eds. *Blacks and German Culture.* Madison: University of Wisconsin Press, 1986.

Grosse, Pascal. *Kolonialismus, Eugenik und bürgerliche Gesellschaft in Deutschland 1850–1918.* Frankfurt: Campus, 2000.

———. "Kolonialismus und das Problem der 'Rassenmischung' in Deutschland: Zur Geschichte der anthropologischen Psychology 1920–1940." In *Psychology im soziokulturellen Wandel—Kontinuitäten und Diskontinuitäten* edited by Siegfried Jäger et al., 75–85. Frankfurt, 1995.

Grunde, Harald. *Eine von uns: Als Schwarze in Deutschland geboren.* Wuppertal: Peter Hammer, 2000.

Hoffmann, Helmut. "Illegitimate Negro Children in German Elementary Schools." *Journal of Negro Education* 23, no. 2 (1954): 180–82.

Höhn, Maria. *G.I.s and Fräuleins: The German-American Encounter in 1950s West Germany.* Chapel Hill: University of North Carolina Press, 2002.

Hopkins, Leroy. "Einbürgerungs-Akte 1154: Heinrich Ernst Wilhelm Anumu, African Businessman in Imperial Hamburg." In *Die (koloniale) Begegnung. AfrikanerInnen in Deutschland 1880–1945. Deutsche in Afrika 1880–1918,* edited by Marianne Bechhaus-Gerst and Reinhard Klein-Arendt. Peter Lang, 2003.

———. " 'Fred' vs 'Uncle Tom': Frederick Douglass and the Image of the African American in Nineteenth-Century Germany." *etudes germano-africaines* 9 (1991): 67–78.

———. "Speak, So I Might See You! Afro-German Literature." *World Literature Today* 69, no.3 (1995): 533–38.

———. *Who is a German? Historical and Modern Perspectives on Africans in Germany.* Washington: AICGS, 1999.

Hurka, Herbert. "Die Mischlingskinder in Deutschland. Ein Situationbericht auf Grund bisheriger Veröffentlichungen." *Jugendwohl* 6 (1956): 257–75.

Hügel, Ika et al., eds. *Entfernte Verbindungen: Rassismus, Antisemitismus, Klassenunterdrückung.* Berlin: Orlanda Frauenverlag, 1993.

Hügel-Marshall, Ika. *Daheim unterwegs: Ein deutsches Leben.* Berlin: Orlanda Verlag, 1998. Translated by Elizabeth Gaffney under the title *Invisible Woman: Growing Up Black in Germany* (New York: Continuum, 2001).

ISD [Initiative Schwarze Deutsche], ed. *Macht der Nacht: eine schwarze deutsche anthologie.* Munich, 1992.

Jobatey, Francine. "Afro-Look: Die Geschichte einer Zeitschrift von Schwarzen Deutschen." Ph.D. diss., University of Massachusetts, 2000.

Kaupen-Haas, Heidrun and Christian Saller, eds. *Wissenschaftlicher Rassismus: Analysen einer Kontinuität in den Human- und Naturwissenschaften.* Frankfurt: Campus, 1999.

Kesting, Robert W. "Forgotten Victims: Blacks in the Holocaust." *The Journal of Negro History* 77, no. 1 (1992): 30–36.

Kiesel, Doron. "Das Schweigen der Fahrgäste: Zu *Schwarzfahrer* von Pepe Danquart." In *"Getürkte Bilder": Zur Inszenierung von Fremden in Film,* edited by Ernst Karpf, Doron Kiesel, and Karsten Visarius. Marburg: Schüren, 1995.

Kirchner, W. "Eine anthropologische Studie an Mulattenkindern in Berlin unter Berücksichtigung der sozialen Verhältnisse." Ph.D. diss., Freie Universität Berlin, 1952.

Klotz, Marcia. "White Women and the Dark Continent: Gender and Sexuality in German Colonial Discourse from the Sentimental Novel to the Fascist Film." Ph.D. diss., Stanford University, 1994.

Knoll, Arthur J. and Lewis H. Gann, eds. *Germans in the Tropics: Essays in German Colonial History.* New York: Greenwood Press, 1987.

Koepnick, Lutz P. "Colonial Forestry: Sylvan Politics in Werner Herzog's *Aguirre* and *Fitzcarraldo.*" *New German Critique* 60 (1993): 133–59.

Koller, Christian. *"Von Wilden aller Rassen niedergemetzelt:" Die Diskussion um die Verwendung von Kolonialtruppen in Europa zwischen Rassismus, Kolonial- und Militärpolitik (1914–1930).* Stuttgart: Franz Steiner, 2001.

Kraft, Marion and Rukhsana Shamim Askraf-Khan, eds. *Schwarze Frauen in der Welt: Europa und Migration.* Berlin: Orlanda Frauenverlag, 1994.

Kroll, Jürgen. "Zur Entstehung und Institutionalisierung einer naturwissenschaftlichen und sozialpolitischen Bewegung: Die Entwicklung der Eugenik/Rassenhygiene bis zum Jahre 1933." Ph. D. diss., University of Tübingen, 1983.

Krüger, Gesine. *Kriegsbewältigung und Geschichtsbewußtsein: Realität, Deutung und Verarbeitung des deutschen Kolonialkriegs in Namibia 1904 bis 1907.* Göttingen: Vandenhoeck und Ruprecht, 1999.

Krüger-Potratz, Marianne. *Anderssein gab es nicht: Ausländer und Minderheiten in der DDR.* New York: Waxmann, 1991.

Kundrus, Birthe, ed. *Phantasiereiche: zur Kulturgeschichte des deutschen Kolonialismus.* Frankfurt: Campus-Verlag, 2003.

Lawrence, Benjamin Nicholas. "Most Obedient Servants: the Politics of Language in German Colonial Togo." *Cahiers d'Etudes africains* 159 (2000): 489–524.

Lemke Muniz de Faria, Yara-Colette. *Zwischen Fürsorge und Ausgrenzung: Afrodeutsche "Besatzungskinder" im Nachkriegs-Deutschland.* Berlin: Metropol, 2002.

Lennox, Sara, Sara Friedrichsmeyer, and Susanne Zantop, eds. *The Imperialist Imagination: German Colonialism and Its Legacy.* Ann Arbor: University of Michigan Press, 1998.

Lester, Rosemarie K. *Trivialneger: Das Bild des Schwarzen im westdeutschen Illustriertenroman.* Stuttgart: Heinz, 1982.

Lilienthal, Georg. "'Rheinlandbastarde,' Rassenhygiene und das Problem der rassenideologischen Kontinuität." *Medizinhistorisches Journal* 15 (1980): 426–36.

Lotz, Rainer E. *Black People: Entertainers of African Descent in Europe, and Germany.* Bonn: Birgit Lotz, 1997.

Lusane, Clarence. *Hitler's Black Victims: The Historical Experiences of Afro-Germans, Afro-Europeans, African Americans, and Africans during the Nazi Era.* New York: Routledge, 2002.

Martin, Peter. *Schwarze Teufel, edle Mohren. Afrikaner in Bewußtsein und Geschichte der Deutschen.* Hamburg: Junius, 1993.

Massaquoi, Hans. *Destined to Witness: Growing Up Black in Nazi Germany.* New York: William Morrow, 1999. Translated by Ulrike Wasel and Klaus Timmermann under the title *Neger, Neger, Schornsteinfeger: Meine Kindheit in Deutschland* (Bern: Fretz & Wasmuth, 1999).

Müller-Hill, Benno. *Tödliche Wissenschaft: Die Aussonderung von Juden, Zigeunern und Geisteskranken 1933–1945.* Reinbek: Rowohlt, 1984.

Nagl, Tobias. "'Afrika spricht!' Modernismus, Jazz und 'Rasse' im Kino der Weimarer Republik." In *Singen und Tanzen im Film,* edited by Andrea Pollach, Isabella Reicher, and Tanja Widman, 171–86. Vienna: Zsolny, 2003.

———. "'Sieh mal den schwarzen Mann!' Komparsen afrikanischer Herkunft im deutschsprachigen Kino vor 1945." In *Zwischen Stechschritt und Charleston.*

Schwarze im Nationalsozialismus, edited by Peter Martin and Christine Alonzo, 69–90. Hamburg and Munich: Dölling & Galitz, 2004.

———. " '. . . und lass mich Filmen und Tanzen bloß um mein Brot zu verdienen': Schwarze Komparsen und Kinoöffentlichkeit in der Weimarer Republik." In *AfrikanerInnen in Deutschland und schwarze Deutsche—Geschichte und Gegenwart*, edited by Marianne Bechhaus-Gerst. Forthcoming 2004.

———. " 'Von Fremder Rasse durchsetzt.' Anti-schwarzer Rassismus im Kulturfilm des Nationalsozialismus." In *Geschichte und Ästhetik des dokumentarischen Films in Deutschland 1895–1945*, v. 3. Forthcoming 2004.

O'Donnell, Krista. "Poisonous Women: Sexual Danger, Illicit Violence, and Domestic Work in German Southern Africa, 1904–1915." *Journal of Women's History* 11, no. 3 (1999): 31–54.

Oguntoye, Katharina. *Eine Afro-Deutsche Geschichte. Zur Lebenssituation von Afrikanern und Afro-Deutschen in Deutschland von 1884 bis 1950*. Berlin: Hoho Verlag, 1997.

———, May Opitz, and Dagmar Schultz, eds. *Farbe bekennen*. Berlin: Orlanda Frauenverlag, 1986. Translated by Anne V. Adams under the title *Showing Our Colors: Afro-German Women Speak Out* (Amherst: University of Massachusetts Press, 1992).

Opitz, May. *Grenzenlos und unverschämt*. Berlin: Orlanda, 1997. Translated by Anne V. Adams under the title *Borderless and Brazen* (Trenton, N.J.: Africa World Press, 2002).

Pfaffenberger, Hans. "Farbige Kinder im Heim—ein Prüfstein." *Unsere Jugend* 5, no. 12 (1953): 533–36.

———. "Hilfe für unsere Mischlingskinder—aber wie?" *Neues Beginnen. Zeitschrift für Arbeiterwohlfahrt*, no. 8 (1955): 113–15.

———. "Zur Situation der Mischlingskinder." *Unsere Jugend* 8, no. 2 (1956): 64–71.

Piesche, Peggy. "Black and German? East German Adolescents before 1989—A Retrospective View of a 'Non-Existent Issue' in the GDR." In *The Cultural After-Life of East Germany: New Transnational Perspectives*, edited by Leslie Adelson. Washington: AICGS, 2002.

Pommerin, Reiner. *"Sterilisierung der Rheinlandbastarde:" Das Schicksal einer farbigen deutschen Minderheit 1918–1937*. Düsseldorf: Droste, 1979.

Popoola, Olumide and Beldan Sezen, eds. *Talking Home: Heimat aus unserer eignene Feder—Frauen of color in Deutschland*. Amsterdam: Blue Moon Press, 1999.

Posner, David Braden. "Afro-America in West German Perspective, 1945–1966." Ph.D. diss., Yale University, 1997.

Raphael-Hernandez, Heike, ed. *Blackening Europe: The African American Presence*. New York: Routledge, 2004.

Reed-Anderson, Paulette. *Berlin und die afrikanische Diaspora: Rewriting the Footnotes*. Berlin: Die Ausländerbeauftragte des [Berliner] Senats, 2000.

———. *Eine Geschichte von mehr als 100 Jahren: Die Anfänge der afrikanischen Diaspora in Berlin*. Berlin: Die Ausländerbeauftragte des Senats, 1995.

Reinders, Robert C. "Racialism on the Left. E. D. Morel and the 'Black Horror on the Rhine.' " *International Review of Social History* 13 (1968): 1–28.

Reinemann, John Otto. "The Mulatto Children in Germany." *Mental Hygiene* 37, no. 3 (1953): 365–76.

Regina Riepe and Gerd Riepe. *Du Schwarz, ich weiß: Bilder und Texte gegen den alltäglichen Rassismus.* Wuppertal: Hammer, 1992.

Scully, Pamela. "Rape, Race and Colonial Culture: The Politics of Sexual Identity in Nineteenth-Century Cape Colony." *American Historical Review* 100, no. 2 (1995): 335–59.

Schmidt, Elizabeth. "Race, Sex, and Domestic Labor: The Question of African Female Servants in Southern Rhodesia, 1900–1939." In *African Encounters with Domesticity,* edited by Karen Tranberg Hansen, 221–41. New Brunswick: Rutgers University Press, 1992.

Schmidt-Lauber, Brigitta. *"Die verkehrte Hautfarbe": Ethnizität deutscher Namibier als Alltagspraxis.* Berlin and Hamburg: Dietrich Reimer Verlag, 1998.

Schulte-Althoff, Franz-Josef. "Rassenmischung im kolonialen System. Zur deutschen Kolonialpolitik im letzten Jahrzehnt vor dem Ersten Weltkrieg." *Historisches Jahrbuch* 105 (1985): 52–94.

Sieg, Rudolf. "Häufung von Haufaffektionen bei Mischlingen in Kinderheimen." *Zeitschrift für analytiche Kinderpsychologie, Psychotherapie und Psychagogik in Praxis und Forschung* 10 (1961): 179–80.

———. "Mischlingskinder in Westdeutschland: Eine anthropologische Studie an farbigen Kindern." *Beiträge zur Anthropologie* 4 (1955): 9–79.

———. *Mischlingskinder in Westdeutschland. Festschrift für Frederic Falkenburger.* Baden-Baden: Verlag für Kunst und Wissenschaft, 1955.

Simon, Alfons. *Maxi, unser Negerbub.* Bremen: Gesellschaft für Christlich-Jüdische Zusammenarbeit, 1952.

Smidt, Karen Boge. " 'Germania führt die deutsche Frau nach Südwest': Auswanderung, Leben und soziale Konflikte deutscher Frauen in der ehemaligen Kolonie Deutsch-Südwestafrika 1884–1920." Ph.D. diss., Universität Magdeburg, 1995.

Smith, Helmut Walser. "The Talk of Genocide, The Rhetoric of Miscegenation: Notes on Debates in the German Reichstag Concerning Southwest Africa, 1904–1914." In *The Imperialist Imagination: German Colonialism and Its Legacy,* edited by Sara Friedrichsmeyer, Sara Lennox, and Suzanne Zantop, 107–24. Ann Arbor: University of Michigan Press, 1998.

Solf, Wilhelm Heinrich. *Kolonialpolitik: Mein politisches Vermächtnis.* Berlin: Reimar von Hobbing, 1919.

Somerville, Siobhan. "Scientific Racism and the Emergence of the Homosexual Body." *Journal of the History of Sexuality* 5, no. 2 (1994): 243–66.

Sozialwissenschaftliche Forschung und Praxis für Frauen e.V. *Geteilter Feminismus: Rassismus, Antisemitismus, Fremdenhass.* Beiträge zur feministischen Theorie und Praxis 27. Köln: Eigenverlag des Vereins Beiträge zur Feministischen Theorie und Praxis, 1990.

Tautz, Birgit. *Colors: Signs of Ethnic Difference, 1800–1900–2000.* Amsterdam: Rodophi, 2003.

Thimm, Karen and DuRell Echols. *Schwarze in Deutschland.* Munich: Protokolle, 1973.

Tucker, William. *The Science and Politics of Racial Research.* Urbana, Ill.: University of Illinois Press, 1994.

Thomas Usleber, *Die Farben unter meiner Haut.* Frankfurt: Brandes and Apsel: 2002.

Unabhängiger Frauenverband. "Schwarze deutsche Frauen, Rassismus in der Sprache, weiße Frauen mit schwarzen Kindern." Special issue of *Weibblick* 13 (1993). Berlin: Unabhängiger Frauenverband, 1993.

van der Heyden, Ulrich and Joachim Zeller, eds. *Kolonialmetropole Berlin: Eine Spurensuche*. Berlin: Berlin-Edition, 2002.

van Onselen, Charles. "Witches of Suburbia: Domestic Service on the Witwatersrand, 1890–1914." In *New Ninevah*, vol. 2 of *Studies in the Social and Economic History of the Witwatersrand, 1886–1914*, 49–60. Johannesburg: Ravan Press, 1982.

Walther, Daniel. "Creating Germans Abroad: White Education in German Southwest Africa." *German Studies Review* 24, no. 2 (2001): 325–52.

Weingart, Peter, Jürgen Kroll, and Kurt Bayertz. *Rasse, Blut und Gene: Geschichte der Eugenik und Rassenhygiene in Deutschland*. Frankfurt: Suhrkamp, 1992.

Wildenthal, Lora. *German Women for Empire, 1884–1945*. Durham, N.C.: Duke University Press, 2001.

———. "Race, Gender and Citizenship in the German Colonial Empire." In *Tensions of Empire: Colonial Cultures in a Bourgeois World*, edited by Frederick Cooper and Ann Laura Stoler, 263–86. Berkeley: University of California Press, 1998.

Willbold, Gabriele. "East German Black." In *Fringe Voices: An Anthology of Minority Writing in the Federal Republic of Germany*, edited by Antje Harnisch, Anne Marie Stokes, and Friedemann Weidauer, 120–22. New York: Berg, 1998.

Zantop, Suzanne. *Colonial Fantasies: Conquest, Family, and Nation in Precolonial Germany, 1770–1870*. Durham, N.C.: Duke University Press, 1997.

Zöllner, Abini. *Schokoladenkind: Meine Familie und andere Wunder*. Hamburg: Rowohlt, 2003.

CONTRIBUTORS

ANNE ADAMS is associate professor of Africana Studies and Comparative Literature at Cornell University. Her current research focuses on evolving conceptions of the African diaspora. She is the translator of two works by May (Opitz) Ayim: *Showing Our Colors: Afro-German Women Speak Out*, coedited with K. Oguntoye and D. Schultz (University of Massachusetts Press, 1991); and *Blues in Black and White* (Africa World Press, 2003). Other articles on Afro-Germans as part of the African diaspora include "*afro look—magazine of blacks in germany*: an Africanist Analysis" (2004).

RUSSELL BERMAN is Walter A. Haas Professor in the Humanities at Stanford University. He has published several books on German cultural studies, most recently *Enlightenment or Empire: Colonial Discourse in German Culture* (University of Nebraska Press, 1998) and *Cultural Studies of Modern Germany: History, Representation and Nationhood* (University of Wisconsin Press, 1993). His article, "DuBois and Wagner: Race, Nation, and Culture Between the United States and Germany," appeared in *German Quarterly* 70 no. 2 (1997).

TINA M. CAMPT is associate professor of Women's Studies at Duke University. Trained as an historian of modern Germany and a feminist oral historian, she theorizes processes of racialization, gendering, and subjecthood in the history of black Germans during the Third Reich. Campt is author of *Other Germans: Black Germans and the Politics of Race, Gender and Memory in the Third Reich* (University of Michigan Press, 2004) and was coeditor with Michelle M. Wright of a special issue of the journal *Callaloo* (2003) entitled "Contested Black Voices: Critical Readings of the Black German Experience." She is currently working on a project on memory and the African diaspora in Europe.

FATIMA EL-TAYEB is assistant professor in the Department of Literature at the University of California at San Diego. She has published a book,

241

Schwarze Deutsche. "Rasse" und nationale Identität 1890–1933 (Campus Verlag, 2001), and a number of articles on the history of black Germans. Her recent work is on transnational identity concepts among European ethnic minorities. She is now working on a book on the role of ethnicity in postwar German popular culture and is co-organizing an international, interdisciplinary study group on Black Europe funded by the Volkswagen Foundation. Together with Angelina Maccarone, she coauthored the script for the film, *Alles wird gut* (Everything Will Be Fine, 1997) and the novelization (1999) of the film.

HEIDE FEHRENBACH is associate professor of History at Northern Illinois University. She is author of *Cinema in Democratizing Germany* (University of North Carolina Press, 1995) and coeditor of *Transactions, Transgressions, Transformations: American Culture in Western Europe and Japan* (Berghahn Books, 2000). Her book, *After the Racial State: Black G.I.s and "Colored Occupation Children" in Postwar Germany and America*, will be published by Princeton University Press in 2005. Recent essays include "Rehabilitating Father*land*: Race and German Remasculinization," *Signs* 24, no. 1 (1998); "Of German Mothers and 'Negermischlinge': Race, Sex, and the Postwar Nation" in *The Miracle Years*, ed. H. Schissler (Princeton University Press, 2001); and "Afro-German Children and the Social Politics of Race after 1945" in *German History from the Margins*, ed. Neil Gregor, Nils Roemer, and Mark Roseman (Indiana University Press, forthcoming).

RANDALL HALLE is associate professor in the Department of Modern Languages and Cultures at the University of Rochester. He is the author of *Queer Social Philosophy* (University of Illinois Press, forthcoming) and coeditor of *Light Motives: German Popular Cinema in Perspective* (Wayne State University Press, 2003). His articles include " 'Happy-ends' to Crises of Heterosexual Desire: Straight-Gay Relationships in Recent German Films," *Camera Obscura* (Spring 2000) and "German Film Aufgehoben: Ensembles of Transnational Cinema," *New German Critique* (2003).

LEROY HOPKINS is professor in the Department of Foreign Languages at Millersville University. His publications include the following: "Speak, So I Might See You! Afro-German Literature" in *World Literature Today*, 69, no. 3 (1995); coedited with C. Aisha Blackshire-Belay and David McBride, *Crosscurrents: African Americans, Africa, and Germany in the Modern World* (Camden House, 1998); and *Who is a*

German? Historical and Modern Perspectives on Africans in Germany (AICGS, 1999). Recently he has written "Einbürgerungs-Akte 1154: Heinrich Ernst Wilhelm Anumu, African Businessman in Imperial Hamburg," in *Die (koloniale) Begegnung. AfrikanerInnen in Deutschland 1880–1945. Deutsche in Afrika 1880–1918*, ed. Marianne Bechhaus-Gerst and Reinhard Klein-Arendt (Peter Lang, 2003). In 2004 "Searching for the Father(land): The Dilemma of Afro-German Literature" will appear in the Festschrift for Frank Trommler. Hopkins is on the board of the Black German Historical Society.

PATRICIA MAZÓN is associate professor in the Department of History at the State University of New York at Buffalo. Her publications include *Gender and Modern Research University: The Admission of Women to German Higher Education, 1865–1914* (Stanford University Press, 2003), *"Fräulein Doktor*: Literary Images of the First Female University Students in Fin-de-Siècle Germany," *Women in German Yearbook* 16 (2000), and "Germania Triumphant: The Niederwald National Monument and the Liberal Moment in Imperial Germany," *German History* 18:2 (2000). Her current research interests lie in gender and the public sphere in Germany.

TOBIAS NAGL received his M.A. in Film Studies and Comparative Literature from Indiana University at Bloomington. He is now completing his doctorate in the Department of Media Studies at the University of Hamburg with a dissertation on race and representation in Weimar cinema entitled, "Die unheimliche Maschine: Rasse und Repräsentation im Weimarer Kino." He has worked as a freelance critic, translator, cultural activist, and newspaper editor and published widely on popular culture, race, and German cinema. His most recent publication is " '. . . und lass mich filmen und Tanzen bloß um mein Brot zu verdienen:' Schwarze Komparsen und Kinoöffentlichkeit in der Weimarer Republik," in *AfrikanerInnen in Deutschland und schwarze Deutsche—Geschichte und Gegenwart*, ed. Marianne Bechhaus-Gerst and Reinhard Klein-Arendt (Münster: Lit, 2004).

KRISTA MOLLY O'DONNELL is associate professor in the Department of History at William Paterson University. She recently published "Poisonous Women: Sexual Danger, Illicit Violence, and Domestic Work in German Southern Africa, 1904–1915," *Journal of Women's History* 11, no. 3 (1999). She is the chief editor, with Nancy Reagin and Renate Bridenthal, of *The Heimat Abroad: The Boundaries of Germanness* (University of Michigan Press, forthcoming 2005).

Currently, she is completing a book manuscript entitled, "Women and Empire: Gender and Community in German Southwest Africa, 1890–1933."

REINHILD STEINGRÖVER is assistant professor in the Department of Humanities at the Eastman School of Music at the University of Rochester. She received a Ph.D. in German and Comparative Literature from the State University of New York at Buffalo. She is the author of *Einerseits und Andererseits. Essays zur Prosa Thomas Bernhards* (Peter Lang, 2000). She has published articles on Thomas Bernhard, Schopenhauer, Kerstin Hensel, contemporary German women's theater, and DEFA film. Her English translation of Kerstin Hensel's *Tanz am Kanal* (1993) is under consideration for publication. She is currently working on a book-length manuscript entitled "Last Features: DEFA's Lost Generation."

NAME INDEX